907.1173   149441
   Per

      Perkins.
      The education of historians
      in the United States.

Learning Resources Center
Nazareth College of Rochester, N. Y.

THE EDUCATION OF HISTORIANS
IN THE UNITED STATES

THE CARNEGIE SERIES IN AMERICAN EDUCATION

The books in this series have resulted from studies supported by grants of the Carnegie Corporation of New York, and are published by McGraw-Hill in recognition of their importance to the future of American education.

The Corporation, a philanthropic foundation established in 1911 by Andrew Carnegie for the advancement and diffusion of knowledge and understanding, has a continuing interest in the improvement of American education. It financed the studies in this series to provide facts and recommendations which would be useful to all those who make or influence the decisions which shape American educational policies and institutions.

The statements made and views expressed in these books are solely the responsibility of the authors.

THE EDUCATION OF HISTORIANS IN THE UNITED STATES

DEXTER PERKINS, Chairman
JOHN L. SNELL, Director

and

Committee on Graduate Education of the
American Historical Association
Jacques Barzun, Fred Harvey Harrington, Edward C. Kirkland,
Leonard Krieger, and Boyd C. Shafer

GREENWOOD PRESS, PUBLISHERS
WESTPORT, CONNECTICUT

Library of Congress Cataloging in Publication Data

Perkins, Dexter, 1889-
    The education of historians in the United States.

    Reprint of the ed. published by McGraw-Hill, New York, issued in the Carnegie series in American education.
    Includes bibliographical references and index.
    1. History—Study and teaching (Higher)—United States.
2. Historians—United States. I. Snell, John L., joint author. II. American Historical Association. Committee on Graduate Education. III. Title. IV. Series: (The Carnegie series in American education.)
[D16.3.P4 1975]   907'.11'73   74-25597
ISBN 0-8371-7881-9

The authors acknowledge with thanks permission to quote from the following publications: to AMERICAN COUNCIL ON EDUCATION, publisher of Theodore C. Blegen and Russell M. Cooper (eds.), *The Preparation of College Teachers* (1950); to McGRAW-HILL BOOK COMPANY, INC., publisher of Bernard Berelson, *Graduate Education in the United States* (1960); to UNIVERSITY OF PENNSYLVANIA PRESS, publisher of Hayward Keniston, *Graduate Study and Research in the Arts and Sciences at the University of Pennsylvania* (1959).

Copyright © 1962 by the McGraw-Hill Book Company, Inc.

All rights reserved. This book, or parts thereof, may not be reproduced in any form without permission of the publishers.

Originally published in 1962 by McGraw-Hill Book Company, Inc., New York

Reprinted with the permission of McGraw-Hill Book Co.

Reprinted in 1975 by Greenwood Press,
a division of Williamhouse-Regency Inc.

Library of Congress Catalog Card Number 74-25597

ISBN 0-8371-7881-9

Printed in the United States of America

FOREWORD

This book, it is hoped, will be one of a series on the historical profession. Discussions concerning this study of the graduate education of historians began during the winter of 1956–1957, following the Presidential Address of Professor Dexter Perkins in St. Louis at the annual meeting of the American Historical Association. The association, with funds from the Carnegie Corporation of New York, sponsored the study through its Committee on Graduate Education composed of Dexter Perkins, chairman, Jacques Barzun, Fred Harvey Harrington, Edward C. Kirkland, Leonard Krieger, and Boyd C. Shafer. In September, 1958, with a generous grant of leave from Tulane University, Professor John L. Snell became director of the study. With the committee's counsel and following its general plan, he collected most of the materials for this book through hundreds of questionnaires, dozens of visits to universities, interviews with both teachers and students, and other intensive research. Professor Snell wrote Chapters 2 to 9, Professor Perkins wrote Chapter 1, and Chapter 10 contains the Recommendations of the Committee.

Washington, D.C.

> Boyd C. Shafer
> Executive Secretary
> American Historical Association

ACKNOWLEDGMENTS AND SOURCES

This study has been conducted under the auspices of the American Historical Association, and has been made possible by a generous grant from the Carnegie Corporation. The author of Chapters 2 to 9, Professor Snell, is grateful to Tulane University for granting him a leave of absence for his work as director of the study. He is also indebted to Mrs. Virginia Ktsanes, Mrs. Kenneth Vines, Mrs. Charles P. Roland, and Robert Mitchell for assistance in the tabulation and analysis of data from questionnaires; to Mrs. James B. Kemp for typing the final manuscript; to Maxine Pybas Snell for her unstinting work as his secretary; and to members of the committee who gave encouragement, stylistic help, good advice, and freedom to complete the assignment they gave him in 1958: to discover and describe—as objectively as possible—practices and problems in graduate training in history and suggestions for their improvement.

All members of the committee wish to express their thanks to the historians who filled out questionnaires, answered letters, and granted more than two hundred interviews during the course of this study.

A special word of thanks should be offered here to Joe Spaeth of the National Opinion Research Center for a report on graduate students in history, based upon a larger study of graduate students undertaken by the NORC; to John K. Folger and Kenneth M. Wilson of the Southern Regional Education Board for data on recent Ph.D.s in history; to John L. Chase of the Office of Education, who provided useful data on fellowships for graduate study; to Paul M. Allen, who made available drafts of a study of graduate education prepared for the American Association of Colleges for Teacher Education; and to Bernard Berelson for advice and data from his own more general study of graduate education.

The footnotes to Chapters 2 to 9 provide an extended bibliography of the studies by others that were used in preparing this study. There would be little advantage in repeating here the references that each chapter contains. The major sources for the information presented in Chapters 2 to 9—usually without footnotes—are the questionnaires and interviews noted in the appendixes.

CONTENTS

Foreword   v

Acknowledgments and Sources   vii

1. INTRODUCTION: AS SEEN BY THE CHAIRMAN   1

2. DO WE NEED MORE COLLEGE TEACHERS?   15

   The Growth of Doctoral Training in History. Future Need for Ph.D.s in History. Variations in Supply and Demand. Summary.

3. GRADUATE STUDENTS IN HISTORY   37

   Ability and Preparation. Academic and Social Origins. Financing Graduate Study. Career Plans. Recruiting. Summary.

4. HISTORY IN THE COLLEGES   62

   The Importance of Teaching Ability. Scholarly Qualifications of Teachers. Working Conditions. What History Is Taught? Methods of Teaching. History Majors. Summary.

5. THE MASTER'S DEGREE   87

   Admission, Screening, and Basic Requirements. The Master's Thesis. Other Variations. The Uses of the Master's Degree. Proposed Reforms: For Secondary School Teachers. Proposed Reforms: For College Teachers. Summary.

6. PH.D.-TRAINING INSTITUTIONS   108

   Which Institutions Offer the Ph.D. in History? Faculties and Fields. Undergraduate Education. Teaching Conditions. Research and Teaching. Library Resources. Summary.

CONTENTS

7. DOCTORAL STUDY IN HISTORY — 141

What Is Studied: Field Requirements. Forms of Study. Examinations. Summary.

8. MAJOR CRITICISMS OF PH.D. TRAINING — 160

Preparation for College Teaching. Breadth and Specialization. Training for Research Scholarship. Protracted Ph.D. Study. Summary.

9. EXPERIMENTS WITH TEACHER TRAINING AND TIGHTENED PROGRAMS — 188

Teacher Preparation. Reducing the Ph.D. "Stretch-out." Summary.

10. RECOMMENDATIONS — 200

Attracting and Admitting Graduate Students. Undergraduate Preparation. The Master's Degree. Shortening Ph.D. Training. Striking a Balance. Preparation for Teaching. Discovering Teaching Capacity. Fostering and Rewarding Good Teaching.

APPENDIXES — 213

Index — 233

TABLES

2-1. Increase in History Doctoral Production, 1881–1952
2-2. Recent Production of Ph.D.s in History, 1953–1960
2-3. Recent Production of Ph.D.s in History and Comparable Disciplines, 1953–1959
2-4. Total Ph.D. Production in Selected Social Sciences, 1926–1957
2-5. Bachelor's, Master's, and Doctoral Degrees in History, 1948–1959
2-6. Predicted Quantitative Trends in Graduate Education in History, 1959–1970, Based upon Increases in Live Births
2-7. Regional Variations in Production of 1,482 Ph.D.s, 1955–1960
2-8. Regional Distribution of Ph.D. Candidates in History in 80 Universities, 1958–1959
2-9. Ph.D.s in History by Geographical Areas of Specialization, 1873–1959
2-10. Anticipated Faculty Appointments and Ph.D. Candidates in Various Fields of History, 1958–1959
3-1. Inadequacies of Undergraduate Preparation for Graduate Study in History Reported by 182 History Ph.D.s of 1958
3-2. Leading Baccalaureate Sources of History Ph.D.s, 1936–1956
3-3. Social Origins of Graduate Students, 1958–1959
3-4. Financial Conditions of Graduate Students, 1958–1959
3-5. Stipends Held by Graduate Students in Selected Disciplines, 1958–1959
3-6. Career Aims of 2,754 Graduate Students, 1958–1959
3-7. Persons Influencing Decision to Undertake Graduate Study in History by 182 Recent Ph.D.s
4-1. Good and Poor Teachers: Appraisals by 182 Recent History Ph.D.s
4-2. Appointment of History Teachers with Less than the Ph.D. in 502 Colleges, 1958–1959

4-3. Teaching Loads of 1,007 History Teachers in 126 Better Colleges, First Term of 1958–1959
4-4. Average Sizes of History Classes at Various Levels in 126 Colleges, 1956–1957 and 1958–1959
4-5. Enrollment Changes in History Courses in 126 Four-year Colleges, 1948–1958
4-6. Changes in History Courses Offered by 502 Four-year Colleges, 1948–1958
4-7. History Courses Most Often Offered among 502 Colleges and 51 Junior Colleges, 1956–1958 (2 Years)
4-8. Variations in History Offerings by Types of Four-year Colleges (Sample of 376 Institutions)
4-9. Comparison of Selected Forms of History Instruction by Types of Colleges, 1958–1959
5-1. Thesis Requirements in Colleges and Universities Offering the Master's Degree in History, 1958–1959
5-2. Relative Strength of Master's Training in 77 Universities and 87 Colleges 1958–1959
6-1. Growth of Doctoral Programs in History by Selected Five-year Periods, 1881–1945
6-2. Production of 3,133 Ph.D.s by 79 Universities Awarding the Doctorate in History, 1948–1958 (11 Years)
6-3. 41 Universities That Were First Choices for Graduate Study by One or More of 202 Woodrow Wilson Fellows in History, 1960, plus 15 Other Universities Chosen by Fellows in 1958 or 1959
6-4. Size of History Faculties in 80 Institutions Offering the Ph.D. in History, 1958–1959
6-5. Scholarly Publication by 1,121 Members of Ph.D.-training History Faculties in 77 Institutions, 1958–1959
6-6. Foreign Travel and Study of 674 Specialists in History of Foreign Areas, 77 Ph.D.-training Institutions, 1958–1959
6-7. Ph.D.s in Various Fields of History Awarded by 29 Institutions in the East, 1955–1959 (5 Years)
6-8. Ph.D.s in Various Fields of History Awarded by 17 Institutions in the South, 1955–1959 (5 Years)
6-9. Ph.D.s in Various Fields of History Awarded by 17 Institutions in the Midwest, 1955–1959 (5 Years)
6-10. Ph.D.s in Various Fields of History Awarded by 11 Institutions in the West, 1955–1959 (5 Years)
6-11. Percentages of 77 Ph.D.-training Institutions Offering Courses in Various Fields of History at Three Levels

6–12.	Types of Courses Reported at Least Three Times as Added or Dropped, 1948–1958, in 77 Ph.D.-training History Departments
6–13.	Notable Enrollment Increases and Decreases, 1948–1958, in Various Types of Courses in 77 Ph.D.-training History Departments
6–14.	History Majors, 1956 and 1958, in 71 Institutions Offering Ph.D. Training in History
6–15.	Various Forms of History Instruction Offered by 77 Ph.D.-training Institutions, 1958–1959
6–16.	Teaching Loads of 1,121 Members of History Faculties in 77 Ph.D.-training Universities, First Term, 1958–1959
6–17.	Average Sizes of History Classes at Various Levels in 77 Ph.D.-training Institutions, 1956–1957 and 1958–1959
6–18.	Factors Reported by History Ph.D.s of 1958 as Causes of Neglect of Ph.D. Candidates by Graduate Faculty
6–19.	Strength of Library Resources of 85 Universities Offering Ph.D. Training in History, 1960
7–1.	Number of Books Recent History Ph.D.s Believe They Were Expected to Read in Various Fields of History
7–2.	Average Lengths of Doctoral Dissertations of 1957–1958 in Various Disciplines
8–1.	Criticisms of Graduate Schools by About 2,780 History Graduate Students, 1958–1959
8–2.	Evaluations by 152 History Ph.D.s of 1958 of Their Doctoral Training as Preparation for College Teaching Positions
8–3.	Reasons Why 182 History Ph.D.s of 1958 Undertook Graduate Study
8–4.	Frequency of Recommendations for More Specific Teacher Training from 126 Selected Four-year Colleges
8–5.	Time Lapse between Start of Graduate Study and Award of Degree to 182 Ph.D.s in History of 1958
8–6.	Ages of 181 Ph.D.s of 1958 upon Award of the Degree
8–7.	Comparison of Faculty Guidance Received by Graduate Students in History and Other Disciplines (Sample of 2,764 Students), 1958–1959

Chapter 1
INTRODUCTION: AS SEEN BY THE CHAIRMAN

Historians, like most scholars, are not given to analyzing the social import of their subject. Intrigued with the job they are doing, and in most cases subject to little external criticism, they rarely ask themselves precisely what they conceive their service to society to be. Yet the question is one that cannot be avoided. It was with a view to answering it that the American Historical Association appointed a Committee on Graduate Study in History, and that the Carnegie Corporation generously provided the funds for an investigation of current practices, with a view to improvement and progress.

We shall not face up to our problems as historians unless we clearly apprehend that history is a special type of discipline, and that its utility must be measured in other ways than those applied to science, or even to economics or the arts. No other subject, except possibly philosophy, embraces the whole story of man. While, in the nature of the case, the historian must confine his special research to a restricted area, he is at all times under a special compulsion to see life whole. If he is equal to the demands of his high calling, he must, as he studies the past, relate one area of activity to another, for example, the history of foreign policy to the history of ideas, the history of the business cycle to the movements of politics, the story of religion to the cultural media in which it finds expression. If he becomes too narrow a specialist, he misses some of the fundamental values of his profession.

In the second place, it is to be remembered and emphasized that most historians are teachers. This is not to say that training in history does not offer opportunities for employment in other fields. Of course it does. But the statistics of our investigation dramatize the fact that the vast majority of those who undertake graduate work in history are preparing for a teacher's career, and that many of those who are not teaching would be glad to do so.

Again, we must clearly recognize that in history, more than in most disciplines, the teacher must transcend his materials. The facts of history can be dead as Marley and the doornail until they are put to use. The data of history can be well nigh meaningless until thoughtfully interpreted. The teaching of history will be effective in so far as it communicates, not facts alone, but the wisdom, experience, and insight that lie behind the facts. "The value of history," wrote one of the greatest of American historians, Carl Becker, "is, indeed, not scientific, but moral; by liberalizing the mind, by deepening the sympathies, by fortifying the will, it enables us to control, not society, but ourselves; it prepares us to live more humanely in the present, and to meet rather than to foretell, the future."

It is with these general principles in mind that we here examine graduate preparation in history.

We must also, of course, take account of some of the practical problems that confront us today. The place of history in the curriculum is vulnerable in a world which has so many pressing immediate problems. Other disciplines can, as of course they should, appropriate relevant areas of the historic past, drawing away from history some of those who ought to profit from its broader values. In a world of rapid change, attention can too easily be fixed upon the immediate, as against the long-term, factors in the life of man. We have seen a process of decline in classical studies; we have seen such important branches of history as ancient and medieval history threatened; there is danger that interest in history will be further narrowed.

Moreover, graduate education in history—and the point of view of the professional historian—has come under sharp attack. Let me state, as the devil's advocate, the case against current historical scholarship. How does it run? The critic would say that a great proportion of our research is of limited interest to the great mass of persons who are interested in history. He recognizes that research is indispensable to the advance of knowledge, and that it is the means by which we stimulate and correct each other. But he would also say that much research is simply the accumulation of new data (sometimes data of restricted significance), rather than the search for new insights. He would contend that it amounts to little more than historians communicating with one another, rather than communicating with that greater audience to whom history may be useful and thrilling. He would go on to say that many historians possess very meager literary gifts. We have not, thank Heaven, like some other disciplines, invented a specialized vocabulary that gives to simple thoughts the appearance of profound learning and erects a barrier to understanding, or suggests profundity where there is really superficiality. But even so, the critic says, few historians collect a wide company of readers, and the history that is read, that is lively and entertaining and influential, is not the history that the mass of historians write.

It is not in meticulous research, says the critic, but in the classroom that history takes hold. There it is possible to communicate the larger aspects of history. There it is possible to give scope to wider views, and broader interpretations out of which the deeper values of history may be drawn.

One radical point of view is expressed by such an experienced educator as Earl J. McGrath of Columbia Teachers College. Professor McGrath believes that the present training for the doctorate is ill-adapted to the preparation of effective teachers. To meet the problem he would provide two divergent educations, one for those who propose to enter the classroom and another for those who intend to engage in research.

To go further with the case against current methods of training historians, in our investigations we discovered evidences of malaise at the increasing impersonality of graduate study. The aspirant for the degree, it is alleged, is rarely in any close rapport with his mentor. He is often left to himself. If it be true, as James B. Conant has asserted, that where there is a great scholar there is a great teacher behind him, our graduate methods, the critic laments, fall short of adequate preparation either for the classroom or the work of research.

Having raised these various questions, let me now proceed to discuss them in terms of what the committee has learned and in terms of the principles agreed upon. First of all, let me say that the committee emphatically repudiates some of the ideas of Professor McGrath. The aim of the doctoral program is the preparation of the scholar-teacher. None of us believes that the two functions ought to be separated. The practical situation in the college world runs against such doctrine. So, too, does the ideal which, in the field of history especially, should be promoted by graduate training.

Good college teaching is possible only when the teacher is well trained in the methods of research. It is possible only when the teacher constantly seeks to enrich his knowledge of his subject. Without the spirit of scholarship, teaching degenerates into routine. It becomes dead and lifeless or superficial, and even meretricious. It sets a bad example for those whom the teacher teaches. On the other hand, exclusive, or even exaggerated, attention to research for those who are also teachers presents dangers of its own. It makes for indifference to the work of the classroom. It can, and sometimes does, destroy that friendly and stimulating relationship between teacher and student which is at the heart of education. It may reduce history to a mere display of technique rather than illumine it as a great humanistic discipline. It often restricts the researcher to communication with specialists in his own field, to the neglect of the immense values to be derived from history by undergraduates and laymen.

Let us, then, reassert the fundamental fact. We are, to a large degree, preparing teachers. We are preparing teachers, moreover, who will in most cases have to teach, not some narrowly restricted area of their own choosing, but relatively broad courses, dealing with fields in which the knowledge is so wide that they cannot hope to get to the bottom of every problem, in terms of intensive and "definitive" research. We are preparing these people, for the most part, to teach not in the largest universities, but in a host of other institutions where the work of the classroom ranks higher in importance than sustained and minute research.

The problem is to see to it that, in our justified zeal for scholarship, we do not neglect in our training for the doctorate the immense values to be drawn from history for the students who sit in our classes—for the large numbers of these students who are not headed for the career of a professional historian, but who can and will learn from the wisdom of the past in precisely the way Becker described the process in the quotation I have cited.

The chapters that follow demonstrate that the demand for well-trained persons prepared for the teaching of history will grow. It will not grow at the astronomical rate that has sometimes been assumed. But even if we merely maintain the present ratio between Ph.D.s and those without the degree in the history departments of the country, there will be an increasing demand. And if the ratio of Ph.D.s is to be increased, the demand, of course, will be larger still.

How shall we meet this demand? Will it be through larger numbers in the graduate schools of high prestige, or through the adding of doctoral programs? The committee has not attempted to give a categorical answer to this question. There are dangers in the enlargement of the present graduate schools, and especially the danger I have already mentioned, the danger of neglect of the student, the danger of impersonality. The danger increases, with the increasing tendency to draw off the best scholars, and often the best scholar-teachers, into extended research projects. On the other hand, it is extremely unwise for institutions to enter upon doctoral training with inadequate resources. On this subject we speak with definiteness on page 201 of our report.

But first of all, as our report shows, we come back to the question of effective teaching or a more intimate concern for those whom we teach at the undergraduate level. Here, after all, is where the recruiting is done. Here is where enthusiasm for the life of the scholar is engendered. Here is where the fire is kindled, never to be put out. I do not mean to say that there are not many persons who become historians without the personal stimulus of an inspiring teacher. I *do* mean to say that an inspiring teacher makes a difference, and I can think, as we all can, of teachers who, without ever writing anything very important themselves, have sent many of their students on to graduate school.

There is a great advantage in catching the prospective historian early. If we take an intense personal interest in the brightest of our undergraduates, we shall be able to help them in very practical ways to accelerate their careers toward the doctorate. If we have some contact with them by the time they begin to concentrate, we shall be able to see to it, for example, that they start their language preparation. To take another example, almost any American historian needs some training in economics. If we know about these recruits for our discipline in time, we can see that they receive such training. We can see, too, that they start with some broad conceptions of history, and some wide knowledge, and do not undertake our discipline with the idea that they can operate only in a restricted area in time, space, and spirit.

This question of early recruiting is discussed in more detail in the recommendations that conclude this report. I emphasize the matter here because it seems to me vital. We need to feel warmly toward those in our classes, to put forth our best efforts to inspire them, to help them, to guide them. I heard a distinguished professor a year ago express a thinly veiled scorn for undergraduates. Nothing could be more shortsighted. These undergraduates are the people from whom we must do our recruiting; they are essential to us; in the last analysis we cannot live without them, even from the narrow professional point of view. And in a broader sense, most of us exist in order to educate these undergraduates.

But let us again turn from this matter to the actual training for the doctorate. Have we not fallen into a routine which we accept without analysis? Have we seriously considered whether our procedures really meet the needs of the situation? Do we really think that there is nothing to be done to improve them?

Our report has a good deal to say on this subject. We find that a very frequently expressed desire is for broader training. This desire is legitimate. Indeed, it is fundamental. In our graduate training, if it is to fulfill its purpose, we must maintain standards of exactitude, of precision, of faithfulness to the spirit of research on the one hand, and respect for and interest in the larger view of history on the other. The problem is not simple. The materials in which the historian works are growing at an awesome rate, making more and more difficult—especially for the historian of relatively recent times—that "definitive" interpretation for which we all strive. The man does not exist who can give a general course in American history, basing it on an examination of all the materials in the monumental and highly useful *Harvard Guide to Historical Literature*. What then are we to do in preparing young men and women to teach such a course, as many of them will be expected to do? We shall want them to set an exacting standard for themselves in accumulating knowledge of this subject. But we must also encourage them to see their subject in the large, to look, not only for data, but for insights; to seek for suggestive generalizations—bold, but not too bold; to infuse not only learning but enthusiasm into their lectures; to approach their subject with some fundamental intellectual and moral attitude of their own. For history is in the last analysis an "interpretation"; and the undergraduates whom most doctors of philosophy will teach will remember not the facts, but the interpretation. In particular they will hope to see in the teacher broad interest, wide tolerance, sensitiveness to beauty and goodness, a vivid appreciation of men and events, and an enthusiasm for communication as well as for knowledge.

In theory, the training for the doctorate has never neglected this breadth of training in history itself. The general examination, or the qualifying examination as it is sometimes called, if properly organized, should meet this need. It should, and does normally, cover a substantial variety of fields. It is probably true, as our report suggests, that these fields are not always carefully chosen, and that more guidance of candidates is necessary. It may be that the fields are not always chosen with regard to the realities of employment in our profession, that is, in some proper relationship to the subjects which are most in demand, and which the candidate for the doctorate is most likely to teach. But there is no reason why they cannot be. Nor is there any reason why the examination itself should test the examinee's zest for minutiae and not his ability to grasp the essentials in a fairly wide area of knowledge.

But this, it may be, is not enough. We are suggesting various expedients for giving the student breadth. I attach substantial importance to our recommendation that the aspirant for the degree be familiarized with the classics of historical writing. It will be found, almost invariably, that these classics illustrate the primary values of historical study, that they deal with large subjects, not small ones, that they are remarkable for their insights, not merely for the accumulation of the data, that they bear the stamp of the author's personality, and have color and form. It will also be found that they have literary quality.

I believe, and I think this is implicitly included in the recommendations of the committee, that it would be helpful if every student had a course, or possibly a half course, in the philosophy of history. There is, of course, no philosophy of history that has eternal validity or that commands universal assent. The value of the study of this field lies in the invitation it offers to audacity, a virtue not much practiced in our profession. We need to play with large ideas from time to time, not because such diversion is a means to absolute truth, but because it is invigorating and stimulating. In seeking the definitive, we often overlook the value of the unproven thesis, the incompletely substantiated theory, in exciting thought and spurring to research. Many of Frederick Jackson Turner's ideas on the frontier have come under heavy attack. But few men have done more to give to younger scholars new fields for speculation, or have promoted the progress of history more effectively by their own writing.

But breadth of training is not in itself enough to prepare the doctoral aspirant for the classroom. The truth is that the conventional Ph.D. program does not really adequately prepare the student for the thing that he will be doing most of his life—that is, it does not teach him how to teach.

I know that there are those who will say that teachers are born, not made. There is, of course, some truth in this view. You cannot make a silk purse out of a sow's ear. But if we are careful in our selection of our graduate students, there ought not to be many sows' ears among them. They will have the aptitude to learn something about teaching if we provide them with the opportunity.

There are certain elements of good teaching that can, indeed, be easily stated. It is elementary to speak so that you can be heard —though I have seen distinguished scholars who have not absorbed this simple fact. It is elementary that one does not read a lecture, that there is, in fact, no more certain way of draining a theme of interest than to divorce oneself from one's audience and cling devotedly to a manuscript, with head lowered except for an occasional peering over one's glasses at the victims—though I have seen real savants who have not learned this. It is elementary to give emphasis to the important by the tone of the voice, and perhaps by repetition. Young men need to be told these things, and if they are told them, they are likely to remember them.

But it is clear where this leads. It leads to the principle that those who are to be prepared for teaching should have some chance to practice teaching under observation. As matters stand today, such instruction as graduate students perform is often thought of as a potboiler. I visited one distinguished university a few years ago at which it was freely confessed to me by the older members of the teaching staff that they never troubled to visit the section meetings of the young assistants in their classes, or even to inquire from the undergraduates how things were going. To ignore this duty not only is unfair to the individual but tends to denigrate the teaching function itself. It leads the student to believe that what is really important is his research, and that it does not matter much what goes on in the classroom.

But there is more to the matter than this. The technique of the classroom is not the same technique as that required for writing a thesis in a narrow field. Classroom teaching means scholarship in action. A lecture is not a report in a seminar. It demands that one take a fairly large subject, organize the material with due regard to emphasis, draw the appropriate stimulating generalizations from the materials, and present the human story with a zest that commands attention and arouses enthusiasm. Similarly, conducting a discussion session is not the same thing as the presentation of elaborate data in writing. It demands skill in answering questions, in controlling and directing debate, in bringing out the most relevant and important conclusions. Do those of us who teach graduate students really know whether or not these prospective teachers can do these things? If we don't, shouldn't we? Have we not a clear obligation to give them some training from this point of view? After all, all of them will teach, not all of them will write, and many of those who do write will not write much.

Our report, while laying stress on this matter, goes far beyond this. The graduate schools will place more emphasis on teaching when there is a clearer demand for good teachers from the colleges, the junior colleges, and, yes, the universities also. And not only where there is a clearer demand, but where there is a substantial and intimate interest. We suggest, therefore, not only that appointing authorities ask specific questions about the teaching capacity of a prospective appointee, but that they make every effort to see him teach. If it is thought that it is too much of an ordeal for the candidate to ask him to teach before a class, there is always the possibility of inviting him to talk more informally to some student group—a history club, for example. Furthermore, after he has been appointed, he should be helped. The administrative officers ought to know whether he is fulfilling his function or not. Too often, says one of my friends in the profession, in recommendations for promotion good teaching is taken for granted. Praise on this point is *pro forma*, not usually based on knowledge. Our report contains many interesting suggestions on this matter. In my own view, the key question is supervision and visitation. There exists, among both novices and experienced teachers, much prejudice with regard to this question, and indeed it is easily understandable that young instructors should resent carping criticism and that older men should not wish to seem officious in their interest in their younger colleagues. The question is one of spirit. Given the right attitude, the visiting of a first-year teacher ought to be easy. Where the relationship between the older and the younger members of a history department is warm and friendly, a little coaching will seem the most natural thing in the world.

But there is more to the matter than that. Of fundamental consequence is the importance, not the lip service, given to effective teaching by administrators, in our colleges as well as in the graduate schools. Do they think chiefly of publication, and of publication on a quantitative basis? Do they assess publication in terms of the significance of what is published, or without regard to this criterion? Is a badly written article on a minute subject given the minor importance it deserves, or does it count just about as much as the published development of a new theme with insight and skill? I ask these questions; I do not answer them. I would, however, plead for a fuller recognition of the truly distinguished teacher, even if his literary output is small. There are men who go on learning all their lives but who never get down to putting their knowledge on paper. There are scholars—I use the word advisedly—whose range of interests is so broad that they cannot bring themselves to the kind of investigation that is so much esteemed in the academic world. There are scholars—again I use the word advisedly—who diffuse wisdom in their classes, wisdom that is the fruit of reflection and experience, but who have a meager output in terms of highly specialized scholarship. In my long teaching career I have lectured in something like seventy American colleges. I have gone away from many of them convinced that we think too little of the values of history in terms of the classroom, too little of the men who make the classroom a place of joy, as distinguished from the productive scholars who care little for communication in any form.

These questions relate to one other aspect of our training for the doctorate. The training is too long, takes too many years out of the scholar-teacher's life. Because it is long, it is too often not completed in regular consecutive sessions of university work. The result is that the young teacher finds himself suffering from schizophrenia. He wants to teach and teach well. He also wants to get his degree. He ends, all too often, by teaching none too well. It would have been better had he not been subjected to this divided loyalty.

Professor Snell has shown that the average time taken to achieve the doctorate in history is more than seven years. Some of the obstacles to a briefer training may be beyond our reach. Early marriage, large families (possibly too large families while training is going on), and the necessity to earn a living often prolong doctoral training. But one of the principal sources of the difficulty lies in the Ph.D. dissertation, in the selection, very often, of a subject so massive that it requires years of preparation, that it necessitates extensive travel, that it becomes not a trial run, but a finished piece of scholarship on a level that only a few can attain. In historical study, unlike the sciences, men mature slowly in their discipline. We would, I think, be better advised if we thought of the thesis as a demonstration of capacity for intensive research, rather than as an ambitious attempt to cover a wide field. Were the thesis so regarded, it might be a more joyous experience than it often is. The choice of a really lively topic, capable of being explored, say, in a year's time, might emphasize to the student the fact that he is being trained, not chained to a task that often becomes increasingly distasteful and destroys the zeal for research itself. This more modest requirement would excite to further learning, not exhaust interest in it. It would establish a healthier sense of proportion as to research itself. It would make it possible for the prospective Ph.D. to complete his job in a reasonable time, and free him for those first exacting years when his first duty—and it is to be hoped his deep pleasure—is to learn to master the job of the classroom.

From time to time I am told that interest in teaching, as distinguished from research, is on the decline and will continue to decline. I doubt it. My doubt is now confirmed by our report. Our graduate students often complain that they are not prepared for their vocation. Young men and young women undergraduates thrill as they have always thrilled to the man who makes the past live, who brings to the business of communication the same enthusiasm that he brings to the enlargement of his own knowledge and the pursuit of deeper scholarship.

We ought never to surrender the desire to know more, and to know more deeply. But we must take care, in our developing scholarship, that we do not become mere bloodless technicians, examining the trivial for our own delectation, sacrificing the deeper values of history for the lesser ones.

Let me seize the opportunity here afforded to say a word more about what some of these deeper values are. The mass of mankind and the great majority of our students are interested most of all in human personality. The tendency of contemporary historical study, a useful tendency if not carried too far, is to put the accent on ideas and systems and concepts of social movements. In doing this let us not forget *the man*. We learn much from the great figures of the past, from their virtues, from their accomplishments, yes, from their mistakes. If history is philosophy teaching by example, it is by the example of the individual that it communicates some of its most precious lessons. Let us never forget this.

The second point I would emphasize is the value of history as a means of understanding another age or another society: of entering with sympathy into that age or that society. It is possible to become so enthralled with the data that the larger view is lost. But there is no more useful intellectual exercise than to seek to enter fully into the life of the past, to interpret it sympathetically, with its presuppositions and prejudices clearly held in view. Nor is there anything more valuable than really to understand another country and its outlook, not merely to talk about it, but to seize its *Geist*, its spirit.

The third point I would emphasize is that the very essence of history lies in the establishment of perspective. The historian here contributes not only to his own profession, but to every intelligent human being; he liberates the individual from the preoccupations of the moment and teaches us all to place ourselves and our age in relation to other persons and other times. "History is never more valuable," wrote William Edward Hartpole Lecky almost a hundred years ago, "than when it enables us, standing as on a height, to look beyond the smoke and turmoil of our petty quarrels, and to detect in the slow developments of the past the great permanent forces that are steadily bearing nations onwards to improvement or decay."

The list of the values to be found in history might be further extended. There is humor in history; that we must never lose sight of. There is chance in history, which ought to reconcile us to the fortuitousness of success and failure, and which serves to illumine the human story. There is drama in history, and we ought to look for the drama. But to go further would be unduly to embroider the theme. The essence of the matter is simple. Let us, in the search for deeper knowledge, never neglect the challenge to achieve new insights, and wider horizons than those which spring from highly specialized research. Let us inspire our graduate students to do the same. Let administrators and department heads encourage boldness and audacity. Let those who teach, and those who select teachers, assure themselves that the pageant of the past will never lose its color, that learning will be followed by insight, that a noble profession will never give up to a few what was meant for the many.

Chapter 2

DO WE NEED MORE COLLEGE TEACHERS?

For amost every day in 1960 a Ph.D. in history was being awarded in the nation. How does this output compare with total Ph.D. production in all fields? How does it compare with previous output of history Ph.D.s? Does it meet or exceed present needs? How much must the production record of 1960 be bettered to meet the needs of the 1960s for fully trained professional historians? These questions this chapter seeks to answer.

Predicting the need for Ph.D.s in any field is an uncertain business. In 1945 one of the best studies of Ph.D. programs that have been undertaken conjectured that "after war shortages in doctoral personnel are made up, it is likely that for the next score of years society will demand a relatively small number of . . . doctors of philosophy." [1] Yet, by 1958–1959 the production of Ph.D.s stood at 284% of the level of 1939–1940 [2] and as early as 1955 anxieties about overexpansion had given way to fearful predictions that too few Ph.D.s would be available to educate the students of the 1960s. How were new teachers to be found in sufficient numbers? Predictions of academic crisis became commonplace and a few distin-

---
[1] Ernest V. Hollis, *Toward Improving Ph.D. Programs* (Washington, 1945), 122, 200.
[2] Bernard Berelson, *Graduate Education in the United States* (New York, 1960), 32.

guished ones were published.[3] Salaries rose as the demand for teachers exceeded the supply. Disconcertingly, however, qualifications asked of new college teachers in some academic disciplines went down.[4]

Private foundations and the Federal government responded to the obvious need for action by sharply increasing the amount of scholarship and fellowship aid. Without the Woodrow Wilson Fellowships, the National Defense Fellowships, and other programs an academic crisis in the early 1960s would almost certainly have developed.[5] A crisis in the late sixties is still possible.

THE GROWTH OF DOCTORAL TRAINING IN HISTORY

The first step in estimating future supply-demand relationships in history is to determine how many Ph.D.s have been needed in the past. And Archbishop Fénelon's advice to the heir of Louis XIV still holds good: "It is not enough to know the past; it is necessary to know the present."

The awarding of Ph.D.s in history began in 1882 when John Franklin Jameson at Johns Hopkins and Clarence Bowen at Yale received the degree. The next decade was one of rapid expansion. Herbert Baxter Adams at Johns Hopkins alone trained 38 Ph.D.s in history. In that ten-year period of beginning, seven institutions awarded Ph.D.s in history. Hopkins awarded somewhat more than half the national total during the eighties, and did so again in the five-year period, 1891–1895.[6] Meanwhile, a good many American

[3] Committee of Fifteen (F. W. Strothmann, ed.), *The Graduate School Today and Tomorrow: Reflections for the Profession's Consideration* (New York, 1955), 7; Grayson L. Kirk and others, "The Education of College Teachers," in the *Fifty-third Annual Report, The Carnegie Foundation for the Advancement of Teaching* (New York, 1958), 11.

[4] See, e.g., *New York Times,* January 11, 1959; Ray C. Maul, "Will New College Teachers Be Adequately Prepared?" *Educational Record,* XL (October, 1959), 326–329, especially 327.

[5] In 1960 Berelson, *Graduate Education,* 79, suggested that the statistics confront the nation with a problem but not a crisis. He was immediately challenged by Earl J. McGrath. See *New York Times,* November 6, 1960.

[6] William B. Hesseltine and Louis Kaplan, "Doctors of Philosophy in History: A Statistical Study," *American Historical Review,* XLVII (July, 1942), 766, 772–773. See also Francesco Cordasco, *Daniel Coit Gilman and the Protean Ph.D.* (Leiden, 1960).

historians were earning the Ph.D. in European universities. By 1927 Marcus W. Jernegan could estimate that there were "about six hundred Ph.D.'s in history living in the United States and that the annual increase is fifty or more." [7]

This is no place to tell in detail how annual production of Ph.D.s in history had been increased to "fifty or more," or how the rate was doubled, tripled, and more than sextupled during the next three decades. Table 2-1 shows the increase. Annual production

TABLE 2-1
INCREASE IN HISTORY DOCTORAL PRODUCTION, 1881–1952

Year	Approximate No. of institutions offering Ph.D.s in history	Average annual No. of history Ph.D.s in each period	Total No. of Ph.D.s in U.S. each year	Percentage of all doctorates accounted for by history Ph.D.s
1881–1882	5	2	46	4.3
1891–1892	13	10	190	5.3
1901–1902	18	19	293	6.5
1911–1912	22	27	500	5.4
1921–1922	30	50	836	6.0
1931–1932	46	133	2,654	5.0
1941–1942	58	151	3,168	4.8
1951–1952	65	258	6,139	4.2

SOURCE: Statistics are from: William B. Hesseltine and Louis Kaplan, "Doctors of Philosophy in History: A Statistical Study," *American Historical Review*, XLVII (July, 1942), 772–773; U.S. Department of Health, Education, and Welfare, *Earned Degrees Conferred by Higher Educational Institutions, 1957–1958* (Washington, 1959), table 6; U.S. Department of Health, Education, and Welfare (Louis H. Conger, Jr., and Marie G. Fullam, eds.), *Projection of Earned Degrees to 1969–70* (Washington, 1959), pamphlet OE-54002, tables 1 and 3; A. J. Brumbaugh (ed.), *American Universities and Colleges*, 5th ed. (Washington, 1948), tables 1–3; and Mary Irwin (ed.), *American Universities and Colleges*, 8th ed. (Washington, 1960), 1146.

[7] W. Stull Holt, "Historical Scholarship," in Merle Curti (ed.), *American Scholarship in the Twentieth Century* (Cambridge, Mass., 1953), 86–87; Marcus W. Jernegan, "Productivity of Doctors of Philosophy in History," *American Historical Review*, XXXIII (October, 1927), 20.

since 1951-1952 has fluctuated sharply. Because production was swelled by returning veterans in the years just after World War II, the increase during the last ten years has been somewhat less rapid than in previous decades (see Table 2-2). The average annual production of history Ph.D.s in the period 1953-1960 was about 319. Comparison with the social sciences, with Education, and with English shows that in some related disciplines Ph.D. production through 1959 was somewhat like that in history but that increases in other fields were even larger (see Table 2-3). Yet history has

TABLE 2-2

RECENT PRODUCTION OF PH.D.s IN HISTORY, 1953-1960

Academic year ending	No. of Ph.D.s in history	No. of Ph.D.s in all fields	% of all doctorates accounted for by Ph.D.s in history
1953	301	8,309	3.6
1954	355	8,996	3.9
1955	310	8,840	3.5
1956	259	8,903	2.9
1957	314	8,756	3.6
1958	297	8,942	3.3
1959	324* (350)	9,360	3.5
1960	342† (365)	9,869	3.5

* Tabulations by the Office of Education for the academic year 1958-1959 show 9,360 Ph.D.s in all fields, 324 of them in history. Our own survey of history departments brought reports of 350 Ph.D.s in history in the calendar year 1959.

† Estimate based on reports by chairmen of history departments.

SOURCE: History and general statistics through 1958 are provided by Walter Crosby Eells in Mary Irwin (ed.), *American Universities and Colleges*, 8th ed. (Washington, 1960), 1146; U.S. Department of Health, Education, and Welfare, *Earned Degrees Conferred, 1958-1959: Bachelor's and Higher Degrees* (Washington, 1961), 31, 35. The 1960 statistics were provided by Mabel C. Rice, U.S. Office of Education.

TABLE 2-3

RECENT PRODUCTION OF PH.D.S IN HISTORY AND COMPARABLE DISCIPLINES, 1953-1959

Discipline	Ph.D.s awarded, 1953, and changes (in % of 1953)							
	1953		1954	1955	1956	1957	1958	1959
	No.	%						
History	301	100	118	103	86	104	99	108
Political science	164	100	93	110	124	95	104	116
Sociology	157	100	117	106	108	85	96	100
English	328	100	109	104	116	107	102	114
Economics	223	100	110	109	132	141	140	99
Education	1,357	100	110	108	117	133	151	119

SOURCE: The Education statistics were taken from: American Association of Colleges for Teacher Education, "Preliminary Report of an Inquiry into Conditions Affecting the Pursuit of Doctoral Degrees in Education: Administrator's Phase," mimeographed report issued by the School of Education, University of Denver, 1959 (p. 1.18). Other statistics for 1953-1958 used in this table are those of Walter Crosby Eells in Mary Irwin (ed.), *American Universities and Colleges*, 8th ed. (Washington, 1960), 1146. Statistics for 1959 were provided by the U.S. Office of Education.

continued to produce more Ph.D.s than any of the social sciences (see Table 2-4).

Prospects for an increase in doctoral production in history depend upon the number of students in residence, currently and in the near future. Recent trends in the award of bachelor's and master's degrees in history are shown in Table 2-5. In history as in other fields there was a "post-G.I. Bill" slump. The popularity of the master's degree in history dropped substantially after 1948 but increased after 1956. The marked increase in 1959, which augurs well for doctoral production in the early 1960s, apparently was due to the national fellowship programs. It is also encouraging to note the large absolute increase in bachelor's graduates in history. History's percentage of all bachelor's degrees in the nation has held its own and even slightly increased in recent years. All in all, the

TABLE 2-4

TOTAL PH.D. PRODUCTION IN SELECTED SOCIAL SCIENCES, 1926–1957

Period	History		Economics		Political science		Sociology		All fields
	No.	% of total	No.	% of total	No.	% of total	No.	% of total	Total No. of Ph.D.s
1926–1937 (12 years)....	1,448	5.6	1,410	5.4	524	2.0	490	1.9	25,871
1938–1947 (10 years)....	1,219	4.8	1,185	4.7	475	1.9	604	2.4	25,381
1948–1957 (10 years)....	2,830	3.8	2,254	3.0	1,501	2.0	1,329	1.8	74,497
Total......	5,497	4.4	4,849	3.8	2,500	2.0	2,423	1.9	125,749

SOURCE: Data provided by Walter Crosby Eells in Mary Irwin (ed.), *American Universities and Colleges*, 8th ed. (Washington, 1960), 1146. Cf. Marshall E. Dimock and Claude E. Hawley (eds.), *Goals for Political Science*, report of the committee for the Advancement of Teaching of the American Political Science Association (New York, 1951), 247–249.

possibilities of increased doctoral production in history are present.

The possibilities will not fully materialize, however, unless more women are encouraged to undertake doctoral studies. Some 30% of the current undergraduate history majors are women; but—for whatever reason[8]—in the period 1920–1950 women accounted for only about 14% of the Ph.D.s awarded in all disciplines. A study of 2,562 active historians in 1952 showed that 13% were women. The percentage today probably is no higher, for of the new Ph.D.s in history 10% in 1956–1957, 11% in 1957–1958, and 14.8% in 1958–1959 were awarded to women. Thus, if any sure lesson can be drawn from the development of doctoral training in history in the United States it is that 13% to 15% of the history Ph.D.s—probably no more—will be women.[9]

[8] Logan Wilson, in *The Academic Man: A Study in the Sociology of a Profession* (London, New York, and Toronto, 1942), 137, suggests one.

[9] J. F. Wellemeyer, Jr., "Survey of United States Historians, 1952, and a Forecast," *American Historical Review*, LXI (January, 1956), 341; Walter Crosby Eells, "Earned Doctorates in American Institutions of Higher Education, 1861–

TABLE 2-5

BACHELOR'S, MASTER'S, AND DOCTORAL DEGREES IN HISTORY, 1948-1960

Academic year ending	Bachelor's degrees in history		Master's degrees in history		Ph.D. degrees in history		Advanced degrees in history per 100 bachelor's degrees in history	
	No.	% of all bachelor's degrees	No.	% of all master's degrees	No.	% of all doctoral degrees	Master's	Ph.D.
1948	9,245	3.4	1,566	3.7	162	3.9	16.9	1.7
1955	9,540	3.3	1,199	2.0	310	3.5	12.6	3.2
1956	10,540	3.4	1,114	1.9	259	2.9	10.6	2.4
1957	11,692	3.4	1,256	2.0	314	3.6	10.7	2.7
1958	12,883	3.5	1,397	2.1	297	3.3	10.8	2.3
1959	13,742	3.6	1,643	2.4	324 (350)*	3.5	11.9	2.3
1960	14,753	3.8	1,794	2.4	342	3.5	12.2	2.3

* See note under Table 2-2.
SOURCE: Based upon data in the following volumes of the serial publication of the U.S. Department of Health, Education, and Welfare, *Earned Degrees Conferred by Higher Educational Institutions:* for the statistics on production in *1947–1948* (Washington, n.d.), table D; for *1954–1955* (Washington, 1956), table 3; for *1955–1956* (Washington, 1958), table 7; for *1956–1957* (Washington, 1958), table 5; for *1957–1958* (Washington, 1959), table 6; and for *1958–1959* (Washington, 1961), 31, 35, 38. Statistics for 1960 by Mabel C. Rice, U.S. Office of Education.

Another lesson that may be drawn is that 7 out of 8 Ph.D.s in history in the 1960s will be college teachers of history. In 1939 probably no more than two-thirds of the history Ph.D.s of 1931–1935 were engaged in teaching in universities, colleges, and junior colleges, but others would have been teaching if they could have found positions. Fletcher Wellemeyer has shown that "over 80 per cent" of the historians of 1952 were "engaged in teaching." *Of the history Ph.D.s of 1958, 88% held academic posts by the*

1955," *Higher Education*, XII (March, 1956), 110; U.S. Department of Health, Education, and Welfare, *Earned Degrees Conferred by Higher Educational Institutions, 1956–1957* (Washington, 1958), 12; *1957–1958* (Washington, 1959), 8; and *1958–1959* (Washington, 1961), 173. For literature on the role of women in higher education see Walter Crosby Eells, *College Teachers and College Teaching: An Annotated Bibliography on College and University Faculty Members and Instructional Methods* (Atlanta, 1957), 127–128.

fall of 1959 (including the 3% in nonteaching academic positions).[10]

Because of the high percentage of history Ph.D.s that become college and university teachers year after year, history faculties have a larger share of Ph.D.s than do most other academic disciplines. About 65% of the historians on college and university faculties hold the Ph.D.[11] What is more, there has been no decrease since 1952, when a survey of 2,562 active historians showed that 63% of them had doctoral degrees. This helps explain why most of the historians who were interviewed in 1959 showed little concern about an *immediate* shortage of Ph.D.s in history.[12]

[10] For the 1939 statistics see Hesseltine and Kaplan, "Doctors of Philosophy in History," 775, 789; for 1952 see Wellemeyer, "Survey of United States Historians, 1952," 348; for 1958 see appendix H of this volume for information about a questionnaire completed by 182 Ph.D.s of 1958, of whom 177 answered the question about current occupations. See also National Education Association (Ray C. Maul, ed.), *Teacher Supply and Demand in Universities, Colleges, and Junior Colleges, 1957–58 and 1958–59* (Washington, 1959), 45. In one place Ray C. Maul reports that 90% of history Ph.D.s go into academic work. In another place he suggests 75.8%. The last estimate seems much too low.

[11] See National Education Association, *Research Bulletin*, XXXII (December, 1954), 164, for statistics on faculty in all fields. The statistics on historians have been compiled from questionnaires completed by heads of departments in junior colleges, colleges, and universities. For information on these questionnaires see appendixes A, B, C, and F. Up-to-date statistics on total faculty are not available, and it should be remembered that the percentage of Ph.D.s on college faculties (total fields) has declined since 1953–1954. It should also be noted that the 4,516 history teachers whose degrees were reported to this committee include all the faculties of history departments that offer Ph.D. training. Their very large percentage of Ph.D.s may make our percentage of 68% for the 4,516 somewhat larger than the percentage of Ph.D.s among all history teachers in higher education. Even allowing for this, it seems highly probable that at least 65% of *all* the history teachers in the nation's colleges, junior colleges, and universities have the Ph.D. (The total number of history teachers above the high school level is not known. Perhaps in 1959–1960 there were about eight thousand of them.)

[12] Wellemeyer, "Survey of United States Historians, 1952," 345. For a report on the interviews of some 230 historians in 1959 see appendix E. Separate presentations of data on the percentages of faculty members holding the Ph.D. in junior colleges, colleges, and universities appear in chap. 4, below. They bear out the estimate that at least 65% of the nation's history teachers in higher education hold the Ph.D.

FUTURE NEED FOR PH.D.S IN HISTORY

The basic element of uncertainty in predicting future needs is our inability to know how many persons will seek instruction in colleges and universities in the future. The National Education Association (NEA) and Bernard Berelson agree that 6 million students in 1969–1970 is a reasonable prediction. But no one can know exactly what the teacher-student ratio will be in 1969–1970; another unknown is the annual rate of replacement of existing faculties. The NEA estimates a need for 346,800 new college teachers in the eleven-year period 1959–1970, while Berelson believes that 180,000 new teachers will suffice.

These general estimates provide, therefore, only a broad framework for any prediction of the number of historians needed in the 1960s; yet these are the most up-to-date and best-informed estimates. Other questions arise. Will historians continue to make up 3.4% of the total national faculty in higher education—as in 1959–1960? Will 65% of the history faculty continue to be holders of the Ph.D.—thus maintaining the approximate standard of 1959–1960? Will the Ph.D.s in history who become college and university teachers of history be 85% of all Ph.D.s produced, as in recent years? If the answer to each of these questions is "yes," then the total production of Ph.D.s in history, 1959–1970, must fall between a low of 4,680 and a high of 9,024, depending upon whether Berelson's estimate or that of the NEA is used. Reduced to average annual production, between 425 and 820 history Ph.D.s per year will be needed during the 1960s.[13]

Obviously this gives little help to graduate faculties in history as they plan their Ph.D. programs for the 1960s. Another estimate of the number of history Ph.D.s that will be needed is here suggested, therefore. This one also rests upon certain assumptions: (1) that a rising student-faculty ratio will just about counterbalance any increase in the percentage of college-age population enrolling in college during the 1960s; and, therefore, (2) that the

[13] National Education Association, *Teacher Supply and Demand* . . . *1957–58 and 1958–59*, 50–51; Berelson, *Graduate Education*, 76–78.

new history faculty needed each year will increase in direct proportion to the increase in the number of 18-year-olds in the national population.

It is also possible to predict the increase in the number of entering history graduate students *in the nation* if we assume, further, that students enter at 22 and that their numbers will rise in proportion to the number of 22-year-olds in the national population. Finally, it is possible to predict how many history Ph.D.s are *likely to be awarded* annually if we make the following additional assumptions: (1) that Ph.D.s in history will be awarded the degree at a median age of 31 (the median age of the history Ph.D.s of 1958 was about 33.5); and (2) that their increase will be in direct proportion to the increase in number of 31-year-olds in the nation. Table 2-6 shows the projections that can be made if all these sets of assumptions are accepted.

Table 2-6 can be extremely useful in that it suggests the sharp variability that the trends in live births will impose upon higher education during the 1960s. It cautions against complacency by showing that *a shortage of Ph.D.s in history is likely to make itself felt in 1964*, giving little notice of its coming except for the temporary warning in 1960–1961 resulting from the increased births of 1942 (10.6% more than in 1941). In 1964 the number of 18-year-olds will jump sharply (19.3%) just when the number of 31-year-olds (born in 1933) will reach the lowest level of the whole period 1945–1970. Reports of placement officers in 16 universities[14] show that in most fields of history there is no significant backlog of unemployed Ph.D.s who can help meet the rising demand of the 1960s. The new talent that can be discovered must meet most of the needs of the next decade.

Sustained efforts to recruit superior students will be needed throughout the 1960s, because another sizable increase in live births, that of 1951 (6.3% more than in 1950), will make itself felt in college enrollments in 1969–1970—bringing another increase in the demand for college teachers. Meanwhile, there will be no sub-

[14] For a list of the 16 institutions whose placement officers completed our questionnaire see appendix G.

TABLE 2-6

PREDICTED QUANTITATIVE TRENDS IN GRADUATE EDUCATION IN HISTORY, 1959–1970, BASED UPON INCREASES IN LIVE BIRTHS*

Live births		Probable annual production of history Ph.D.s, assuming 31 is the age at which award is made		History Ph.D.s likely to be needed to meet rising enrollments	Probable entering history graduate students in percentages of 1959–1960 level	
Year of birth	No. (in millions)	Year	No.†	No.‡	Year	Level (in %)§
1928	2.674	1959	350	350	1959	100
1929	2.582	1960	338	387	1960	103
1930	2.618	1961	343	402	1961	102
1931	2.506	1962	328	380	1962	106
1932	2.440	1963	319	370	1963	112
1933	2.307	1964	302	442	1964	124
1934	2.396	1965	314	495	1965	129
1935	2.377	1966	311	471	1966	122
1936	2.355	1967	308	472	1967	118
1937	2.413	1968	316	470	1968	141
1938	2.496	1969	327	499	1969	158
1939	2.466	1970	323	506	1970	151
1940	2.559	....	...	...	....	...
1941	2.703	....	...	...	....	...
1942	2.989	....	...	...	....	...
1943	3.104	....	...	...	....	...
1944	2.939	....	...	...	....	...
1945	2.858	....	...	...	....	...
1946	3.411	....	...	...	....	...
1947	3.817	....	...	...	....	...
1948	3.637	....	...	...	....	...
1949	3.649	....	...	...	....	...
1950	3.627	....	...	...	....	...
1951	3.856	....	...	...	....	...
1952	3.912	....	...	...	....	...

* The projections in this table assume no change in factors encouraging graduate study and completion of the Ph.D. See text for qualifications.
† Annual variations in this column are in proportion to variations in numbers of births, 1928–1939, and thus in proportion to presumed numbers of thirty-one-year-olds, 1959–1970.
‡ Annual variations in this column are in proportion to variations in numbers of births, 1941–1952, and thus in proportion to presumed numbers of eighteen year-olds, 1959–1970.
§ Annual variations in this column are in proportion to variations in numbers of births, 1937–1948, and thus in proportion to presumed numbers of twenty-two-year-olds, 1959–1970.
SOURCE: Live-birth statistics from the National Education Association's *Research Bulletin*, XXXV (October, 1957), 104.

stantial increase in the number of 31-year-olds until 1972. It is desirable, therefore, to find ways to award Ph.D.s to the majority of doctoral candidates before they reach the projected median age of 31, and well before they reach the actual median age of the Ph.D.s in history of 1958, about 33.5.

Yet, it is very important to note that Table 2-6 presents a model projection based on live-birth trends. It shows what might be expected to happen if the factors making for Ph.D. production in 1959 were to be neither increased nor decreased. In actuality, however, the national fellowship programs inaugurated or greatly expanded since 1956 are new factors of major importance. If they continue and increase their financial support for graduate study, the demand for historians in the 1960s can be met. It is noteworthy that the number of Ph.D.s in history granted in 1960—approximately 342—somewhat exceeded the number that might have been expected on the basis of birth trends (338; see Table 2-6). It appears, therefore, that the effect of increased financial support since the mid-1950s is already being felt.

Other qualifications of the yearly trends predicted in Table 2-6 must be noted. Table 2-6 makes the annual peaks and valleys of supply and demand sharper than they will be in reality. It is worthwhile, therefore, to calculate the *average* annual production and need for Ph.D.s for three periods. Our predicted averages fall much closer to Berelson's conservative estimate than to the NEA prediction. They confront historians with a challenge, but one that can be met without encouraging less-than-superior students to undertake graduate study and without encouraging unprepared departments to offer Ph.D. training. The immediate tasks are: (1) to raise average annual production of Ph.D.s from the 319 of 1953–1960 and the estimated 365 of 1960 to an average of 378 per year in the period 1959–1963; and (2) to recruit superior students who can be expected to earn the Ph.D. between 1964 and 1970. About 470 will be needed annually, 1964–1968, and 502 will be needed annually in the period 1969–1970.

It must be emphasized that we have discussed the expected need for new *Ph.D.s,* not the expected need for new college teachers of history. If we speak in terms of new teachers rather than new Ph.D.s, then we must talk in terms of at least 672 annually (Berelson's statistics suggest 556; NEA statistics, 1,073) for the eleven-year period 1959–1970.

Still another point must be emphasized here. The number of new Ph.D.s in history that we have estimated to be needed will result in no increase at all in the percentage of Ph.D.s on history faculties; they will only maintain the standards of preparation already achieved in the 1950s. Is that enough? One of the dismal aspects of many similar estimates of need for new faculty in the 1960s is their tendency to abandon a traditional American determination to raise the qualifications of college teachers. Too often it is suggested that mere preservation of the *status quo* will be triumph enough in the 1960s. It will be a strange and disturbing new epoch in the history of American higher education if the generation of the 1960s is willing to settle for no more than that.

VARIATIONS IN SUPPLY AND DEMAND

Programs for training Ph.D.s in history are too complex to be created suddenly and they can seldom be expanded swiftly. Thus patterns of the production of Ph.D.s in the various regions of the nation and in the diverse fields of history will probably continue for some time to resemble those of the recent past.

In the period 1936–1956 the regions of the nation accounted for the following percentages of all 4,240 history Ph.D.s produced: East, 44%; Midwest, 29%; West, 15%; South, 12%.[15] Table 2-7

[15] National Academy of Sciences-National Research Council (M. H. Trytten and L. R. Harmon), *Doctorate Production in United States Universities, 1936–1956, with Baccalaureate Origins of Doctorates in the Sciences, Arts, and Humanities* (Washington, 1958), table 3.

Throughout this study the following regional classifications will be used: *East:* Maine, New Hampshire, Vermont, Massachusetts, Rhode Island, Connecticut, New York, New Jersey, Pennsylvania, Delaware, Maryland, West Virginia, and the District of Columbia. *South:* Virginia, North Carolina, South Carolina, Georgia, Florida, Alabama, Mississippi, Louisiana, Texas, Oklahoma, Arkansas, Tennessee, and Kentucky. *Midwest:* Ohio, Indiana, Illinois, Michigan, Wiscon-

TABLE 2-7

REGIONAL VARIATIONS IN PRODUCTION OF 1,482 PH.D.s, 1955-1960

Region	Percentage of total reported Ph.D.s				
	1955	1956	1957	1958	1959
East*	43	41	42	47	43
South*	16	18	13	17	14
Midwest*	26	26	33	24	28
West*	15	14	12	12	15

* For definition, see footnote 15 for this chapter.
SOURCE: Based upon questionnaires completed for this study by chairmen of 81 departments offering Ph.D. training in history, 1955-1959. See appendix F.

shows what the regional patterns of productivity have been in recent years. In the production of Ph.D.s in history as in the natural sciences[16] the South lags decisively behind other regions of the nation. Regional variations in current graduate enrollments make it possible to predict that the pattern of Ph.D. production revealed by Table 2-7 will continue into the early 1960s (see Table 2-8).

Differences in production among the various fields of history are of more immediate significance than are regional variations in production. Historians, like other scholars, specialize, and predictions of supply and demand must take cognizance of their specialties. Historians may specialize in the history of one facet of human experience (e.g., in intellectual history or diplomatic history). They also may specialize in a larger or smaller geographical region (e.g., in Russian history, or the history of the South in the United States). Historians specialize, too, in limited periods of history. Thus a Ph.D. candidate may elect to concentrate on the history of

---

sin, Minnesota, Iowa, Missouri, Kansas, and Nebraska. *West:* South Dakota, North Dakota, Montana, Wyoming, Colorado, New Mexico, Arizona, Nevada, Utah, Idaho, Washington, Oregon, California, Hawaii, and Alaska.

[16] R. H. Knapp and H. B. Goodrich, *The Origins of American Scientists* (Chicago, 1952), 45, 53.

TABLE 2-8

REGIONAL DISTRIBUTION OF PH.D. CANDIDATES IN HISTORY IN 80 UNIVERSITIES, 1958–1959

Status of candidates	East		South		Midwest		West		Nation	
	No.	% of total	No.	% of total	No.	% of total	No.	% of total	No.	%
Ph.D. candidates on campus.....	919	47	293	15	469	24	274	14	1,955	100
Ph.D. candidates off campus.....	592	49	162	13	310	26	146	12	1,210	100

SOURCE: Based upon data provided by chairmen of 81 Ph.D.-training departments of history. Unless otherwise noted, the data for subsequent tables were gathered as set frth in appendixes A–K.

Europe since 1789 and more particularly on the *political* history of *France* in the period *1870–1940.*

Historians in the United States have shown a stronger interest in "modern" history (the period since about 1500 A.D.)—and even "recent" history (since about 1900)—than in ancient or medieval history. This is no new trend; of the 1,410 new Ph.D.s of 1929–1939, no less than 92% were specialists in modern history. At least 88%—and probably somewhat more—of the new Ph.D.s of 1955–1959 were specialists in modern history.[17]

More American historians have specialized in the history of their own country than in the history of any other nation. We have moved a long way from the situation of 1890, when Herbert Baxter Adams wrote that he wanted "a fair field for comparative studies in Church and State and the Institutes of Education, with-

[17] A. J. Brumbaugh (ed.), *American Universities and Colleges,* 5th ed. (Washington, 1948), tables 1–3; questionnaires completed by chairmen of 81 history departments that offer Ph.D. training. Henceforth in this study the questionnaires that have already been cited will not be footnoted. When data in the text are not accounted for in the footnotes the reader may assume that they are derived from one or another of the data-gathering tools described in the appendixes.

out being regarded as an American provincial." In the entire period 1873–1935, 57% of all Ph.D.s in history were awarded in American history (including a small percentage in Latin-American history). And 51% of the new Ph.D.s in history in the five-year period 1955–1959 were specialists in United States history.[18]

But it would be a mistake to assume that historians in the United States are especially provincial. More history of foreign areas is taught in the United States than in any other nation in the world. Only in the South is the historical study of foreign areas markedly underdeveloped, and there the study of England and Latin America are exceptions to the prevailing pattern of concentration in United States history.[19] In the nation as a whole a significant number of Ph.D.s in European history have been trained. They accounted for 12% of those who became Ph.D.s in history between 1880 and 1900, 35% of those in the period 1926–1935, and 38% of those in recent years. (Ancient and medieval history and the history of all modern European nations—including England and the U.S.S.R. or Russia—are treated here as "European" history.) The production of specialists in Russian history still appears to be much lower than it should be, although "the past decade has witnessed a virtual revolution in Russian studies."[20] Asian, African, and Latin-American history have almost held their own in the post-1945 period, but it may seem surprising that they have done no more than that in an age of "cold war" and of rising concern about the "uncommitted" or "underdeveloped" countries (see Table 2-9).

One development could change the pattern of Ph.D. production revealed by Table 2-9: if demand in one or another field should rise or fall substantially, in time the production of Ph.D.s would

---

[18] Holt essay in Curti (ed.), *American Scholarship in the Twentieth Century*, 100–101; Hesseltine and Kaplan, "Doctors of Philosophy in History," 776–777; Wellemeyer, "Survey of United States Historians, 1952," 342–344; and data on 1,455 new Ph.D.s, 1955–1959, reported by the Ph.D.-training departments to this committee.

[19] See John L. Snell (ed.), *European History in the South: Opportunities and Problems in Graduate Study* (New Orleans, 1959).

[20] Cyril E. Black and John M. Thompson (eds.), *American Teaching About Russia* (Bloomington, Ind., 1959), 22–113.

TABLE 2-9

PH.D.s IN HISTORY BY GEOGRAPHICAL AREAS
OF SPECIALIZATION, 1873–1959

Geographical area	Percentage of all new Ph.D.s in history 1873–1935	Percentage of all new Ph.D.s in history 1955–1959
American history (total)	57	55.5
United States	x*	51.0
Latin-American	x	4.6
European history (total)	33	38.4
Modern European	x	24.0
English-British Commonwealth	x	7.9
Medieval	x	5.1
Ancient	x	0.7
Russian-Slavic	x	0.7
Asian-African history	5	3.8
Other history	5	2.3

* Data not available.
SOURCE: Based upon data reported to this committee together with statistics in William B. Hesseltine and Louis Kaplan, "Doctors of Philosophy in History: A Statistical Study," *American Historical Review*, XLVII (July, 1942), 774, 776–777.

be adjusted to meet the new situation. In estimating future needs for history Ph.D.s it is essential to know how demand is now distributed among the various fields of history.

In the fall of 1959, chairmen of Ph.D.-training history departments were asked about the supply and demand for new Ph.D.s, as they had experienced it, in the period 1957–1959. The supply of new Ph.D.s in United States history seems to exceed the demand, say 19% of the respondents; the demand seems to exceed the supply, say 46%. Only 7% of the respondents say that the supply of Ph.D.s exceeds the demand in modern European history; 65% report that demand exceeds supply. Obviously the demand for Ph.D.s in modern European history is less often being satisfied than is the demand for Ph.D.s in United States history. But graduate history departments in all regions of the nation report a shortage more often than a surplus of Ph.D.s. Although more Ph.D.s in history were awarded in 1959 and again in 1960 than in any year since 1954, they did not glut the market. There were more positions than new Ph.D.s in both major fields of history.

What about other fields of history? In November, 1958, the chairmen of 77 Ph.D.-training departments of history and 502 college departments were asked to list the appointments in history they expected to make between 1959 and 1970. Only the returns for the period 1959–1961 were full enough to be useful. The specific fields in which appointments were anticipated are ranked in Table 2-10 according to the frequency with which they were reported. Table 2-10 also shows for comparative purposes the potential supply of Ph.D.s by specifying the fields of specialization among Ph.D. candidates "enrolled and on campus" in 81 Ph.D.-training departments of history in 1958–1959.

In yet another attempt to discover the relation between demand

TABLE 2-10

ANTICIPATED FACULTY APPOINTMENTS AND PH.D. CANDIDATES IN VARIOUS FIELDS OF HISTORY, 1958–1959

Fields of history	No. and % of all anticipated appointments for 1959–1961	No. and % of all Ph.D. candidates in residence, first term of 1958–1959
United States	121 (35%)	957 (55%)
Modern Europe	105 (30%)	483 (28%)
Russia-East Europe	25 (7%)	
Asia and Far East	29 (8%)	59 (3%)
Medieval	21 (6%)	68 (4%)
Latin America	12 (3.5%)	67 (4%)
English-British Commonwealth	10 (3%)	81 (5%)
Ancient	7 (2%)	19 (1%)
Africa	1 (0.3%)	1 (0.05%)
Other	16 (5%)	0 (0%)
Total	347 (99.8%)	1,735 (100.05%)

and supply in various fields of history, chairmen of Ph.D.-training departments were asked, in November, 1959, to name the fields in which they noted either a current shortage or a current surplus, and those in which they expected the shortage or surplus to continue. It appears from these reports that good positions for new Ph.D.s in some fields of United States history, in English-British Commonwealth history, and in Latin-American history may be difficult to find during the next several years. On the other hand, an increased number of able Ph.D.s in all fields should have no difficulty in finding college teaching positions of one type or another during the 1960s.[21]

SUMMARY

The picture of the coming decade that we have painted looks very different from different perspectives. To the graduate student or the young Ph.D. it shows positions available and reasonably rapid professional advancement likely in most fields of history. To those responsible for securing qualified faculty members it shows a shortage of qualified teachers in these fields of history.

Several things could change our basic predictions. The estimates given in Table 2-6 assume that conditions will be those of peacetime; that a substitute doctorate—specifically for college teachers and cheaper than the Ph.D.—will not be offered;[22] that the one-year master's degree will not become an acceptable qualification for a permanent college teaching position;[23] that historians will not teach radically larger classes than those they were teaching in

[21] See American Council of Learned Societies *Newsletter*, X (June, 1959), 3–4, on the shortage of specialists in the history of religions.

[22] The Committee of Fifteen refused to endorse the idea of a second doctorate. The following recent renewal of the idea has won very little sympathy among historians: Earl J. McGrath, *The Graduate School and the Decline of Liberal Education* (New York, 1959). Berelson cautiously suggests that it "might be tried," but he admits that "only college presidents and people from departments of education favor it" (Berelson, *Graduate Education*, 250–251, 90).

[23] See also Berelson, *Graduate Education*, 91, and chap. 5, below.

1959–1960; and that television sets will not be widely used in history classrooms as substitutes for teachers.[24] Different assumptions would lead to lower estimates of the number of Ph.D.s in history that will be needed. Different assumptions have not seemed warranted.

Prediction of the future need for Ph.D.s involves many variables. The two best general estimates of need for Ph.D.s—those by Berelson and the NEA—differ widely, as we have shown. Using our own method of calculation (explained on pages 23–26) we conclude that we will need an average of 378 Ph.D.s per year, 1959–1963; 470 per year, 1964–1968; and 502 per year in 1969 and 1970. The probable growth of junior college and other professional demands for Ph.D.s, which were not included in our calculations, may well create a need for many more Ph.D.s than has been suggested here.[25] An increase over the present percentage of teachers who hold the Ph.D. would also require more Ph.D.s than have been predicted.

[24] On the methods being used to meet increasing enrollments and teacher shortages see U.S. Department of Health, Education, and Welfare (Clarence B. Lindquist), *College and University Faculties: Recent Personnel and Instructional Practices* (Washington, 1959), 21–23. Many history departments already have higher student-faculty ratios than were suggested as desirable by Beardsley Ruml and Donald H. Morrison, *Memo to a College Trustee: A Report on Financial and Structural Problems of the Liberal College* (New York, 1959). For a thoughtful justification of large classes see Eric A. Walker, "Quality in Quantity," *Educational Record*, XL (April, 1959), 129–136. For a cogent criticism of large classes see Bruce R. Morris, "Faculty Salaries, Class Size, and Sound Education," *American Association of University Professors Bulletin*, XLV (June, 1959), 196–202. On the pros and cons of educational television a large body of literature already exists. For bibliography see Walter Crosby Eells, *College Teachers and College Teaching*, 195–203. See especially John C. Adams and others, *College Teaching by Television* (Washington, 1958). A special "Committee on Utilization of College Teaching Resources" of the Fund for the Advancement of Education recommends teaching by television, large classes, small classes, and—for good measure—no classes (independent study): *Better Utilization of College Teaching Resources* (New York, 1959).

[25] See, e.g., T. C. Holy and others, *A Study of Faculty Demand and Supply in California Higher Education, 1957–1970* (Berkeley and Sacramento, 1958), especially 16–25, 52–54, 59–61.

The demand for Ph.D.s in history is not evenly distributed. In 1959 there appeared to be a slight surplus of Ph.D.s in some fields of American history and a very slight surplus in British and Latin-American history. In other fields increasing numbers of Ph.D.s would help meet existing shortages. Regardless of fields and to a degree true of few other disciplines, Ph.D.s in history are headed toward teaching. This fact is of the utmost importance in the training process, and much will be said of it hereafter.

Can the required number of Ph.D. candidates be found? If our estimate of actual 1960 production as 365 is accurate, only a slight increase is needed to meet the expected demand of 1961-1963. Thanks to the Woodrow Wilson and National Defense Fellowships there is likely to be no serious shortage of Ph.D.s in some fields of history before 1964.

The needed increase in number of Ph.D.s for the years 1964-1970 (and, we repeat, such an increase is desirable), will be accomplished in most fields of history gradually and without emergency measures. What is especially needed now are (1) some acceleration of Ph.D. training and (2) more attention by historians to recruiting students for graduate study.

Chapter 3

GRADUATE STUDENTS IN HISTORY

"A basic aim of our society is to help each individual to fulfill the promise that is in him."[1] This is an American dream, and changes in world affairs have made it an American necessity. It is in the interest of the individual and of the nation that students capable of undertaking graduate study be discovered and encouraged, in history no less than in other fields. For as Lord Acton so aptly put it, history "must be our deliverer not only from the undue influence of other times, but from the undue influence of our own, from the tyranny of environment and the pressure of the air we breathe."[2]

Already large numbers of college students are going on to graduate study. One out of forty persons who earn bachelor's degrees earns a Ph.D.; in 1900 only 1 in 60 did so.[3] Some 270,000 to

---

[1] Carnegie Foundation for the Advancement of Teaching, *Education of the Academically Talented* (reprinted from the 1958–1959 *Annual Report* of the Carnegie Foundation for the Advancement of Teaching), 1.

[2] John Emerich Edward Acton, *Lectures on Modern History* (London, 1907), 33.

[3] Hans Rosenhaupt, *Graduate Students: Experience at Columbia University, 1940–1956* (New York, 1958), 4.

300,000 students are engaged in graduate study, perhaps as many as 8,500 of them majoring in history.[4] Are sufficient numbers of the superior graduate students studying history? Who are the graduate students? Are they offered sufficient financial assistance? What are their career ambitions? Answers to these questions show why historians must recruit students of superior ability for graduate study in history. They also suggest some of the basic conditions that must be considered in recruiting.

ABILITY AND PREPARATION

There are no certain standards of measurement to show the quality of graduate students in history in comparison with those in other fields. In one attempt to discover the ability and preparation of history graduate students, the new Ph.D.s of 1958 were asked to report how their graduate faculties had evaluated their talent for scholarship. More than half (56%) report that they were "rated high." Only 1 out of 8 says "average" or less than average. But many of the Ph.D.s came to graduate school with less than adequate preparation: two-fifths report that they were rated higher during the last year of graduate study than during the first year. Only 1% were rated higher the first year than the last.

The lack of precise standards for measuring scholarly promise makes it inevitable that some students will be admitted to graduate study who will not attain the Ph.D., much less distinction in their professions. Undergraduate grades and scores on admission examinations are helpful but not infallible indices of scholarly potentiality.[5] A study of eminent scientists has concluded that high—

[4] Berelson, *Graduate Education,* 129, estimates the total number of graduate students in 1959 to be 278,000. Eighty Ph.D.-training history departments report the following number of graduate students in 1958–1959: 3,256 master's candidates; 1,555 on-campus doctoral candidates; and 1,210 off-campus doctoral candidates (a total of 6,021 graduate students). Many other graduate students attend institutions that offer the master's degree but not the Ph.D.

[5] See, e.g., Kenneth E. Clark, *America's Psychologists: A Survey of a Growing Profession* (Washington, 1957), 117.

"but not the highest"—intelligence in combination with the greatest degree of persistence will achieve greater eminence than highest intelligence with less persistence.[6]

Ph.D. training attracts students of high intellectual ability. IQ scores of graduate students in law, medicine, and the Ph.D. programs currently differ no more than four points (124 to 128).[7] Elbridge Sibley in 1948 warned that "relatively large numbers of mediocre and inferior students" were being admitted to graduate study in the social sciences, but he concluded that the graduate student bodies in the social sciences were "not greatly inferior in previous scholastic achievement . . . to those in natural science departments."[8]

Judged by grades, history is currently getting a large share of the better students, but not as many as some other disciplines. In an extensive survey of seniors and graduate students in 1957-1958, history graduate students ranked in the upper fifth of their high school classes somewhat more often than did the total sample, but less often than physics and English students. A-average college seniors in history were planning to undertake graduate study as often as the total sample, but a much larger percentage of the A-average physics students (86%; history, 55%) planned graduate study.[9]

Another way to estimate the quality of history graduate students is to compare test scores on the Graduate Record Examination (GRE). These show that history is getting fewer of the best students than graduate faculties in history should hope to attract. A 1952 study of the average scores on the GRE of seniors in 11 colleges showed that in the verbal tests the literature (564), physics

[6] The 1953 conclusion by Anne Roe is quoted by R. W. Gerard (with M. L. N. Bach), *Mirror to Physiology: A Self-Survey of Physiological Science* (Washington, 1958), 75.

[7] Berelson, *Graduate Education*, 154.

[8] Elbridge Sibley, *The Recruitment, Selection, and Training of Social Scientists* (New York, 1948), 29-31, 38-39, 128.

[9] George L. Gropper and Robert Fitzpatrick, *Who Goes to Graduate School? A Study of the Decision to Enter Graduate Training* (Pittsburgh, 1959), 46, 48, 50. There were 221 history students in the sample.

(531), and psychology (527) majors ranked higher than those in history (517). The history majors ranked higher than the other social science majors.[10] (Woodrow Wilson Fellows in the sciences in 1958–1959 "wrote better essays than the candidates in the humanities and social sciences."[11]) A survey of the GRE scores of 910 senior history majors of 1955–1957 shows that the mean score in history was 561. One-fourth (24%) scored higher than 640. An equal number scored lower than 500.[12] Thus graduate schools admitting history students in 1955–1957 with scores of less than 520 on the verbal test (24%) and less than 500 on the history test were admitting persons relatively weak in preparedness for graduate study.

Specific inadequacies of undergraduate training often trouble graduate students in history. Table 3-1 shows the types of undergraduate training that Ph.D.s of 1958 report as "greatly inadequate." One can safely conclude that potential graduate students in history need better preparation than many have been getting in historiography and the methods of historical research as well as in languages.

There are other shortcomings. The core of undergraduate preparation for graduate study in history is a major in history for 3 out of 4 graduate students in history, and this is good.[13] But history

[10] See Educational Testing Service, *Graduate Record Examinations Scores for Basic Reference Groups* (Princeton and Los Angeles, n.d.), tables 1–6, 9; Sibley, *The Recruitment, Selection, and Training of Social Scientists*, 29–31; ETS, *National Program for Graduate School Selection: Score Interpretation Handbook for Deans and Advisers, November, 1959* . . . (Princeton and Los Angeles, n.d.), 14–16. See also mimeographed report by Gerald V. Lannholm and Barbara Pitcher, "Mean Score Changes on the Graduate Record Examinations Area Tests for College Students Tested Three Times in a Four-year Period," prepared in 1959 for the Educational Testing Service (Princeton), which provided us with a copy.
[11] Woodrow Wilson National Fellowship Foundation, *Report for 1959* (n.p. [Princeton?], n.d. [1960?]), 69.
[12] ETS, *National Program for Graduate School Selection*, 14–19.
[13] This proportion is based upon data from 312 recent Ph.D.s in history. Of the 312, 169 are from our sample of 1958 Ph.D.s. The data on 143 other Ph.D.s in history were provided by the Southern Regional Education Board through the courtesy of Dr. John K. Folger.

TABLE 3-1

INADEQUACIES OF UNDERGRADUATE PREPARATION FOR GRADUATE STUDY IN HISTORY REPORTED BY 182 HISTORY PH.D.s OF 1958

Order of inadequacy	Type of preparation	Number reporting "greatly inadequate"	% of total reporting "greatly inadequate"
1	Use of a second foreign language as a research skill	98	54
2	Preparation in philosophies of history and historiography	78	43
3	Preparation in historical research methods	55	30
4	Use of one foreign language as a research skill	32	18
5	Preparation in any special field of history	29	16
6	General preparation in history	17	9
7	Organizing and writing papers	16	9
8	Development of ability to work independently	11	6
9	General preparation in humanities and social sciences	8	4

graduate students need more undergraduate study in related disciplines than they commonly acquire. A recent study of graduates of four large colleges and universities in three southwestern states[14] shows that no more than 12% of the history majors in any institution took any course in anthropology. In 2 of the 4 institutions almost two-thirds of the history majors took no economics, half or

[14] Paul A. Brinkner, "Our Illiberal Liberal-Arts Colleges," *Journal of Higher Education*, XXXI (March, 1960), tables 2–3 and pp. 136–137.

more took no psychology, and more than one-third took no philosophy. Obviously, large numbers of history majors are not being as liberally educated as they should be for graduate study in history.[15] Preparation in foreign languages, writing and organizing ability, and a general background of liberal education—these are just the qualities graduate faculties in many fields would like students to have when they begin graduate study.[16] History faculties do not differ in this respect. Even for a specialized field like Russian history, the best undergraduate background for graduate study is said to be "general preparation in the social sciences and humanities, sufficient grounding in a single discipline to permit the beginning of disciplinary work at the graduate level without delay, and adequate language preparation." [17]

ACADEMIC AND SOCIAL ORIGINS

Where do graduate students in history come from? Four out of five Ph.D.s in history earn their highest degree at an institution other than the one that awarded the bachelor's degree. In their search for perspective in time and space they come to graduate school from all types of colleges.

Academic legend holds that small colleges are more productive of graduate students than large universities. Statistics support the legend. A 1959 study of 143 recently graduated Ph.D.s in history in the South shows that they hold baccalaureate degrees from 103 institutions, most of them quite small.[18] The Woodrow Wilson Fellows of 1945–1960 were graduates of no less than 560 colleges, and a study of 7,000 younger "scholars" (new Ph.D.s and holders of graduate scholarships in all fields) in 1953 found that they had

[15] *Ibid.*, 136.
[16] Berelson, *Graduate Education*, 141.
[17] Black and Thompson (eds.), *American Teaching About Russia*, 39.
[18] Data provided by Southern Regional Education Board through the courtesy of Dr. John K. Folger. The statement that 80% of Ph.D.s receive their degrees at an institution other than their undergraduate institution is based upon Wellemeyer, "Survey of United States Historians, 1952," 347.

graduated from 562 colleges. Two small colleges—Swarthmore and Reed—produced the highest number of scholars per 1,000 graduates (61 and 53 respectively) according to the 1953 survey.[19] On the other hand, while most teachers' colleges are relatively small, their productivity of scholars per 1,000 graduates (only 2.5) has been lower than universities and liberal arts colleges.[20] The distinction of the faculty and quality of the students are more important factors than size.

Most history graduate students will, in fact, be graduates of the larger institutions. All but 4 of the 25 largest undergraduate producers of history Ph.D.s between 1936 and 1956 were large institutions. The five institutions that most often awarded *bachelor's* degrees to the history Ph.D.s of 1936–1956 are themselves graduate schools that rank among the six largest producers of history Ph.D.s. The lesson is clear that Ph.D.-training departments can find many of the graduate students of the 1960s in their own undergraduate colleges.

Table 3-2 shows institutions that awarded bachelor's degrees to seven or more of the history Ph.D.s of 1936–1956. These 138 institutions accounted for two-thirds of the scholars who won the Ph.D. in history, 1936–1956.

History graduate students are to be found in every cultural, economic, and social stratum of America. Few women earn Ph.D.s, and yet 10% of the 1958 Ph.D.s in history were women. One Negro and two Orientals were in the sample of 182 (two other persons failed to respond to our question about racial origin). Two-thirds (63%) came from Protestant families. In religious background another 20% were Catholic, 13% were Jewish, and 4% were of some other faith, but many of the 1958 Ph.D.s have departed from the religious attachments of their families. Two-thirds of the Ph.D.s

---

[19] Woodrow Wilson National Fellowship Foundation, *Report for 1959*, 11; Robert H. Knapp and Joseph J. Greenbaum, *The Younger American Scholar: His Collegiate Origins* (Chicago, 1953), 11, 16, 70.

[20] *Ibid.*, 77. Apparently institutions with 3,000–5,000 students are the undergraduate colleges of a disproportionately large number of "Significant Contributors" in psychology. Cf. Clark, *America's Psychologists*, 121.

Table 3-2
Leading Baccalaureate Sources of History Ph.D.s, 1936–1956

No.	Institution	No.	Institution	No.	Institution
153	Harvard and Radcliffe (8)	18	Oregon	10	Southwest Missouri State
119	California (Berkeley)	18	Syracuse	9	Augustana (Ill.)
		18	Wayne State	9	Central Missouri State
99	Yale	17	Boston U.		
77	Chicago	17	Brown	9	Colgate
75	Columbia	17	Georgetown	9	Earlham
74	CCNY	16	Baylor	9	Grinnell
69	UCLA	16	DePauw	9	Hamilton
68*	Wisconsin	16	Oklahoma	9	Haverford
67	Princeton	15	Emory	9	Howard
62	Stanford	15	Kansas	9	Knox
52	Texas	15	Western Reserve	9	Louisiana State
51	Michigan	14	Arkansas	9	Rice
48	Illinois	14	Cincinnati	9	Richmond
46	Minnesota	14	Davidson	9	San Jose
42	Amherst	14	Mississippi	9	Tulane
38	Dartmouth	14	Mount Holyoke	9	Walla Walla
36	North Carolina	14	Rutgers	8	Allegheny
31	Oberlin	14	St. Johns (N.Y.)	8	Clark
30	Northwestern	14	Southern California	8	Denver
30	U. of Washington	14	Southern Illinois	8	Georgia
29	Brooklyn	14	Vanderbilt	8	Gettysburg
29	Pittsburgh	13	Washington and Lee	8	Kentucky
28	State U. of Iowa	13	Wheaton (Ill.)	8	Michigan State
28	St. Louis	12	Bowdoin	8	Morningside
26	Catholic	12	Carleton	8	New Mexico
25	Indiana	12	Iowa State Teachers	8	North Texas State
25	Swarthmore			8	Union College (Nebr.)
24	Alabama	12	Occidental		
23	George Washington	12	Reed	8	South Carolina
23	Johns Hopkins	12	Wake Forest	8	Vermont
23	Ohio State	11	Birmingham-Southern	7	Butler
23	Wesleyan			7	Concordia Seminary
22	Cornell	11	Bryn Mawr	7	Creighton
22	Rochester	11	Dickinson	7	Franklin and Marshall
22	Boston College	11	Florida		
21	Colorado	11	Hunter	7	Hiram
21	Missouri	11	Loyola (Ill.)	7	Hobart
21	Nebraska	11	Northeast Missouri State	7	Indiana Central College
21	Pennsylvania				
21	Wellesley	11	Pomona	7	Manhattan
21	Williams	11	Temple	7	Millsaps
21	Wooster	11	Utah	7	U. of Notre Dame
20	Duke	11	Washington U. (Mo.)	7	Ohio Wesleyan
20	Miami U.	10	Fordham	7	St. Olaf
20	Smith	10	Gonzaga	7	Wabash
20	Vassar	10	Maine	7	West Virginia
19	Virginia	10	Penn. State	7	Western Kentucky State
18	NYU	10	Southern Methodist		

SOURCE: Constructed from the statistics in National Academy of Sciences-National Research Council (M. H. Trytten and L. R. Harmon), *Doctorate Production in United States Universities, 1936–1956, with Baccalaureate Origins of Doctorates in the Sciences, Arts, and Humanities* (Washington, 1958), 70–141.

of 1958 were married males, and 44% had children—most of them fewer than four but some with more than four. Only 1% were under twenty-six years of age when the Ph.D. was awarded. Three-fourths had passed their thirtieth birthday and 35% their thirty-sixth.

This profile of graduate students in history is warped somewhat —but not much—by the fact that the persons providing the data had fully completed graduate study and were older than most graduate students. The main features of the profile are reinforced, and comparison with graduate students in other disciplines is made possible, by an independent study of graduate students conducted by the National Opinion Research Center (NORC) in 1958–1959.[21] Thus history students seem to retain a religious affiliation more often than those in other disciplines. Notably more Catholic graduate students are found in history than in other disciplines. History students more often than others tend to come from the New England region. Married students are slightly less common in history than in other disciplines, and history students who are married do not differ significantly from other married students in the number of children they have: 26% of the history students reported having at least one child. Finally, in comparison with others, twice as many of the history students (12%) are forty years of age or more and somewhat fewer (26%) are under twenty-four.

Berelson and others have shown that Ph.D. candidates tend to come from somewhat lower economic-social-cultural levels than medical and law students.[22] Ph.D. candidates in various disciplines

[21] Joe L. Spaeth, "Graduate Students in History," a mimeographed report prepared by the National Opinion Research Center, University of Chicago, for the American Historical Association. The NORC survey included about three hundred graduate students in history. Its sample seems to contain a disproportionately high percentage of Catholic institutions (see appendix I).

[22] Berelson, *Graduate Education*, 134; Sibley, *The Recruitment, Selection and Training of Social Scientists*, 40; Gropper and Fitzpatrick, *Who Goes to Graduate School?*, 50–51, 55. Gropper and Fitzpatrick report median annual income of fathers of graduate students in history in their large sample of 1957–1958 was $5,600; fathers of law students, $8,300.

tend to be much alike in this respect.²³ Class origin seems to have little effect upon scholarly promise in one's field of specialization. The level of education of one's parents is a more important factor, but a recent study of psychologists showed that the parents of 39% of a sample of "significant contributors" went beyond the high school level, while the parents of 42% of a sample of undistinguished psychologists had also gone beyond high school.²⁴

Table 3-3 shows the educational and social background of history graduate students in comparison with others in the NORC study and with a separate sample of graduate students in Education. Some historians may well conclude from Table 3-3 that graduate students from "better" families must be recruited in the interest of maintaining the professional prestige of academicians. But recruiting cannot be limited to any class. Indeed, most college history teachers will be found in the future where they are now being found, in families that do not rank by education, occupation, or income in the uppermost prestige levels of American society. This has especially important implications for the financing of the graduate education of historians.

FINANCING GRADUATE STUDY

In 1948 Elbridge Sibley showed that graduate students in the natural sciences held grants more often than those in the social sciences, and that the natural science grants tended to be larger. Six years after Sibley wrote, the National Science Foundation confirmed his findings. The NSF study showed further that only 1 out of 5 (21%) history graduate students held stipends, "a lower proportion than in most social sciences," and that the median stipend for history students with grants was $930—"among the lowest in social sciences." ²⁵

²³ See Wilson, *The Academic Man*, 19.
²⁴ Clark, *America's Psychologists*, 106–107.
²⁵ Sibley, *The Recruitment, Selection, and Training of Social Scientists*, 113–126; National Science Foundation, *Graduate Student Enrollment and Support in*

TABLE 3-3

SOCIAL ORIGINS OF GRADUATE STUDENTS, 1958–1959

Criterion	History sample	Total NORC sample	Education sample
Father:			
Failed to complete high school....	40%	40%	63%
Earned bachelor's degree.........	31%	30%	15%
Earned higher degree(s)..........	18%	18%	8%
In "low prestige" occupation.....	55%	54%	(about 55%)
In "elite" occupation............	21%	19%	(about 20%)
Mother:			
Failed to complete high school....	37%	37%	63%
Earned bachelor's degree.........	18%	17%	8%
Earned higher degree(s)..........	2%	5%	2%
Graduate students:			
% meeting half or more of undergraduate expenses by own earnings......................	30%	32%	x*
% for whom no undergraduate expenses were met by parents....	38%	30%	x*

* Data not available.

SOURCE: Data on social background of history graduate students in comparison with others taken from Joe L. Spaeth, "Graduate Students in History," mimeographed report prepared by the National Opinion Research Center, University of Chicago, for the American Historical Association, 1958–1959. The data on graduate students in Education are from American Association of Colleges for Teacher Education (J. Marlowe Slater and others), "Inquiry into Conditions Affecting Pursuit of the Doctoral Degree in the Field of Education," a mimeographed report made available to the AHA committee through the courtesy of Dr. Paul M. Allen, tables XV–XXI.

American Universities and Colleges, 1954 (Washington, 1957), 92–93. A comprehensive study of fellowships for graduate study undertaken by John L. Chase in 1959 showed the following numbers, governmental and private, in the nation: *Humanities:* 1,139 (17%); *Social Sciences:* 1,043 (15%); *Natural Sciences:* 4,578 (67%); *Education:* 56 (1%). Grants by individual institutions were not included in this survey. For a reliable published guide see Virginia Bosch Potter, *Fellowships in the Arts and Sciences, 1960–61*, 3d ed. (Washington, 1959).

The general observations of 1948 and 1954 must be altered in only one respect in 1960: because of expanded institutional grants, the Woodrow Wilson Fellowships, and the National Defense Fellowships, the financial difficulties of beginning graduate students have been somewhat alleviated. About 15% of the Woodrow Wilson Fellows in recent years have undertaken graduate study in history. With 167 Fellows in 1959-1960 and 202 in 1960-1961, history ranks second only to English in numbers of Woodrow Wilson Fellowships. It appears that 72 (4.8%) of the 1,500 National Defense Fellowships for graduate study in 1960-1961 were allocated for study in history.[26]

While additional financial support for beginning graduate students is needed, the scarcity of aid is now felt much more severely in the final stages of Ph.D. work, when the candidate must devote a year or more to research and the writing of a dissertation. Fulbright grants for study abroad help a limited number of students at the dissertation level. But many others look unsuccessfully for aid at this stage, especially to defray the costs of travel in doing research. Some travel for dissertation research was reported by 85% of the Ph.D.s in history of 1958. Even in the seven Ph.D. programs that ranked highest in prestige in a questionnaire survey of 1959 (see page 226, below) Ph.D. candidates find it necessary to leave the campus to complete dissertation research. Thus 57% of the 1958 Ph.D.s in history from California, Chicago, Columbia, Harvard, Princeton, Wisconsin, and Yale report "considerable" or "extensive" travel. Yet only half the Ph.D.-training departments report that students are sometimes given grants if travel is required because of "significant gaps in library holdings."

Another serious deficiency in financing graduate study is the lack of help available for summer study. Since the stipends now granted do not provide for summer work, many students must interrupt their studies to earn a livelihood. The result is a break in the continuity of training and delays in progress toward the Ph.D.

[26] Woodrow Wilson National Fellowship Foundation, *Report for 1959*, 29; announcement of fellowships dated Jan. 5, 1960, by U.S. Department of Health, Education, and Welfare.

Even the initial financing of graduate study remains troublesome for most graduate students, for there are many more students who are capable of earning a Ph.D. than there are grants to go around. Only about 1 out of 8 of the nominees for Woodrow Wilson Fellowships in recent years have won them, though the officials of the Woodrow Wilson program report that "the majority of the almost 9,000 nominees . . . deserve encouragement, and most of them actually do not have enough money to go to graduate school." [27] While about 274 Woodrow Wilson and National Defense Fellowships were available for graduate study in history in 1960–1961, they supported only a fraction of the first-year history graduate students (probably about two thousand in the Ph.D.-training departments alone).[28]

Financial need is, of course, a relative condition. It is important to emphasize, therefore, that graduate students in history are stipend-poor in comparison with other graduate students, especially those in the natural sciences. (The term "stipend" here means a grant that is not to be repaid and that involves either no services at all or only services that contribute to professional training, e.g., part-time research and teaching.) The NORC study of graduate students in 1958–1959 speaks of the "disadvantaged position" of history students as "the group with fewest academic sources of income available to them." Table 3-4 compares the financial status of some three hundred history students with that of students in other disciplines in the NORC survey.

Data released in mid-1961 by Dr. John L. Chase of the U.S. Office of Education show that grants made by individual universities (139 reporting) to graduate students in the social sciences and humanities were on the average several hundred dollars lower than grants to students in other disciplines. These data (which include tuition fellowships) reported a total of $1,482,357 was available in the nation for history fellowships in 1959–1960. This is enough to provide 927 fellowships of $1,600 for study in history. More money was available for graduate study in chemistry, physics, mathematics,

[27] Woodrow Wilson National Fellowship Foundation, *Report for 1959*, 71.
[28] The Ph.D.-training departments in 1958–1959 reported 3,256 master's candidates in residence. Perhaps 2,000 of them were first-year students.

TABLE 3-4

FINANCIAL CONDITIONS OF GRADUATE STUDENTS, 1958-1959

Financial condition	History sample (about 300)	Other social sciences (about 640)	Total sample (about 2,750)
Holding scholarship.....................	36%	37%	35%
Holding teaching assistantship or fellowship.............................	18%	21%	28%
Holding research assistantship..........	2%	17%	16%
Having no income from stipend (excluding veteran's benefits)....................	66%	45%	39%
Having tuition plus $1,000 or more from nonduty stipend......................	21%	22%	24%
Receiving financial aid from parents.......	24%	23%	22%
Receiving some income from investments..	19%	12%	14%
Holding a job.........................	43%	40%	35%
Job only source of support..............	33%	24%	21%
Having no savings available.............	27%	24%	24%
Own automobile.......................	60%	67%	67%
Not very worried about immediate financial condition............................	48%	51%	53%
Optimistic about long-run financial condition..................................	29%	44%	42%
Expect to need 7 years or more to get Ph.D.	47%	40%	38%

SOURCE: Data from Joe L. Spaeth, "Graduate Students in History," mimeographed report prepared by the National Opinion Research Center, University of Chicago, for the American Historical Association, 1958-1959.

English-and-dramatic-art, psychology, and Education. Fields except those just cited received less fellowship aid than history (and all of them except agriculture-forestry produced fewer Ph.D.s in 1958). History, with 3.5% of the 1959 Ph.D.s in all fields, obtained 4.2% of the fellowship aid; political science, with 2.0% of the Ph.D.s, got 2.8% of the aid; mathematics, with 2.7% of the Ph.D.s, got 7.1% of the aid.[28a]

[28a] John L. Chase, *Doctoral Study: Fellowships and Capacity of Graduate Schools.* (Washington, 1961), 18, 48, 64-65.

TABLE 3-5

STIPENDS HELD BY GRADUATE STUDENTS IN
SELECTED DISCIPLINES, 1958-1959

Discipline	% of all students in discipline holding one or more stipends	% of stipend students with stipends of $2,000 or more for 9 months
Botany	89	53
Chemistry	79	63
Physics	78	60
English	53	29
Sociology	49	29
Philosophy	47	45
Economics	45	44
Political science	45	30
History	34	27

SOURCE: Compiled by National Opinion Research Center, University of Chicago: Joe L. Spaeth, "Graduate Students in History," Mimeographed report prepared for the American Historical Association, 1958-1959.

Table 3-5, compiled by the NORC, shows even more vividly how inadequately graduate study in history is financed.[29] Other NORC statistics show that history students compare favorably with others in the holding of scholarships but less often hold teaching and—especially—research assistantships.

The result is that great numbers of history graduate students must work full time—often in nonacademic services. A survey of 143 recent Ph.D.s in history by the Southern Regional Education

[29] This is borne out by Gropper and Fitzpatrick, *Who Goes to Graduate School?*, 51. It is possible that both this and the NORC survey fail to report instructorships held by some history students who might not think of them as "stipends." But the number of these instructorships is not great enough to alter very significantly the relative financial condition of graduate students as reported in tables 3-4 and 3-5. The general NORC report, completed in 1960, confirms the conclusion that history students in 1958-1959 were probably receiving "the least support of any field of study in graduate school." (From James A. Davis and others, "The Financial Situation of American Arts and Science Graduate Students," mimeographed report, National Opinion Research Center [Chicago, 1960], 82.)

Board (SREB) has shown that 89% did one year or more of full-time work during the period between award of A.B. and Ph.D. and that *half (51%) worked full time for six years or more between A.B. and Ph.D.* The periods worked by history Ph.D. candidates—mostly as college teachers—were on an average longer than the periods worked by Ph.D. candidates in all but one other discipline (English) among more than 15 disciplines covered in the SREB survey.

Full-time work is the major delaying factor in prolonged Ph.D. programs. Of the 1958 Ph.D.s who were thirty-six years of age or more upon award of the degree, half (52%) cite full-time work as the chief cause of delay. Objective statistics support their opinion: 54% of the total sample of 1958 Ph.D.s report that they worked full time for more than one academic year between beginning graduate study and award of the Ph.D.; and 73% of those who finished after thirty-five years of age report having done so. Prolonged part-time work also takes its toll. Part-time teaching by graduate students is valuable experience, but the delay in Ph.D. programs that is caused by more than one or two years of it is undesirable.

Altogether almost two-thirds of the history Ph.D.s of 1958 (65%) report having done full-time or part-time work as independent teachers, leaders of discussion sections, or assistants in grading papers while working toward the Ph.D. Another 9% served as research assistants. Others performed a wide variety of services as library assistants, dormitory counselors, assistant editors, professional writers, machinists, recreation supervisors, piano teachers, grocery clerks, operators of businesses, preachers, or in a number of other capacities. At least one Ph.D. of 1957 found lodging in a District of Columbia jail (in return for services!) in order to carry out research at the Library of Congress.

Even with part-time or full-time work, almost one-third (30%) of the history Ph.D.s of 1958 emerged from graduate school in debt. They most often borrowed from their families; but 6.6% of the total sample of 182 Ph.D.s borrowed money from commercial agencies, and 5.5% borrowed from their graduate schools. Two out of five (44%) of those who borrowed obtained noninterest

loans, but 20% paid interest at 5% or more. Two-thirds (66%) could repay their loans in installments "whenever possible."

Will Durant has pungently suggested that more than a revival of antiquity was needed to make the Renaissance, that "first of all it took money—smelly bourgeois money."[30] It will take more of the same to meet the demands of graduate education in history during the next decade. The need for stipends for research and teaching assistantships has already been suggested. The armed services could appropriately provide fellowships if they were to send many of their new ROTC officers to graduate schools for their required active duty assignments; graduate study in history and other social sciences would be excellent training for future intelligence and staff officers. Graduate schools that have not already done so need to make noninterest loans available to graduate students.

The graduate schools, the national foundations, and the Federal government might all consider the merits of establishing a system of "loan-scholarships" in which a large portion of loans to students would be canceled upon successful completion of the Ph.D. Such grants would have the advantage of being equally available to students in all disciplines. They would provide strong incentive to complete the Ph.D. and to complete it with all proper speed. Some graduate faculty members fear that students would not be attracted by loan-scholarships, but experience at Tulane University with noninterest loans (with no part canceled) suggests that this fear is partly without foundation.[31] The attitude of the 1958 history Ph.D.s toward the loan-scholarship idea is also reassuring. They were asked if they would have borrowed money for a year of full-time work on the Ph.D. dissertation, with no interest, 30% of the indebtedness to be canceled upon successful completion of the Ph.D. degree and repayment of the outstanding indebtedness within ten years after borrowing the money. Two-thirds of the respondents answered "yes" to this question.

[30] Will Durant, *The Renaissance: A History of Civilization in Italy from 1304–1576 A.D.* (New York, 1953), 67.
[31] Berelson, *Graduate Education*, 243.

Loan-scholarships should not take the place of service-free fellowships for the best Ph.D. candidates in history; on the contrary, more of them are urgently needed. Berelson has predicted that "the main costs of graduate study over the next years will . . . have to be borne by the Federal government." [32] He will be proven right unless the graduate schools and the national foundations make even more generous provisions for financing graduate education than they have made in the past.

CAREER PLANS

The career plans of history graduate students as well as the modest incomes of their families must be considered in any discussion of ways to finance graduate study. Three-fourths of the history graduate students surveyed by the NORC in 1958–1959 report academic careers as their first choices, and as was reported in Chapter 2, 88% of the history Ph.D.s of 1958 actually filled academic positions. Our data are confirmed by a separate study of 143 recent Ph.D.s in history conducted by the Southern Regional Education Board: 89% were employed by colleges or universities and 3% were employed by other educational institutions. While faculty salaries have improved in recent years, they cannot now attract sufficient numbers of superior students unless stipends for graduate study are offered.

The *kinds* of college careers the graduate students want are even more noteworthy than the numbers that hope to become teachers. Only one-fifth aim at positions in large universities; slightly more than half (53%) want careers in liberal arts colleges. While 19% prefer research to teaching, 57% describe teaching as "intrinsically more satisfying" than research.[33] In response to another question in

---

[32] *Ibid.*, 245. See also David D. Henry, "The Role of the Federal Government in Higher Education," *Educational Record*, XL (July, 1959), 197–202; John A. Perkins, "Financing Higher Education: Perspectives and Possibilities," *Educational Record*, XL (April, 1959), 99–112.

[33] It is interesting to note that a good many persons who leave college teaching for other careers actually take decreases in salary in doing so. See John W.

TABLE 3-6

CAREER AIMS OF 2,754 GRADUATE STUDENTS, 1958–1959

Career	History (290), in %	Humanities (513), in %	Social sciences (649), in %	Biological sciences (366), in %	Physical sciences (366), in %	Total sample (2,754), in %
Teaching undergraduates....	44	47	16	18	15	25
Teaching graduate students..........	17	18	13	10	14	14
Research............	16	13	28	60	56	38
Academic administration.....	4	1	4	2	1	2
Other careers........	21	22	39	9	14	21

SOURCE: Joe L. Spaeth, "Graduate Students in History, mimeographed report prepared by the National Opinion Research Center for the American Historical Association, 1958–1959.

the NORC survey, graduate students in history and other disciplines described their career choices. As Table 3-6 shows, undergraduate teaching attracts the history and humanities students far more than those in the social and natural sciences.

RECRUITING

The need to recruit graduate students more systematically and energetically is implicit in much of this chapter. That need has been recognized by virtually all disciplines. A study of political science pointed to the problem in 1951; physiologists in 1958 called recruiting the "serious deficiency" of training in their disciplines; the president of the American Bar Association has warned fellow lawyers that legal study is failing to attract its rightful share of students because of competition from the sciences, engineering, and medicine; and the Association of Medical Colleges has ex-

Gustad, "The Choice of a Career in College Teaching," a mimeographed report prepared in 1958 for the Southern Regional Education Board, 18. We are indebted to the author for providing a copy of the report.

pressed concern about a 33% drop in the number of applicants for admission to medical schools since 1950. History faculties would do well to consider the consequences reported by the medical schools: "The ratio of acceptances has risen, resulting in a disturbing decline in the quality of those admitted. This, in turn, has led to a higher rate of failure." [34] Unless historians recruit, they are likely to be left only the students that other disciplines do not want, students uninspiring to teach and often unable to complete the Ph.D. degree.

The tasks of recruiting and advising potential historians about particular grants and graduate schools must be shared by those who teach and counsel high school and college students. Table 3-7 shows the persons who "directly or indirectly" influenced the de-

TABLE 3-7

PERSONS INFLUENCING DECISION TO UNDERTAKE GRADUATE STUDY IN HISTORY, 182 RECENT PH.D.s

Person	Yes	No
Teacher in a small college	68	114
Teacher in a large university	55	127
High school teacher	30	152
Father	18	164
Mother	16	166
Teacher in elementary or junior high school	7	175
Grandparent	2	180
Uncle	2	180
Another relative	4	178
Friend of the family	5	177
Another person	20	162

[34] The concern of the medical colleges is reported in the *Journal of Higher Education*, XXXI (March, 1960), 163. See also, on recruiting: Dimock and Hawley, *Goals for Political Science*, 263; Gerard, *Mirror to Physiology*, vii, 12, 191–192; report of address by John D. Randall, president of the American Bar Association, in the New Orleans *Times-Picayune*, May 7, 1960. See also: Berelson, *Graduate Education*, 245–247. Trustees of the Carnegie Foundation for the Advancement of Teaching, "The Education of College Teachers," 7; Strothmann and others, *The Graduate School Today and Tomorrow*, 9–11.

cisions of Ph.D.s of 1958 to undertake graduate study in history. The struggle for survival in graduate study would be conducted on a higher level, attrition there would be lower, and the interests of the profession would be served if professors of history played a more active part than they do in choosing those who seek professional education. It would be especially helpful if students interested in graduate study could be persuaded to begin their preparation by the end of the sophomore year of undergraduate study.

Interesting students in graduate study and advising them about grants and graduate schools are important beginnings in a recruiting program. A third task, that of the careful selection of students for admission, must be assumed by the graduate faculties. Elsewhere Jacques Barzun has written that "in the exertions of Intellect those who lack the muscles, co-ordination, and will power can claim no place at the training table, let alone on the playing field."[35] The great majority of historians on graduate faculties who were interviewed by the director of this study agreed that the admission of first-year graduate students was not sufficiently rigorous, and that it should be made more so.

It is, of course, impossible to devise a system that will guarantee the success in graduate school of every student who is admitted. As one critic has pointed out, available tests "cannot measure either a student's motivation or his ability to withstand the ordinary pressures, shocks, and temptations of life."[36] But the most fundamental obstacle to selectivity in most institutions has been the relatively small number of applicants. Thus more active recruiting would be the basic step and the chief hope for raising the quality of graduate students in history even if larger numbers of students were not needed. As Berelson has suggested, the way to get better students is to get more applicants.[37]

[35] Jacques Barzun, *The House of Intellect* (New York, 1959), 94–95.

[36] Sibley, *The Recruitment, Selection, and Training of Social Scientists*, 22; George Williams, *Some of My Best Friends Are Professors: A Critical Commentary on Higher Education* (New York, 1958), 135.

[37] Berelson, *Graduate Education*, 145. For suggestive material on recruiting students for teaching see Ruth E. Eckert and others, "College Faculty Members

Undergraduate teachers in both colleges and universities readily recognize the specifically historical qualities of mind that a graduate student in history should possess. He certainly needs to have learned that change is the one immutable law of history and the unique subject matter of history courses; that most historical change has been gradual rather than revolutionary. He should also know that historical changes are accomplished by multiple causes, whether he is concerned with the fall of the Roman Empire or the outcome of the Yalta Conference. While sensitive to the dominant features of an age, he should give full allowance to the complex character of every historical period, whether colonial America, the era of the Industrial Revolution in England, or the Nazi era in Germany. He should show some awareness of the ambiguous legacies that historical forces leave to the future, recognizing that both authoritarian and democratic impulses flowed from Calvinism, Marxism, and the New Deal.

The potential graduate student also should possess some essential personal traits. Remembering Leo Tolstoy's mocking flattery that "history would be an excellent thing if only it were true," [38] he must seek absolute honesty as his indispensable guide to a realistic view of history. It is well for him to be reminded of the noble admonition that "history that is not entirely honest is entirely contemptible, degrading to the writer and fraudulent and pernicious in its influence upon public opinion." [39] If he has shown a certain balance of courage, tolerance, and modesty, then so much the better; for he should early begin to do what Alfred North Whitehead once said a professor should do: "exhibit himself in his own true character—that is, as an ignorant man thinking, actively utilizing his small store of knowledge." [40]

View Their Jobs," *American Association of University Professors Bulletin*, XLV (December, 1959), 513–528.

[38] Quoted by Isaiah Berlin, *The Hedgehog and the Fox* (New York, 1957), 25.

[39] William Harbutt Dawson, *The German Empire, 1867–1914, and the Unity Movement*, 2 vols. (New York, 1919), I, x.

[40] Alfred North Whitehead, *The Aims of Education and Other Essays* (New York, 1929), 58.

Obviously these traits in students cannot be bought; but students who possess them cannot be expected to use their rare qualities in sacrificial rites lasting a lifetime. The most important weapon historians could use in recruiting superior undergraduates would be a drastic improvement in faculty salaries. A second would be outstanding college teaching. The teacher of history must exemplify the mental qualities he hopes to find in the best of his students. Informal advice and inspiration from individual professors has been helpful in the past and will be helpful in the future.

More systematic efforts to recruit students can also be made. Dickinson College invites speakers in various fields to lecture to undergraduates about careers in teaching. Harvard University in 1958 created a faculty committee on teaching as a career. Some graduate schools send faculty members to visit colleges in their regions in order to discuss graduate training with able students. High school students can be made aware of the possibilities of college teaching as a career.[41] The development of programs for superior college students can aid in recruiting future college teachers.[42] Through history clubs able students can be made aware of the possibilities of graduate study and careers as teachers of history. Service as undergraduate research or teaching assistants is known to have influenced the decision of many students to undertake teaching as a career, and these assistantships might well be expanded.[43]

[41] Cf. Dimock and Hawley, *Goals for Political Science*, 243; Gerard, *Mirror to Physiology*, 191-192. High school teachers can do much to "recruit" potential graduate students by making history challenging, intellectually exciting, and meaningful. The publications of the American Historical Association's Service Center for Teachers of History can help in this. See, e.g., W. Burlie Brown, *United States History: A Bridge to the World of Ideas*, one of the booklets in the AHA series (Washington, 1960). Asked to name persons who influenced their decisions to undertake graduate study in history, one-sixth of the Ph.D.s of 1958 named "a high school teacher."

[42] See, e.g., George R. Waggoner, "The Development of Programs for the Superior Student in Large Universities," *Educational Record*, XL (October, 1959), 319-325.

[43] Gropper and Fitzpatrick, *Who Goes to Graduate School?*, 44; Woodrow Wilson National Fellowship Foundation, *Report for 1959*, 69.

Programs that reach many students have been operated at the University of Pittsburgh and at Tulane University in recent years. In these institutions multiple committees of faculty members identify, encourage, and advise undergraduate students who show promise as scholars during their freshman, sophomore, or junior years. Early attention to the possibilities of a teaching career enables students to achieve proper undergraduate preparation for graduate study. Furthermore, as a result of these recruiting programs it is possible to recommend the best-prepared seniors for the various scholarship competitions. Officials of the Woodrow Wilson program have expressed the hope that the "Pittsburgh Plan" might become a model for similar recruiting efforts, "especially at larger universities." [44]

SUMMARY

History faculties are getting some very good graduate students, but they have no cause to be complacent. The best graduate students are too often attracted to disciplines that offer more lucrative stipends for study and financially more profitable careers.

Graduate students in history come from upwards of six-hundred colleges, some large and some small. They have diverse socio-cultural backgrounds and their families seldom have high incomes. Because of these factors and the relatively low salaries that have been offered in the past to teachers—which most of them become—history students need stipends to finance graduate study. It is of the greatest importance that additional financial support for fellowships, research assistantships, and teaching assistantships be found. Loan-scholarships would be helpful supplements, but they alone are not sufficient. History students should be offered as generous support for graduate study as students in other disciplines are given, for the significance of their work is not to be denied.

[44] The Tulane program is cited as exemplary by Berelson, *Graduate Education*, 246, and by Frederick W. Ness, *The Role of the College in the Recruitment of Teachers* (Washington, 1958), 62-63. For an account of the somewhat similar plan at Pittsburgh see Woodrow Wilson National Fellowship Foundation, *Report for 1959*, 49-50.

An age of striking accomplishments in science and technology must have scholars and citizens who face the past without fear as well as those who fearlessly face the future, unless it wishes to confront tomorrow with only the cheap courage that arises from unreason and lack of knowledge.

Without adequate financial support for graduate study in history, greater efforts by historians to recruit graduate students are likely to be both embarrassing and relatively unsuccessful. But if increased financial aid and higher professional salaries than have been common in the past can be won, the number and quality of graduate students in history can easily be increased to meet the needs of the 1960s.

"Why," Boyd Shafer has asked, "should anyone take up a profession that pays . . . less in a lifetime than a cheap ballad singer gets for one hastily-made platter of vulgar songs?" He provided a large part of his answer when he added: "And yet, . . . teachers . . . are paid for doing what they want most of all to do: teaching, reading, research, writing, continuing to learn."

We owe it to our students to tell them that there are many ways of being made rich by one's work.[45]

[45] Boyd C. Shafer, "The Teacher and the Taught," an address delivered at Dickinson College in 1959.

Chapter 4
HISTORY IN THE COLLEGES

The colleges are the academic destination as well as the academic origin of many graduate students. Fifty-three per cent of the history graduate students of 1958–1959 aspire to teach in liberal arts colleges. Seven out of ten of the Ph.D.s in history in the nation actually do teach in colleges and junior colleges.[1]

How do the colleges discover teaching talent and how important is it to them? How well trained are their faculties? What are their working conditions? What kinds of history do they teach? What teaching methods do they use? What special attention do they give to history majors? The graduate faculties need to know the answers to these questions. In attempting to find them, this study has relied upon letters from 134 college executives and questionnaires completed by the chairmen of history departments in 126 "better-than-average" four-year colleges, 376 "typical" colleges (some very good ones and a great many more that are not outstanding in prestige), and 51 junior colleges (see Appendixes A, B, C, and D).[2]

[1] Our survey of 3,072 members of history faculties holding the Ph.D. shows that 62% teach in colleges and junior colleges. The sample included virtually all Ph.D.-training faculties but failed to include a large number of college and junior college faculties. Thus it is probable that 70% is a more accurate estimate of history Ph.D.s in the colleges than 62%.

[2] Our samples include 56% of all the colleges and universities that in 1957–1958 granted bachelor's degrees in history, and 12% of those that granted them in "social science."

About 28% of the 1,937 institutions of higher learning in the United States

THE IMPORTANCE OF TEACHING ABILITY

There can be no doubt that the college executives, in appointing new Ph.D.s in history, want capable teachers. Two-thirds of the college officials consulted in this study rate evidence of teaching competence as more important than promise in research scholarship when they consider candidates for teaching positions. The three qualities they most often mention are "good personal traits," actual teaching experience, and evidence of enthusiasm for one's field and for teaching. Recent history Ph.D.s agree that these are valuable traits. Table 4-1 shows the qualities that were most often rated as good and as bad traits by the history Ph.D.s of 1958.[3]

All graduate schools can comment to a potential employer on the strengths and weaknesses of their Ph.D. candidates in some of the qualities mentioned in Table 4-1. But graduate faculties that have not observed the capacity for teaching of their candidates cannot very well comment on a number of the traits in which college employers are interested. The president of a state college writes that "the qualifications with which we are most concerned are the ones that are the most difficult on which to find specific

---

may be called "junior colleges." About 4% offer the Ph.D. degree in history. The remaining 1,306 institutions are four-year colleges (many of which offer master's degrees). These may be grouped by the following types: 7% are primarily teacher preparatory colleges; 16% are professional or technical schools; and 998 (76%) are public, private, or sectarian liberal arts colleges. These 998 —we will call them colleges of a *"general type"*—make up 52% of all the 1,937 colleges and universities in the nation.

About 26% of all the institutions of higher learning in the United States are private and nonsectarian; another 25% are Protestant; 14% are Roman Catholic; and 0.3% are Jewish. The remaining 35% are public institutions. Our samples represent all of these types of institution, as tabulated by the U.S. Office of Education (Theresa Birch Wilkins, ed.), *Education Directory, 1957–1958*, Part III of *Higher Education* (Washington, 1957), 1–11.

[3] For suggestive comments on the qualities of good and poor teachers in the schools see David G. Ryans, *Characteristics of Teachers: Their Description, Comparison, and Appraisal, A Research Study* (Washington, 1960), 343–367.

TABLE 4-1

GOOD AND POOR TEACHERS: APPRAISALS BY 182 RECENT HISTORY PH.D.s

Qualities considered good*	Qualities considered poor*
1. Knowledge of history	1. Inability to communicate
2. Enthusiasm for history	2. Inability to arouse interest of students in history or enthusiasm for it
3. Ability to communicate ideas and facts	
4. Ability to inspire interest in and enthusiasm for history	3. Lack of skill as formal lecturer
	4. Lack of general knowledge
5. Intellectual curiosity	5. Lack of enthusiasm for history
6. General knowledge	6. Lack of intellectual curiosity
7. Exacting standards	7. Low standards
8. Sympathetic treatment of students	8. Dogmatism
	9. Lack of knowledge of history
9. Personal qualities	10. Preoccupation with research to the neglect of teaching
10. Skill as formal lecturer	

* Listed in order of the frequency with which these qualities are mentioned by the history Ph.D.s of 1958.

evidence." [4] Letters from graduate faculties, often vague about the teaching capacity of candidates, are rated by one-third of the college departments as "not especially helpful."

Thus, in a large majority of the colleges, one, two, or three candidates are interviewed by the screening authorities before an appointment is made. In a few cases—six or seven college executives mention this—the candidate is asked to teach a class, give a lecture, or conduct a seminar. Several colleges and universities have developed more or less formal and intensive orientation programs for newly appointed instructors. These include the Air Force Academy, Amherst College, Hunter College, East Carolina College, Southern Illinois University, Colgate University, Temple Univer-

[4] On this lack of evidence about teaching capacity see comments by L. S. Woodburne, *Faculty Personnel Policies in Higher Education* (New York, 1950); M. R. Trabue, "Characteristics Desirable in College Teachers," *Journal of Higher Education*, XXV (April, 1954), 201–204. For additional literature on the evaluation of teachers see Eells (ed.), *College Teachers and College Teaching*, 151–164.

sity, Occidental College, and the State University of South Dakota. Probably many other institutions have special programs for new teachers during which their capacities for classroom teaching can be discovered or developed.[5]

About 17% of the college executives report that it is standard practice to carry out direct observation of new teachers in their classrooms, and two-fifths of the responding departments say this is *sometimes* done. The president of a large Eastern institution writes that "each non-tenure appointee is visited at least once a semester by each of our five Executive Committee members." Some others admit that departmental chairmen use less reliable devices in "getting a line" on the new teacher. About one-third of the college executives and four-fifths of the history departments state that formal or informal student ratings play a role in evaluation of teachers. Most indirectly, enrollment trends are taken as evidence of student attitudes; 37% of the history departments report that enrollments are usually regarded as one index of a teacher's competence.

SCHOLARLY QUALIFICATIONS OF TEACHERS

It is obvious that the colleges are in search of good teachers. What they hope for has been eloquently described in ideal terms by Harry J. Carman: "teachers who are persons of attractive personality, insight, sensitiveness, and perspective . . . moral strength, a sense of beauty of spirit, the seeing eye, the watchful soul, the inquiring mind . . . teachers who are free of conventional prejudices and fears, and who are articulate and skilled in conversation . . . [and who] derive great satisfaction from assisting students to see the relationship between learning and life."[6] But even these qualities

---

[5] A strong argument can be made that the college is obligated to provide in-service training for the new teacher. See Elmer Ellis, "Making Competent Teachers of New Instructors," *Journal of Higher Education*, XXV (April, 1954), 204–206.

[6] In Theodore C. Blegen and Russell M. Cooper (eds.), *The Preparation of College Teachers: Report of a Conference Held at Chicago, Illinois, December*

alone are not enough. The college executives also want solidly trained research scholars. Thus 29% consider capacity for research scholarship more important than teaching capacity in appointing new instructors, and all of the 65% who consider teaching competence more important than capacity for research scholarship emphasize that they look for *both* these traits. This is in harmony with the reports of department heads on the criteria used in making appointments.

How successful are the college executives and department heads in their search for scholar-teachers? The number of historians, the degrees they hold, and their years of experience are not guarantees of scholarly competence; rather they are valuable indices of it. Using these indices it is possible to compare the strength of history faculties in junior colleges, "typical" four-year colleges, and four-year colleges of higher prestige.

The most obvious difference in the status of history among these institutions is in the average number of historians per institution. The 126 better colleges report 1,103 historians as members of their regular faculties in 1958–1959, an average of 8.8 historians per college. The random sample of 376 four-year colleges report 4.9 historians per college, and the junior colleges report an average of 3.8 per institution. Quantity is not always a valid index of quality, but the departments with larger numbers of historians can offer courses taught by specialists in more areas of history than small faculties can competently teach.

How well qualified are the teachers of history? Notwithstanding the fact that two-thirds of the students who enroll in junior colleges expect to transfer to four-year institutions (one-third actually do so[7]), the junior college history teachers are much less often fully

---

8–10, 1949, *Sponsored by the American Council on Education and the U.S. Office of Education* (Washington, 1950), 18. *Ibid.*, 62, offers a more prosaic but useful statement of the qualities of a good teacher. For other suggestive statements about the qualities of excellent teachers see Knapp and Goodrich, *Origins of American Scientists*, 249–258; list by M. R. Trabue in *Journal of Teacher Education*, II (June, 1951), 136.

[7] For this and other data on junior colleges see Leland L. Medsker, *The Junior College: Progress and Prospects* (New York, 1960), 97.

trained Ph.D.s than are the instructors of either the typical or the better four-year colleges. The master's degree is the highest held by two-thirds of the history instructors in the junior colleges in our sample. It is heartening to note, however, that those faculty members who hold the Ph.D.—22%—are twice as numerous as those who have only the bachelor's degree.[8] The situation in the four-year colleges is much better. No less than 58% of the faculty members in the history departments in our sample of typical colleges and 71% of those in our sample of better colleges hold the Ph.D.

Other differences can be shown in the scholarly potential of the history faculties in the two samples of four-year colleges. We asked: "Can a teacher who does not have the doctor's degree be appointed to your history faculty?" Flat "yes" answers were reported by 62% of all 502 four-year colleges, as Table 4-2 shows. But 30%

TABLE 4-2

APPOINTMENT OF HISTORY TEACHERS WITH LESS THAN THE PH.D. IN 502 COLLEGES, 1958–1959

Group	% saying "yes"					% saying "yes, but only temporarily"				
	Nation	East	South	Midwest	West	Nation	East	South	Midwest	West
Sample of 376 typical colleges.......	67	72	75	59	56	30	26	22	36	41
Sample of 126 better colleges..........	47	47	53	42	45	46	47	37	52	50
Total sample of 502	62	66	69	55	52	34	31	26	39	44

of the "typical" four-year colleges and 46% of the better-known colleges say "only as a temporary measure."

The better the college, the more likely that its instructors are teaching in the field of history in which they specialized in graduate school. In 55% of the typical four-year colleges at least one

[8] See National Education Association, *Teacher Supply and Demand . . . 1957–58* and *1958–59*, 33–34.

history instructor in 1957–1959 taught "chiefly" outside his major field of history in graduate school (an example would be that of a specialist in modern European history teaching chiefly United States history). But only one-eighth of all the instructors in the better colleges were teaching "chiefly" outside their major fields. Half the departments in these better colleges report that they do not appoint instructors to teach chiefly outside their major fields of graduate study. In the junior colleges, on the other hand, nine-tenths of the departments we surveyed reported at least one history instructor teaching chiefly outside his major field of history.

One form of experience—travel in the area of specialization—is especially important for those faculty members who teach the history of foreign areas. Two-fifths (42%) of the history instructors in the better colleges teach "primarily" the history of foreign areas. Of these, 70% have "travelled or studied in the area of their specialization within the last ten years"; and three-fifths (59%) of them have done so "within the last five years." (Fewer in the South and Midwest; more in the East.) More than 1 out of 10 (12%) of those who teach the history of foreign areas in these colleges are foreign-born. Only 17% have "never travelled in the area of their specialization." (Cf. pages 117–118, below.)

Berelson has stated that the liberal arts colleges—"except for a few at the top"—cannot expect to attract "the top doctoral product."[9] But our data suggest that all but the weakest four-year colleges can expect to attract Ph.D.s in history. The qualifications of the history faculties of America's colleges look very good on paper.

WORKING CONDITIONS

Berelson has succinctly catalogued the unattractive working conditions of some four-year colleges: "low salaries, poor libraries . . . , high teaching load, little research opportunity, poorer students, poorer colleagues, extracurricular demands and restrictive

[9] Berelson, *Graduate Education*, 224.

atmosphere, dead-end career line, etc."[10] Though Berelson overstates the obstacles to scholarly teaching in the colleges and mentions none of their advantages, his diagnosis deserves at least as much attention as others that blame graduate school specialization exclusively for the "decline of liberal education" in America.[11] In truth, low salaries do make it difficult for many colleges to attract the best products of the graduate schools and hurt the professional spirit of those appointed to the poorly paid positions.[12] The libraries of American colleges are hampered by financial limitations, and libraries are of direct concern to teachers of history. The average library budget for books and periodicals in a random sample of "typical" colleges in 1958–1959 was $20,737 (all disciplines) and the average holding of the 10 libraries was 99,322 volumes.[13] One college, in proportion to its size among those most often selected by winners of National Merit Scholarships in 1959 and 1960,[14] spent only $21,030 for books and periodicals *in all disciplines* in 1958–1959; and its total library holdings of 80,000 volumes served an enrollment of 1,745 students. Library holdings are especially inadequate in the history of foreign areas.[15]

More directly, the heavy teaching loads in most colleges cause history instructors to give hostages to fortune as teachers. Well-

[10] *Ibid.*

[11] McGrath, *The Graduate School and the Decline of Liberal Education, passim.*

[12] The data for comparison of salaries are available in the *American Association of University Professors Bulletin*, XLVI (June, 1960), 156–193. See also Eckert and others, "College Faculty Members View Their Jobs," 525; Louis A. D'Amico, "Salaries of College and University Professors by Rank, Institutional Size, and Control," *Educational Record*, XLI (October, 1960), 300–305.

[13] The data were found in Irwin (ed.), *American Universities and Colleges*, 8th ed., under the descriptions of the sample colleges. The sample of typical colleges included: Elmira, Franklin and Marshall, Kent State, Loyola (Los Angeles), Macalester, Maryland State Teachers (Frostburg), Mississippi College, University of Richmond, Wells, and Whitman.

[14] National Merit Scholarship Corporation, *Recognizing Exceptional Ability Among America's Young People: Fourth Annual Report, 1959* (Evanston, Ill., n.d. [1960?]), 19.

[15] See, e.g., Robert F. Byrnes (ed.), *The Non-Western Areas in Undergraduate Education in Indiana* (Bloomington, Ind., 1959), 19.

trained, experienced teachers should be able to do fine jobs of teaching in an assignment of two separate courses, three sections, and a total enrollment of 70 to 100 students.[16] The controversial report by Beardsley Ruml and Donald Morrison would not have a teacher do more than this.[17] Unfortunately, however, the overwhelming majority of history teachers in the nation's colleges are already doing considerably more. Even in the better colleges, the "normal" load is 12 hours (mean, 11.3), and one-fourth (27%) of the history instructors teach more than 12-hour loads (see Table 4-3).

TABLE 4-3

TEACHING LOADS OF 1,007 HISTORY TEACHERS IN 126 BETTER COLLEGES, FIRST TERM OF 1958–1959

Hours of teaching per week	% of faculty teaching various loads				
	Nation	East	South	Midwest	West
Some but less than 6.....	4	3	2	7	7
6–8	10	12	8	9	9
9–10	14	19	10	9	15
Total under 10........	28	34	20	25	31
11–12	45	42	45	37	55
13–15	22	22	31	23	11
More than 15	5	1	5	14	2
Total over 13.........	27	23	36	37	13

Two-thirds (63%) of the history Ph.D.s of 1958 report that three or more separate course preparations are normally required in their history departments, and this sample included many instructors

[16] See, e.g., H. K. Newburn, "Faculty Personnel Policies in State Universities" (multilithed for limited distribution by President Newburn, Montana State University, October, 1959), 127–129.

[17] Ruml and Morrison, *Memo to a College Trustee*, 27–44. For other literature on class size see Eells (ed.), *College Teachers and College Teaching*, 143–144.

in universities with relatively light loads; 62% of the history Ph.D.s of 1958 were teaching more than 100 students each in 1958–1959, and one-tenth (9%) were teaching more than 200 students each (see also Table 4-4). Only 18% of the history Ph.D.s of 1958

TABLE 4-4

AVERAGE SIZES OF HISTORY CLASSES AT VARIOUS LEVELS IN 126 COLLEGES, 1956–1957 AND 1958–1959

Type of course	National sample of professional and teachers' colleges		Regional averages of liberal arts colleges								National averages, all colleges	
			East		South		Midwest		West			
	1956	1958	1956	1958	1956	1958	1956	1958	1956	1958	1956	1958
Introductory, U.S.	31	30	30	29	35	34	45	37	47	52	37	36
Introductory, other	31	31	27	26	33	34	43	42	42	47	35	36
Advanced undergraduate, U.S.	22	24	22	21	26	24	24	25	20	24	23	24
Advanced undergraduate, other	20	21	19	20	21	23	20	22	20	24	20	22
Advanced undergraduate and graduate	22	19	21	23	19	18	22	23	17	20	21	21
Exclusively graduate students	13	13	15	16	7	8	7	8	7	7	10	10

found positions in departments where the normal teaching load was 9 hours or less per week.

Some critics of research argue that teachers with heavy loads could still teach well if they did not slight students in favor of footnotes and publications.[18] We asked many questions about this

[18] See, e.g., *Carnegie Corporation of New York Quarterly, Supplement* (April, 1960) for comment by Harry Carman; Ruml and Morrison, *Memo to a College Trustee*, 8; McGrath, *The Graduate School and the Decline of Liberal Education, passim*; Theodore Caplow and Reece J. McGee, *The Academic Marketplace* (New York, 1958), 225 and *passim*; Williams, *Some of My Best Friends Are Professors*, 206.

issue. Of the 1958 history Ph.D.s teaching in colleges, only two-fifths (39%) report that some publication is usually required for promotion *to a full professorship* in their colleges. The department heads in an equal percentage of the better colleges report that "some scholarly publication" is usually expected for promotion to a full professorship. Conversely, heads of four-fifths (82%) of the departments in our sample of better colleges report that teaching and other duties consume so much time that they interfere with the development of history teachers as research scholars, and 88% of these department heads told us that the research demanded of faculty members does *not* interfere with teaching.

Other data support the conclusion that history teachers seldom sacrifice good teaching for research. Three-fourths (74%) of the history Ph.D.s of 1958 say that in their institutions good teaching is *demanded,* and two-fifths (39%) say it is demanded even "more than research and writing." Only 18% say good teaching is demanded "considerably less" than research and writing or that it simply is "not demanded." Conversely, only 6% of the 1958 Ph.D.s report that the amount of publication expected by their institutions is "unreasonable"; 39% say *no* publication is required for promotion in their institutions.

In some of the colleges the history faculties need to be engaged in more research than is now possible. For condemnations of research in the colleges usually ignore the fact that there are other students than undergraduates in many of them. A large percentage of the better colleges in our sample offer master's degrees in history (see Chapter 5, below). As a result, 44% of the history teachers in the better colleges and 23% of those in the more typical colleges teach graduate students as well as undergraduates. In the combined sample of 502 colleges, some graduate-level teaching is done by 42% of the 1,852 history faculty members holding the Ph.D. degree. These percentages must be remembered in considering the proper emphasis to place upon research scholarship in the graduate training of college teachers. It is going too far to argue that historians who are "not actively engaged in contributing to their own knowledge and testing the results of their own researches by frequent publication are failing in their duty to their college, their students, and their profession." [19] But there seems to be little basis for the widespread belief that college teachers live under such great pressure to do research that they neglect their teaching. In point of fact, heavy work loads handicap their efforts both as scholars and as teachers.

Several things can be done to promote scholarly teaching in the colleges. When the teaching-hour burden is heavy and very large numbers of students must be taught by one person, a good many colleges provide student assistants or secretarial help to the faculty. One institution in our sample of better colleges reports that each history teacher is provided with 20 hours of secretarial assistance per week. Classes are often scheduled to provide some free time for scholarly effort by instructors. Half the better colleges report the availability of research grants or sabbaticals with pay, but only 3.3% of the total history faculty in these 126 colleges are reported to have been on full-time leave in the first term of 1958–1959. At this rate each professor can expect a year's leave every 33 years, or half a year every 16.5 years! Ph.D.-training departments can help in this matter by inviting doctoral graduates teaching in the colleges to return for temporary assignments during a summer, a term, or a full academic year. Many of the wealthier colleges might well take note of the example of Parsons College (Iowa), which offers its faculty members 1 term in 3 free for postdoctoral study or research. In other colleges committee service can be restricted by making certain that only those committees that are needed are retained, by preventing those that exist from being unnecessarily large, and by making certain that faculty committees are spared administrative duties and allowed to concentrate upon their true functions: the formulation and supervision of policy. Finally, heavy teaching loads can be made more palatable where they cannot be reduced by allowing history teachers to concentrate their labor in fields to which they have given their years of specialization and their professional affections.

[19] Hesseltine and Kaplan, "Doctors of Philosophy in History," 790.

WHAT HISTORY IS TAUGHT?

The most striking fact about history courses in the colleges in recent years is their prevalence and their expansion. In 1958–1959 almost one-third of the colleges in our sample were requiring more history for graduation than ten years earlier; only 6% of them were requiring less. Enrollments in history in 1958–1959 in the better colleges were up 9% over the 1956–1957 level.

The types of history courses that are most commonly reported as graduation requirements are Western civilization, modern European history, or world history; 54% of the four-year colleges in our samples report one of these courses as a requirement. The present emphasis on American history represents the major change since World War II. Surveying 690 colleges and universities during the war, Benjamin Fine found that only 18% required a course in American history for graduation. At about the same time a special committee of the American Historical Association, the Mississippi Valley Historical Association, and the National Council for the Social Studies reported that "American history is now taught with sufficient frequency." [20] Yet today United States history or American civilization is reported as a requirement by 39% of the colleges, or more than twice as frequently as in 1942.[21]

There have been changes not only in requirements but also in history offerings and enrollments during the last decade, but the

[20] Committee on American History in Schools and Colleges of the American Historical Association, the Mississippi Valley Historical Association, and the National Council for the Social Studies (Edgar B. Wesley, director), *American History in Schools and Colleges* (New York, 1944), 42, 118.

[21] A survey of 200 institutions by the U.S. Office of Education (1959) has shown that 48.7% require one or another history course for graduation. No other social science is so often required. Thus in terms of the number of students enrolled and the average number of semester hours taken per student, history ranks higher than any other social science. See Jennings B. Sanders, *Social Science Requirements for Bachelor's Degrees: A Study of Anthropology, Economics, History, Political Science, and Sociology in General Graduation Requirements* (Washington, 1959), 20, 65.

Table 4-5

Enrollment Changes in History Courses
in 126 Four-year Colleges, 1948–1958

Type of history course	% of colleges reporting enrollments 20% higher in 1958 than in 1948	% of colleges reporting enrollments 20% lower in 1958 than in 1948
United States	54	19
Medieval and modern European (including Western civilization)	41	16
English-British Commonwealth	13	8
Russian-East European	10	2
World	8	2
Asian (Near and Far East)	6	0
Ancient	6	3
Latin-American	5	9
Other history courses	25	6

Table 4-6

Changes in History Courses Offered
by 502 Four-year Colleges, 1948–1958

Type of history course	% of colleges reporting courses added	% of colleges reporting courses dropped
United States (including state and regional)	22	5.0
Modern European (including national)	20	4.0
Asian (Near and Far East)	19	1.0
Russian-East European	18	0.4
Cultural-intellectual	11	0.2
English-British Commonwealth	7	2.6
Latin-American	5	3.6
Economic	5	1.2
Ancient	3	2.0
Medieval	2	2.4
Military	0.6	0.0

changes only reinforce the traditional Western-world orientation of history offerings (see Tables 4-5 and 4-6). The history of non-Western areas in the colleges looks much stronger in terms of courses added than in terms of enrollment increases. And courses arranged by topics rather than by periods or areas have become increasingly common during the last ten years, especially courses in cultural, intellectual, and economic history. United States history is offered by virtually all the colleges and junior colleges. Western civilization is taught by one-third (31%) of the junior colleges, modern European history by one-fourth (25%), and world history by one-fifth (22%). Diversity is, as might be expected, more characteristic of the four-year colleges. More than nine-tenths of them teach courses in modern European history, and the others almost invariably offer either Western civilization or world history. More than two-thirds teach courses in British and medieval history. Colleges in the South give less than average attention to the history of foreign areas. Colleges in the Midwest offer a greater variety of courses than do those in other regions of the nation. The types of history vary also by types of colleges (see Tables 4-7 and 4-8).

It is important to note what history the colleges fail to teach, or teach less commonly than would be thought desirable. As Stull Holt has noted, military history was severely neglected before World War II, but since 1941 has been avidly cultivated at the level of creative scholarship.[22] Yet, as Tables 4-7 and 4-8 show, courses in military history are still rarely taught by the history departments in the colleges. The danger for new learning in ancient history is a real one; few American students develop the linguistic skills to specialize in ancient history in doctoral studies. Yet, while enrollments are often small, ancient history remains one of the more generally taught subdivisions of history in the colleges, as Tables 4-7 and 4-8 show.[23] To provide faculties capable of teach-

[22] See Holt's essay in Curti (ed.), *American Scholarship in the Twentieth Century*, 105.
[23] Cf. *ibid.*, 100.

TABLE 4-7

HISTORY COURSES MOST OFTEN OFFERED AMONG 502 COLLEGES
AND 51 JUNIOR COLLEGES, 1956–1958 (2 YEARS)

Field of history	% of Junior colleges reporting each type of history	% of four-year colleges reporting each type of history				
		% in Nation	% in East	% in South	% in Midwest	% in West
1. United States	92	96	97	97	95	95
2. Modern European	25	89	92	91	90	87
3. English-British Commonwealth	12	75	71	86	81	67
4. Medieval	14	71	73	68	78	64
5. Western civilization	31	69	68	68	67	77
6. Diplomatic	2	62	65	60	69	61
7. Ancient	10	61	60	58	72	54
8. Russian or U.S.S.R.	4	55	55	47	60	61
9. Latin-American	10	54	48	58	56	52
10. Far Eastern (including Indian)	8	51	52	39	58	61
11. Economic	16	48	46	51	50	48
12. Cultural-intellectual	6	45	48	39	46	51
13. State	27	40	37	55	29	51
14. Constitutional	0	39	39	31	44	46
15. Historiography	0	35	34	32	38	41
16. Methodology	0	34	32	30	40	39
17. General education or broad survey course	6	30	29	23	28	41
18. Religious	14	29	29	22	38	26
19. Social	2	27	35	16	28	21
20. World	22	25	21	29	26	25
21. Interdisciplinary course	8	24	23	23	26	34
22. Near Eastern	2	20	20	18	20	23
23. Philosophies of history	0	15	17	11	19	16
24. History of science	0	9	15	6	7	5
25. African	0	6	5	6	6	8
26. Military	4	5	7	7	1	2

TABLE 4-8

VARIATIONS IN HISTORY OFFERINGS BY TYPES OF FOUR-YEAR COLLEGES (SAMPLE OF 376 INSTITUTIONS)

Type of history course	% of total sample	% Professional colleges	% Teachers' colleges	% Colleges for Negroes	% Catholic colleges	% General colleges
United States............	97	83	95	90	98	99
Modern European.......	91	58	85	90	94	95
English-British Commonwealth.......	77	25	67	81	60	91
Medieval..............	74	37	57	81	86	76
Western civilization.....	69	75	55	67	79	68
Diplomatic.............	64	33	67	43	66	68
Ancient................	64	29	45	67	69	68
Latin-American.........	54	12	67	57	55	56
Far Eastern............	52	17	72	24	39	61
Economic..............	50	37	40	62	55	50
Russian................	50	12	50	29	47	58
State..................	43	33	75	52	33	41
Cultural-intellectual.....	41	29	32	43	55	39
Constitutional..........	36	8	22	43	55	33
Methodology...........	35	12	32	43	42	34
Religious..............	33	25	12	29	54	30
Historiography.........	33	4	15	43	36	37
General education or survey course.........	30	33	35	24	26	32
World.................	27	25	37	38	24	26
Interdisciplinary course..	24	33	17	33	29	22
Social.................	23	8	20	10	34	22
Near Eastern...........	20	4	25	10	16	23
Philosophies of history..	15	4	12	14	18	16
History of science.......	9	21	2	0	15	8
African................	6	4	5	14	5	5
Military...............	4	21	0	0	5	3

ing the history of non-Western areas—which is lagging—the authors of an Indiana survey have recommended joint appointments of one specialist by two or more colleges. The principle of sharing instructors among several colleges can also be used to staff courses in other areas of history. The principle has been applied with good results in the cooperative programs of Amherst–Mount Holyoke–

Smith–University of Massachusetts in the East and Claremont–Occidental–Whittier–Redlands in California.[24]

The graduate schools need to train more specialists in the history of the non-Western areas, but Tables 4-7 and 4-8 show very clearly that most history Ph.D.s are desired in the traditional areas of study. In the nation as a whole, it appears, two-fifths (41%) of the college history enrollments are in United States history. Half (49%) of the enrollments are in European and English history, leaving 10% for all other areas.[25]

A number of questions can be raised about the level at which history courses are taught. Why should 46% of the colleges that offer medieval history teach it only at the introductory level and an equal number (43%) only at the advanced undergraduate and graduate levels? Which is right? Are both equally appropriate? Similar questions can be asked about ancient history, English history, Far Eastern history, Russian history, and Latin-American history. Why should courses that are essentially broad surveys be reserved so exclusively for the advanced levels of college curricula? And is it not conceivable that a combined course in historical method and historiography—an introduction to the nature of history—should be the introductory course offered by college history faculties instead of the now common survey? This would give a

[24] Byrnes (ed.), *The Non-Western Areas in Undergraduate Education in Indiana*, 21, 29, 30, and *passim*. The inadequate offering of courses in the history of non-Western areas has prevailed not just in Indiana but in most parts of the nation. See the articles by Jennings B. Sanders in *Higher Education:* VI (Oct. 1, 1949), 31–34; VI (Nov. 15, 1949), 67–70; and VI (May 1, 1950), 201–202. See also Fred Cole, *International Relations in Institutions of Higher Education in the South* (Washington, 1958). The following suggest possibilities and problems involved in intercollege cooperation: Sidney R. Packard, "Academic Cooperation," *Educational Record*, XL (October, 1959), 358–363; C. L. Barber and others, *The New College Plan: A Proposal for a Major Departure in Higher Education* (Amherst, 1958).

[25] Jennings B. Sanders, "College Social Sciences: A Statistical Evaluation with Special Reference to History," *Higher Education*, XI (April, 1955), 109–113. The data we have collected suggest that the distribution of enrollments has not significantly changed since Sanders wrote.

degree of unity to subsequent study in history courses that in many colleges are highly fragmented.[26]

METHODS OF TEACHING

After serving as president of Cornell University, Andrew D. White wryly recalled the kind of history instruction he had received at Yale in the class of 1853: "It consisted simply in hearing the student repeat from memory the dates from 'Putz's Ancient History.' " [27] Now it is the lecture system that is under attack. Because they so often consist of factual lectures, history courses have been described by one critic as "the university's most perfect type of the fact-loaded, idea-absent, academic exercise." [28] Advocates of educational television have answered criticism of its limitations upon ideal teacher-student interaction with the telling rebuttal that "the ideal is rarely achieved by conventional teaching methods." [29] Yet the lecture remains the basic form of instruction in which history courses are most commonly taught, and it is worth strongly defending as a way of alerting students quickly to conflicting historical interpretations and thus stimulating critical thought, and as a medium that can make history "come alive" as probably no other medium can.

Furthermore, it is important to note that lecturing is supplemented by discussion sections in many history departments. Opportunities for semi-independent study are provided for students who are capable of profiting from independence. Parallel reading almost invariably accompanies lectures and textbook study, providing opportunities for semi-independent work; on a great many

[26] McGrath, *The Graduate School and the Decline of Liberal Education*, vi and *passim*, blames the graduate schools too exclusively for the fragmentation of courses in the colleges.
[27] Quoted from Andrew Dickson White's *Autobiography* by W. H. Cowley in "College and University Teaching, 1858–1958," *Educational Record*, XXXIX (October, 1958), 311–326.
[28] Williams, *Some of My Best Friends Are Professors*, 226–229.
[29] C. R. Carpenter in Adams, Carpenter, and Smith (eds.), *College Teaching by Television*, 13–14.

campuses history instructors make use of paperback booklets that present primary sources or varieties of interpretations of historical events, thus laying the basis for term papers or discussion sessions. Some history teachers use movies, slide projectors, musical recordings, art illustrations, and field trips to convey to students the spirit of the age through which they are asked to pass vicariously.

Methods of instruction other than the lecture are varied and, in the better colleges, fairly common. The freshman course in history at Carnegie Institute of Technology, for example, has introduced students to the nature of history and to the study of primary sources,[30] and Antioch College also emphasizes historical method in the introductory history courses.[31] Reed College features small discussion groups, frequent conferences about written work between teachers and individual students, and extensive reading. It has no textbook courses. One-tenth of the 126 better colleges we surveyed require history majors to take either a research seminar, a course in historiography, or a combination of these (see also Table 4-9). Wesleyan University introduces history majors to one-term research seminars during the sophomore year.[32] A few of the better colleges of the nation require all history majors to write senior theses. Honors work involving the writing of senior theses is somewhat more frequently offered to outstanding majors; it is reported by 13% of the typical colleges, and by 28% of the better colleges.

Most colleges expect to make no major changes in their methods

[30] See Department of History, Carnegie Institute of Technology (Edwin Fenton), "Teaching the First Ten Assignments in an Introductory European History Course." (Copies are available at 25¢ each.) See also Paul L. Ward, *A Style of History for Beginners* (Washington, 1959), a publication issued by the Service Center for Teachers of History, American Historical Association.

[31] See Irvin Abrams, "The Historian's Craft and General Education," *Journal of General Education*, IX (October, 1955), 36–41.

[32] For a similar requirement at the junior level see Henry Reiff, "Historiography and Government Research: A Blended Course in History and Government at St. Lawrence University," *Journal of Higher Education*, XXII (March, 1951), 129–137.

TABLE 4-9

COMPARISON OF SELECTED FORMS OF HISTORY INSTRUCTION
BY TYPES OF COLLEGES, 1958–1959

Form of instruction	% of colleges reporting each form of instruction offered during 1957–1958					
	Nation (376)	Professional colleges (24)	Teachers' colleges (40)	Negro colleges (21)	Catholic colleges (85)	General colleges (206)
Tutorial work	7	4	8	14	8	6
Directed readings	34	17	33	43	40	33
Instruction to individual students	11	21	10	10	6	12
Seminar work	48	21	33	52	56	51

of teaching history in order to meet rising enrollments. Three-fifths of the history departments will add new sections of existing courses. Only 2% suggest that they may use television, and less than 1% expect to inaugurate independent study by the students. Two out of five (38%) of the colleges and junior colleges plan to meet future enrollment increases as they have met them in the past, by enlarging sections. This almost certainly means that the lecture will remain the basic form of history instruction in most colleges. Colleges with large enrollments and few history teachers cannot offer special attention to individual students, or to small groups of them, no matter how convinced the history faculties are that this is desirable. The way to more personalized as well as more scholarly history teaching can be found in these colleges only through substantial reductions in the work loads of history faculties.

HISTORY MAJORS

Special faculty attention to students in large introductory courses is understandably unusual. Most historians would agree, however, that it should be commonplace in the education of history majors. While this happy condition does not yet exist, there are encouraging signs that it is coming (see Table 4-9).

The history major almost always requires distribution of course work in at least two fields—most commonly in United States and European history—and 10 of the 126 better colleges specify that majors must study in three or four fields of history. These requirements are especially desirable in departments that offer many highly specialized history courses. To further the integration of historical knowledge and to fill in gaps in reading, a number of colleges offer special courses, seminars, or reading programs.

The typical major program in history in the colleges offers, it must be admitted, much less imaginative and personalized fare and thus less fully prepares students for the kind of work expected by graduate faculties. The major program commonly requires 24 to 30 semester hours of history (reported by three-fourths of the better colleges). In the colleges that offer the general social science major with concentration in history, the requirement is usually 30 to 40 semester hours of courses in the social sciences.[33] Only one content course is usually specified as a requirement for the major in history, and that is the introductory course in United States history. (This is generally required of public school teachers by state law.) The United States history course has been reported to be a requirement for the major in 86% of a sample of 290 institutions.[34] The widespread adoption of this requirement since World War II helps to explain why so many teaching positions have been available for new Ph.D.s in United States history.

Strong or weak, offering personalized attention or mass educa-

[33] Of all the bachelor's degrees granted in 1957–1958 in "history" and in "social science," 60% were granted in "history." And 60% of the 1,342 institutions granting either degree granted the degree in "history." Our samples of the colleges are heavily weighted (86% "history," 14% "social science") in favor of institutions that offer the bachelor's degree with a major in "history." (HEW, *Earned Degrees* . . . *1957–1958*, 37, 175–178, 182–187.)

[34] Jennings B. Sanders, "How the College Introductory Course in United States History is Organized and Taught," mimeographed Circular No. 288, U.S. Office of Education (Washington, Apr. 10, 1951), 14.

tion, the history major program attracts a sizable proportion of the junior and senior students in most liberal arts colleges. In the three-year period 1956–1959 history majors accounted for about 3.5% of all the bachelor's graduates in the nation, and history's share of the total increased slightly each year in that period. The bachelor's degree with a major in history was conferred by 790 institutions in 1957 and by 840 in 1959. The history majors graduating in 1959—13,742—were 30% more numerous than those of 1956.[35] Half the better colleges (52%) report that one-tenth or more of their graduates were history majors. In comparison with majors in other disciplines, the major in history ranked first in number of graduating seniors in one-fourth (26%) of the better colleges, and among the top three majors in three-fourths (77%) of them.

SUMMARY

What emerges from this survey of history in the colleges that is most pertinent to graduate education in history?

It is of first importance for graduate faculties to note that the colleges want historians who are capable teachers. Both the colleges and the universities need to foster good teaching by young historians more than they do.

The training of college teachers should continue to emphasize experience in research scholarship. This training, important for all college teachers, is especially needed by those who teach graduate as well as undergraduate students—2 out of every 5 *college* teachers of history who hold the Ph.D.

It is especially important to note that so many of the history teachers in the colleges have achieved the Ph.D.: 22% of the junior college teachers, 58% of the teachers in "typical" four-year colleges, and 71% of the teachers in the better colleges. These statistics have a direct bearing upon proposals to create new degrees for college

---

[35] The data for all the nation's bachelor's degree graduates were taken from HEW, *Earned Degrees* . . . *1956–1957*, 12, 22, 27; *1957–1958*, 8, 23, 37; and *1958–1959*, 30–31, 35.

teachers. They should also be considered by institutions that are thinking of starting Ph.D. programs.

Both the graduate history faculties and the college administrations will agree that the development of young Ph.D.s as teachers and as scholars is severely handicapped in many colleges by low salaries, inadequate libraries, and heavy teaching loads. And it is to be hoped that college history teachers in the future might be less often expected to teach primarily in fields other than the one in which they have concentrated their doctoral studies. Since it will continue to be necessary for instructors to do some teaching in more than one field of history in a great many colleges, doctoral programs must provide new Ph.D.s with considerable breadth of historical training.

The variety of history courses in the colleges is encouraging. It makes teaching in the colleges attractive to trained historians, and offers a range of education to undergraduates that is to be applauded. But care should be taken to offer history courses to nonmajor undergraduates that suit their broad needs and their limited time for the study of history.

An awareness of the discipline as a whole can be conveyed to undergraduate history majors by requiring a patterned distribution of courses in three or four broad fields of history, by providing a comprehensive reading course for senior majors to fill gaps in coverage, or by the introduction of a comprehensive examination for history majors. In addition, majors ought to be acquainted—the earlier the better—with historical method, changing philosophies of history, and the classics of historical literature. Early competence in foreign languages should be strongly encouraged. Neglect of the non-Western areas should be ended. In 1961 a distinguished committee recommended that: "During their undergraduate years, all students should get at least an introductory acquaintance with some culture other than their own." [36]

In training Ph.D. candidates as teachers, graduate faculties

[36] John B. Howard, Harold Boeschenstein, and others, *The University and World Affairs* (n.p. [New York?], n.d. [1961]), 17, a Ford Foundation report of the Committee on the University and World Affairs.

should take cognizance of the diversity of forms of instruction in the colleges. Formal lectures will continue to constitute the basic method of history instruction, but Ph.D. candidates should also be prepared to lead discussions, direct independent study by students, and conduct small-group tutorials and seminars. Whatever the form of instruction, college history instructors will continue to try to develop in students—majors and nonmajors alike—the capacity for critical thinking and literate expression along with historical understanding. They will find time to become more scholarly teachers through research, while recognizing that their best chance to make an impact on others is offered by the classroom. The history classrooms in American colleges, especially in our nervous era, can be "an abiding influence in the life of the great nation to which we belong and . . . a vital part of life itself."[37]

[37] Dexter Perkins, "We Shall Gladly Teach," *American Historical Review*, LXII (January, 1957), 309.

Chapter 5

THE MASTER'S DEGREE

For about 3 out of 10 college-level teachers of history the master's is the highest degree. In the late 1950s, amidst growing anxieties about the teacher shortage, several proposals were advanced for the creation of special master's degree programs for college teachers. These proposals won quick support from critics of traditional Ph.D. training. The present and future of master's training in history is thus of great concern to all those who appoint college teachers of history, and its future has a direct bearing upon the consideration of proposals to reform Ph.D. training.

The prevalence of master's training must be considered in any contemplation of the present condition and prospects of the degree. Awarded by all the institutions that are engaged in Ph.D. training in history, the master's is for most Ph.D.s a part of doctoral training. One-fourth (26%) of the Ph.D.-training history departments require students who aspire to the doctorate to take the master's degree; only 7% discourage them from taking the master's or are indifferent about it. A survey of 143 recent history Ph.D.s has shown that 98% earned the master's degree; 86% of them earned it in history.[1] In addition to the eighty-odd Ph.D.-training history departments, more than 100 others offer the degree

[1] Data supplied by Dr. John K. Folger of the Southern Regional Education Board.

in history. A total of 196 institutions in the nation awarded the master's degree in history in 1959, many more than in any of the social sciences. (Sociology, with 115 in 1958, was the nearest "rival.") In our sample of four-year colleges, one-fifth of the "typical" institutions offer the master's degree in history. Half the better ones do so. The number of master's programs is likely to grow, for 11% of the "typical" colleges and 8% of the better ones report that they are considering inaugurating them.

The number of persons earning the master's in history has increased each year since 1956; 1,643 master's degrees in history were awarded in 1959 (see Table 2-5 in Chapter 2). Production has developed in recent years in comparison with the 1956 level as follows: 1957, 113%; 1958, 125%; and 1959, 147%.[2] The Ph.D.-training universities awarded two-thirds (67%) of all the master's degrees in history in the nation in 1958, averaging 12 master's graduates each. Three institutions awarded more than 40 and the largest producer—Columbia University—awarded 87 degrees, 1 out of every 16 in the nation. On the other hand, more than one-fourth of all institutions awarding master's degrees in history in 1958 awarded no more than two degrees each.[3]

How is master's training now conducted? What alternatives to it have been proposed?[4] To find out about these matters, questionnaires on master's training were collected from 164 institutions. Together, these institutions awarded four-fifths of all the master's degrees in history in the nation in 1958. They include 77 Ph.D.-training departments of history and 87 departments in colleges that award the master's degree in history.

[2] HEW, *Earned Degrees* . . . *1956–1957*, 12; *1957–1958*, 23, 37; and *1958–1959*, 30–31, 35.
[3] Production statistics are taken or averaged from HEW, *Earned Degrees* . . . *1957–1958*, 182–187.
[4] Berelson, *Graduate Education*, 185–190, shows that large numbers of academicians favor "rehabilitation" of the master's degree.

ADMISSION, SCREENING, AND BASIC REQUIREMENTS

"At present, requirements for the A.M. vary sharply over the country and as the requirements vary, so does the respect paid the degree."[5] These words from the 1957 report of four graduate deans succinctly summarize the present training of historians at the master's level.

Variations begin with admission of students. Some institutions take almost all applicants who have had undergraduate academic records of at least average quality (C or better). At the same time, students in obscure colleges with almost "straight-A" records find it difficult to gain admission to major centers of graduate study. In a number of the Ph.D.-training history departments visited during this study, lower standards are set for master's candidates than for post-M.A. students. This happens especially in the state universities, which feel obligated to serve secondary education. Partly because many of the history Ph.D.s of 1958 assume this double standard, a majority of them report that admission of master's candidates was "sufficiently rigorous" in the departments where they took Ph.D. training.

Two-fifths (41%) of the 1958 Ph.D.s (and 57% of the graduates of the seven programs highest in prestige) state that "some too many" or "far too many" master's candidates were in residence at their universities "for adequate faculty attention to them." Screening of students generally lacks rigor during the first year of graduate study. Even in such a difficult field as Russian studies, three-fifths of the entering students in five universities, 1946–1956, were awarded master's degrees, and in three of these universities four-fifths or more of the entrants were awarded degrees.[6]

If too few students are now sent away during the first year of

[5] Report by J. Barzun and others to the 58th Annual Conference of the Association of American Universities and the 9th Annual Conference of the Association of Graduate Schools, October 22–23, 1957, published in *Journal of Proceedings and Addresses—1957.*

[6] Black and Thompson (eds.), *American Teaching About Russia,* 61.

graduate study, perhaps the fault lies with faculty grading rather than with departmental policy. For 88% of the Ph.D.-training departments and 85% of the colleges that offer the master's in history already require a minimum grade level of B for successful completion of the master's degree. Standards seem to be slightly less rigorous in the East than elsewhere; only 69% of the Eastern colleges granting master's degrees in history report that they require a minimum grade level of B.

Though forms differ, requirements of credit hours are, in substance, the most uniform of all stipulations for the master's degree. Most departments either require 30 semester hours including 6 hours credit for thesis or 24 hours plus a thesis for which no hour-credit is given. Residence requirements vary but a full academic year or its equivalent in summer terms is stipulated by about four-fifths of the institutions that offer the master's degree in history. There is much more variation in the more significant requirements for the master's degree.

THE MASTER'S THESIS

About three-fourths of all the colleges and universities in our sample still require a thesis for the master's degree in history (see Table 5-1). It is optional in many other departments. Some of the

TABLE 5-1

THESIS REQUIREMENTS IN COLLEGES AND UNIVERSITIES
OFFERING THE MASTER'S DEGREE IN HISTORY, 1958–1959

Characteristic	% of 87 reporting colleges					% of 77 reporting universities				
	Nation	East	South	Midwest	West	Nation	East	South	Midwest	West
Thesis is required...	77	62	77	94	76	75	83	88	50	80
Thesis on a foreign area must be based on sources in language of the area	72	90	59	62	75	69	73	65	57	82

Ph.D.-training faculties that do not require the thesis of all master's candidates nevertheless demand it of those who aspire to the Ph.D. They insist that students need the thesis experience and that the faculty needs the thesis as proof of ability to do Ph.D.-level work. Other departments explicitly discourage the writing of master's theses by would-be Ph.D. candidates. They argue either (1) that the prerequisite experience for doctoral work and the demonstration of ability can both be accomplished in a year of seminar work by master's candidates, or (2) that they can be accomplished during studies at the Ph.D. level. Among the historians interviewed in this study, those who either wish or are willing to eliminate the master's thesis for Ph.D. candidates are somewhat more numerous than the defenders of the thesis requirement.

How much would be lost if the master's thesis were to be abandoned? How serious a scholarly effort do master's theses represent where they are now written? Ideally the thesis should be a "historical work that is exemplary in style and method, based solidly on original sources and interpretatively significant in current scholarship." This is the kind of thesis that Loyola University (Chicago) described in 1959 in announcing the inauguration of the William P. Lyons Master's Essay Award. The Lyons Award offers tangible evidence of the serious belief in some quarters that much would be lost if the master's thesis were to be abandoned.

Both the prestige of the thesis and its training value may be approximately gauged by the amount of faculty time and criticism that is given to the project. One index of faculty effort is suggested by the way in which thesis subjects are chosen. Usually agreement between the student and a major professor is sufficient; only 8% of the Ph.D.-training departments require the deliberation of a faculty committee. The ratio of faculty members to master's graduates is also suggestive. In 1958 the Ph.D.-training universities awarded an average of 7 master's degrees in history for every 10 history faculty members. The colleges on an average awarded between 4 and 5 master's degrees for every 10 members of the history faculty. Thus the college faculties may be able to give more time to the supervision of master's theses than university faculties do.

Still another way to estimate the faculty effort that a master's thesis represents is to ask how many professors must read and pass on a thesis. In more than half (54%) of the Ph.D.-training departments the answer is three or more faculty members. Two readers suffice in one-third of the departments. In 1 out of 8 (12%) a single reader is sufficient. Where a committee is consulted, the timing is significant. In at least 36% of the Ph.D.-training departments the opinions of second, third, or fourth readers are solicited before the student completes a full draft of the thesis. But in at least 45% of the departments the committee members read and pass on the thesis after a complete draft has been written by the master's candidate.

The length of master's theses is not a good test of scholarly quality but it is crudely suggestive of the size of the task. Each department that was surveyed was asked to list the length and titles of three "typical theses accepted since 1956." The lengths of the 267 theses reported range from a low of 56 to a high of 358 pages; 23% are shorter than 100 pages and another 23% are longer than 160 pages. Three-fourths of the theses are less than 160 pages long. It is often difficult to imagine why one topic is treated briefly and another at length. Why should "Horace Maynard: A Tennessee Statesman" get only 56 pages while "Richard Bennett Hubbard, 'The Demosthenes of Texas'" is worth twice as many? But judging by the length of typical theses it seems quite clear that they represent a large investment of time, energy, and money.

Thesis research for would-be Ph.D. candidates in the history of foreign areas can have a special value if it accustoms them to using foreign language sources. A large majority of the reporting departments in the colleges as well as in the universities agree that students should be allowed to write theses on foreign areas only when they are able (and willing) to use the languages of the subject areas, and exceptions are discouraged even in those departments that allow them.

OTHER VARIATIONS

The varieties of thesis and other requirements reflect a fundamental and prevalent uncertainty and disagreement about the purpose of training at the master's level. In twentieth-century America the old European concept of the master's degree as evidence of broad cultural experience has been challenged and modified—some would say corrupted—by attempts to introduce students to the more confining rigors of professional research training. Because of internal differences of opinion, most graduate faculties build both concepts into their rules, often allowing considerable room for flexible interpretation of the regulations. On a smaller scale this happens within a single department: one faculty member aims primarily at the one goal while a colleague seeks the other.

The position of foreign language examinations among requirements for the master's degree is ambiguous. The requirement is sometimes justified on the grounds that it fosters intellectual breadth. Other departments require reading knowledge of a foreign language as a research tool though they may not think its worth as a cultural attribute justifies the price students pay to achieve it. Among both colleges and universities, considered on a regional basis, master's candidates are least often required to pass a foreign language examination in the Midwest. In the nation as a whole almost half the colleges (47%) and universities (48%) require master's candidates to pass an examination in one foreign language.

Potentially the requirement that master's candidates in history take courses in other disciplines is, like the foreign language requirement, adaptable to the needs of either research training or cultural breadth. In practice, however, cultural breadth is the usual justification for this requirement, and it is often linked with the pragmatic argument that students as future teachers must be prepared to give instruction in fields related to history. Yet there is little agreement about requiring work in other disciplines or about the specific nature or purposes of such work. Compromise is inevitable, and it is most often found in the formula that study in other fields shall be "encouraged"; that is, it shall be neither "required" nor "discouraged." In our combined sample of colleges and universities, minorities of almost equal numbers "require" courses in other disciplines (25%) or "discourage" students from taking them (21%). Departments in each of these groups have, though in different directions, taken large steps toward resolving internal differences and defining their purposes; many of the remaining 54% that "encourage" study in other disciplines have not. The students in many of these departments are left to make their own rule.

A majority of students at the master's level, left to their own devices, seem to choose courses of least resistance rather than avidly to seek either of the goals—research prowess or cultural breadth—that might logically justify study in another discipline. They tend to study neither the strange and often difficult methodology of other disciplines that could enrich their research method nor the new content courses that could most broaden their conceptualization of history and their capacity for teaching it. Literature, political science, and economics (especially economic history), the same disciplines most often studied as minors by undergraduate history majors, are the ones most often elected as minors at the master's level. The very circumstance that should cause master's candidates to take work in a relatively neglected discipline such as psychology usually causes or rationalizes their failure to do so: undergraduate prerequisites for graduate courses have not been taken.

One way out of this dilemma is to permit master's candidates to fulfill requirements in another discipline by taking undergraduate survey courses for graduate credit. Perhaps even if this is done—and almost certainly if it is not done—history students who study other disciplines will continue to elect courses most like their own. And unless the faculties clarify their thinking on these matters history students who take courses in other disciplines will take widely varying amounts of work. At present 51% of the university departments that report any requirement of work in other disciplines require only one or two courses; one-fourth require three courses and another fourth require four or more courses.

The variety of practices that has been noted at every stage of master's training appears also in the final testing procedure. Some departments—apparently as many as 15 to 20%—require neither a written nor an oral terminal examination. A few (perhaps 4%) require one or the other of each student (presumably letting him choose between trial by fire and trial by water). A larger number of the departments—almost 20% of those requiring a terminal examination—specify that the examination is to be written; somewhat more (approximately 30%) require both a written and an oral examination; and still more—about half—administer an oral examination only.

The oral examination is required (singly or with a written examination) in about four-fifths of all departments that administer any terminal examination. The oral examination is most often required in the Midwest, least often in the East. In almost two-thirds of the universities but in only 43% of the colleges requiring an oral examination the candidate usually is questioned an hour and a half or longer. Commonly a committee of three examines the candidate. In 46% of the colleges (but in only 16% of the universities) four or more examiners participate, and it is in the South that examining committees are most often this large. The oral examination in almost half the colleges and universities that require it covers course work or fields taken in master's training as well as a defense of the thesis. One out of five demands defense of the thesis and restricts the content examination to the field of the thesis. One-third of the institutions cover courses or fields but demand no defense of the thesis. (Many—probably most —of these institutions do not require students to write theses.)

When the master's candidate has paid his typist (if there was one) and has been congratulated by his oral examination committee (when one has functioned) he may count the months he has invested in the degree. The sums of time, like the other characteristics of master's training, differ greatly from institution to institution. One thing is certain: the "typical" master's candidate needs much more than the advertised period of one academic year to complete the degree. Reports were received from our sample of *colleges* on the length of graduate study required for 182 persons earning master's degrees in history in 1958. In these cases there can be no uncertainty whether the time was spent in master's or doctoral training because none of the reporting institutions offered the Ph.D. The average (mean) period reported was 18 months— two academic years or one and a half calendar years. For one-third (34%) of the national sample of 1958 master's degree winners the degree was based upon more than 18 months of graduate study; only 15% completed the degree in 9 months of study.[7]

This survey of master's training shows that it is futile to talk of what *the* master's degree in history is like. There is no such identifiable thing. There are, instead, dozens of different varieties of master's degrees in history with varying combinations of some or all of the ingredients sketched above. In many institutions the master's is a strong degree. In others it is weak.

One must carefully distinguish between colleges and universities in discussing master's training, but on the surface the college master's appears to be as strong as the university master's (see Table 5-2). The regional strengths and weaknesses of master's training in history are also worth noting. It is current fashion in discussions of the master's degree to point to some regions as the guardians of its purity and to the East as its defiler. Whatever may be true of other disciplines, in history it is insufficient to say that the master's degree has been weakened only in the East, or "east of the Hudson." Among the universities, those in the South give on the whole a strong master's degree and those in the Midwest give weaker ones. Among the colleges, those in the Midwest give a strong degree, closely followed by the West. The institutions

[7] Woodrow Wilson National Fellowship Foundation, *Report for 1959*, 7, shows that only 23% of the Fellows of 1958–1959 had been awarded the master's degree at the end of one year of graduate study.

TABLE 5-2

RELATIVE STRENGTH OF MASTER'S TRAINING IN 77 UNIVERSITIES AND 87 COLLEGES, 1958–1959

Characteristic	% of Institutions reporting	
	Universities	Colleges
B average required	88	85
Thesis required	75	77
Theses more than 100 pp. in length	65	77
Theses on foreign areas required to be based on sources in foreign languages	69	72
Foreign language examination required	48	47
Courses in other disciplines required	27	23
Oral examination required	69	76
Oral examination of 1½ hours or more	63	43
More than 3 faculty members for final oral examination	16	46
Thesis and more than thesis field covered on oral examination	48	41

of the East, which on the whole do give a relatively weak master's degree, nevertheless maintain notably high standards of foreign-language competence.

It must be emphasized that this account has been concerned with the master's degree in *history*—usually reported by departments as a "master of arts" degree, but occasionally reported as a "master of science" degree. This account does not cover the master's degree in social science, a degree that often allows concentration in history and that was awarded by 81 institutions in 1958.[8] It does not cover the master's degree in Education, which sometimes involves concentration in history (more commonly, in social science); nor has it covered the "master of arts in teaching" degree (M.A.T.), which a few universities have inaugurated for secondary school teachers and which allows concentration in history. There has been

[8] HEW, *Earned Degrees* . . . *1957–1958*, 23, 37.

sufficient variety of practice observable in limiting discussion to master's training in history. There is variety also in the uses to which this training is put.

THE USES OF THE MASTER'S DEGREE

Theoretically, standardization of training might be the first step toward standardization of use, and most advocates of reform approach the problem in this way. But in practice the chances are probably even greater that standardization of use will lead to greater uniformity of training. Is the master's degree in history to be offered primarily for secondary teachers of social studies? A clear decision for this alternative would in some institutions call for standardization downward. It would necessitate relatively lax admission standards, the training of very large numbers of students, less rigorous and less individualistic student work, emphasis upon breadth more than upon research training, and in most cases the completion of the master's program in one calendar year at most. Is the master's degree to be offered not for secondary teachers but for college teachers? A clear decision for this alternative would quite generally necessitate standardization upward. The task in this case would be not so much to "rehabilitate" the master's degree as to create a new variety of M.A.

Since the colleges want their teachers to be broadly educated, trained as research scholars, and acquainted with the problems of teaching, it will not do to offer them the master's degree of forty or sixty years ago. A master's degree deliberately designed to meet the needs of college teachers must be a junior Ph.D. if it is to be attempted at all. Since fewer candidates would want it than would want a master's for secondary teachers, fairly high admission standards for such a degree could be established, training could be reasonably individualistic and rigorous, and considerable emphasis could be placed on research training if not on creative scholarship. All this plus the achievement of breadth and possibly some supervised introduction to college teaching would make it difficult to compress the training period into less than two academic years, and part-time students might require three academic years.

Faculties will be more inclined to build programs for a super-master's if they are reasonably certain that the colleges will appoint and promote persons who might earn it. Can they be "reasonably certain" now? Chapter 4 of this study has shown that a good many teachers of history in colleges and very many in junior colleges lack the Ph.D. degree; but this does not mean that they have only the master's degree. Most of them have engaged in post-master's study and many have completed all requirements for the doctorate except the dissertation. Their presence on college faculties cannot be accepted as evidence of general demand in the colleges for persons with only a master's degree.

In an attempt to determine the present uses of the master's degree, departments of history in the fall of 1958 were asked to report on the professional activities of persons to whom they had awarded the master's degree in history that year. This yielded reports on 544 persons, 39% of all 1,397 master's degrees in history awarded in the nation in 1958. Almost two-thirds of the new master's graduates were pursuing doctoral studies. Those who earned university master's degrees much more frequently pursued doctoral studies than did those who earned college master's degrees (74% and 43%). The next most common professional function of master's training in history is to further the qualifications of secondary school teachers: 12% of the university master's graduates and 25% of the college master's graduates found positions in secondary education. Almost half (45%) of those in the total sample who did not undertake doctoral studies found teaching positions in secondary education and about 3% more entered elementary education. Only 2% of the history master's graduates of 1958 are reported to have found college teaching positions, and only 4% more were appointed to junior college faculties. Whatever the future may hold, few persons with only the master's degree in history are now appointed to college teaching positions.

PROPOSED REFORMS: FOR SECONDARY SCHOOL TEACHERS

History departments have an obligation to the schools that they cannot ignore, especially since Soviet as well as American educators are working toward a fifth year of study for secondary school teachers and calling for more emphasis on "solid subject matter content." [9] If the traditional master's degree is to be refurbished for college teachers something must be put in its place for secondary teachers. The substitute must be acceptable to both the secondary schools and the history faculties in colleges and universities. In devising the substitute it will be both pedagogically and strategically wise to recognize the good sense in admonitions by W. H. Cartwright and R. M. Lumiansky that "the whole university rather than any special department or division"—the administration and the academic departments as well as the professors of Education—"must enter actively and cooperatively into the program." [10]

Several colleges and universities—among them Harvard, Yale, Wesleyan University, Brown, Colgate, Mount Holyoke, the University of Massachusetts, Johns Hopkins, Duke, Vanderbilt, and Tulane—have inaugurated the Master of Arts in Teaching (M.A.T.) for secondary teachers. This degree has at least the advantage of clearly defined function. One institution that awards only the M.A.T. as a graduate degree speaks for others in reporting that graduates are placed in "all types of secondary and elementary

[9] On American approaches see, e.g., the following thoughtful articles in the April, 1959, number of *Educational Record* (XL): William H. Cartwright, "The Graduate Education of Teachers—Proposals for the Future," 149, 150; Calvin E. Gross, "A Rationale for Teacher Education," 137, 141; R. M. Lumiansky, "Concerning Graduate Education for Teachers," 145. On Soviet trends see U.S. Office of Education, *Soviet Commitment to Education: Report of the First Official U.S. Education Mission to the U.S.S.R., with an Analysis of Recent Educational Reforms* (Washington, 1959), 85.

[10] Cartwright, "The Graduate Education of Teachers," 154; Lumiansky, "Concerning Graduate Education for Teachers," 145.

teaching positions or administrative posts in these levels." Few, if any, M.A.T.s go on to doctoral studies. Graduates are not appointed to college or junior college positions. But if the professional use of the M.A.T. is clearly defined, its requirements already vary somewhat from institution to institution. The M.A.T. commonly requires more hours of course work than the older master's degree, divides them between the subject-matter field and Education, requires no foreign language examination, and sometimes requires no terminal examination. It can be completed in nine to twelve months.

With the M.A.T. available, is there any compelling reason why Ph.D.-training departments should continue to offer the traditional master's degree in history for secondary teachers? How serious a loss would the secondary schools suffer if the master's degree in history were no longer offered for their teachers? There is no way to know exactly the number or percentage of the new master's-level secondary school teachers of a given year that earn the master's degree *in history*. We can estimate that at most about 1 out of 6 new master's-level teachers of history in the secondary schools in 1958 could have earned the master's degree in history.[11] Since only about half of these earned their degrees in universities, the universities could have provided no more—at the very most—than 1 out of 12 persons who make up the pool of new, master's-level history teachers in secondary schools in a given year. It seems probable that secondary education would suffer no irreparable quantitative damage if the Ph.D.-training history departments should cease offering the master's in history for secondary teachers.

How much of a loss would Ph.D.-training departments suffer if they were no longer to offer the master's degree in history for secondary school teachers? For some institutions the loss would be a very considerable one, especially in summer school enrollments; but already two-thirds of the Ph.D.-training and college history

[11] This assumes that the number of would-be secondary school teachers of history earning master's degrees in 1958 was at least 1,480. Probably about 237 persons who were awarded the master's degree in history in 1958 went into secondary teaching.

departments (65% in the former and 69% in the latter) report that secondary teachers in their institutions tend to seek the master's degree in Education or the M.A.T. rather than the master's degree in history. The colleges and the universities agree that they make their choice chiefly because Education offers a quicker or easier degree, though in some institutions students also choose Education to meet state certification requirements for teachers. This tendency of secondary teachers to shy away from the master's in history enables many of the history departments to maintain higher standards for the master's degree in history than would be possible if they tried to educate large numbers of prospective secondary school teachers.

Some history departments strongly oppose abandoning the master's degree in history for secondary teachers on the grounds that secondary teachers need to gain research training by writing theses. But very many secondary teachers who earn the master's degree manage to do so without writing theses. (Many of the larger history departments offer a choice of degree programs; master's candidates may choose one with or one without the thesis requirement.) The strongest argument against the M.A.T. for history teachers is that it would provide them with fewer content courses than the present master's degree in history. To this complaint advocates of the M.A.T. reply that the new degree offers a way through which some secondary teachers now taking the M.Ed.—and completely lost to historians—might be at least half-saved by the graduate history faculties.

Would students be attracted in large numbers to M.A.T. programs for secondary school teachers? Factors that lie outside the program would determine this, and the basic factor would probably be the prevailing salaries for secondary school teachers.[12]

[12] See Ernest Stabler, "The Master of Arts in Teaching Idea," *The Educational Record*, XLI (July, 1960), 224–229. It may be noted in passing that in the U.S.S.R., where salaries for secondary teachers compare favorably with those for medical doctors, there is no shortage of candidates. On the contrary, only about 1 out of 5 applicants are admitted to teacher-training institutions, according to the U.S. Office of Education, *Soviet Commitment to Education*, 85.

Money can do more than experimentation with master's curricula to staff the secondary school history courses with competent teachers during the 1960s.

PROPOSED REFORMS: FOR COLLEGE TEACHERS

Perhaps a few Ph.D.-training history departments will wish to reform master's training by incidentally awarding the M.A. degree to Ph.D. candidates upon the completion of all requirements for the Ph.D. except the dissertation. This is already being done by Princeton University. No candidate who wants only the master's degree is admitted to graduate study in history at Princeton. Yet by conferring the master's degree only upon students who have completed two to three years of graduate study and who are expected to be able to complete the Ph.D., Princeton has in actuality created a super-master's degree of the kind that has figured in a good many theoretical statements in recent years.

Widespread adoption of the Princeton plan would provide qualified college teachers of history, but if Princeton standards were maintained it would not provide college teachers in greatly larger numbers than can be awarded Ph.D.s. Various plans have been suggested for a master's degree that would prepare larger numbers of college teachers. The Committee on Policies in Graduate Education of the Association of Graduate Schools (AGS) in 1957 proposed a "rehabilitated" year-and-a-half master's program for college teachers that would not necessarily be terminal. "The first year should be exactly like that of the candidate for the Ph.D., since the difference between the degrees should pivot on amount and not on quality. In the third term (the first of the second year), each candidate should take a course directly concerned with the teaching of this subject. This course should be taught only by members of the student's department. . . . In this same term the student would write an essay of 75 to 125 pages, preferably stemming from his seminar of the second term, which need not be the original contribution demanded of the Ph.D. Finally, the student's subject should be named on the Master's diploma." [13]

Similar proposals quickly followed. On November 20, 1957, the Trustees of the Carnegie Foundation for the Advancement of Teaching cited the AGS report of the four graduate deans and, without providing details, called for "a rigorous effort . . . to revitalize the Master of Arts degree and make it a terminal degree for teaching." [14] A. P. Brogan, dean emeritus of the University of Texas graduate school, in the spring of 1958 proposed a master's degree for college teachers that would be completed in twelve months of study in "strictly graduate courses" with emphasis on "seminars and conference work." The Brogan master's would include some introduction to "the methods and the problems of teaching" and a thesis usually less than 100 pages in length, viewed as a training experience but "suitable for publication at least in form." [15]

The year 1959 brought other proposals. In February the dean of a West Coast graduate school, supported by the historian then president of the university, suggested the creation of a new degree, the "diplomate in college teaching." This proposed program would identify potential college teachers and begin their preparation in the junior year of undergraduate study. It would continue for three full academic years and two or three summers. Taking required courses would be minimized and the program would "maximize reliance on self-study, research, conferences, discussions, and creative scholarly achievements." [16] Later in 1959 the principle of beginning the training of college teachers in the junior year of undergraduate study was incorporated in a new proposal by Oliver C. Carmichael, consultant to the Fund for the Advancement of

[13] See footnote 5, above.
[14] Grayson L. Kirk and others, "The Education of College Teachers," 13, 18.
[15] A. P. Brogan, "Tarnishing is an Autocatalytic Reaction: Restoring the Master's Degree," *The Graduate Journal*, I (Spring, 1958), 34–40.
[16] Harry Alpert, "The Diplomate in College Teaching," mimeographed proposal "for discussion purposes only," University of Oregon, Feb. 13, 1959.

Education and former president of the University of Alabama. The program would involve: (1) selection and advice of students during the first two undergraduate years; (2) teaching of one course (one term) by undergraduates; (3) much more reading and writing of research papers during the junior and senior years than is now common; and (4) a master's thesis. The master's thus earned would not necessarily be a terminal degree; on the contrary, the author of this plan suggests that one of its advantages would be "in recruiting Ph.D. candidates," and another would be its acceleration of doctoral training.[17]

Unless the policies of both the colleges and the accrediting associations are changed there will be few jobs for college history teachers with master's degrees representing twelve to eighteen months of graduate study. Officials of all six regional accrediting associations, responding to specific questions, show no sympathy for a one-year master's degree. A two- or three-year master's degree such as that awarded at Princeton will be honored much more readily.[18] But the accrediting officials make it clear that the Ph.D. is the preferred degree for college teachers. One states that "in general staff members who have two years of graduate study are regarded as better qualified than those who hold only the master's degree," but adds that "a two-years' master's degree for college teachers is not to be weighted as satisfactory for a large number of college teachers." One accrediting agency official even wrote that: "A Doctor's degree is accepted as such whether it be a Ph.D. or an Ed.D., a research or a teaching doctorate." While this may be an extreme view, it is clear that it is the doctorate that counts most when a faculty is evaluated by the regional accrediting agency; and there is some reason to believe that the college executives are

[17] Oliver C. Carmichael, "A Three-Year Master's Degree Beginning with the Junior Year in College," *Journal of Higher Education*, XXXI (March, 1960), 127–132.

[18] In substance this is the two-year master's recently proposed by Everett Walters, "A New Degree for College Teachers," *Journal of Higher Education*, XXXI (May, 1960), 282–284.

as prone to demand the doctorate of their faculty members as are the officials of the accrediting agencies.[19]

These circumstances suggest that reservations about any immediate attempt to "rehabilitate" the master's degree in history are in order. Other, graver, questions will occur to many history faculties. It is difficult to see how the kind of historians the colleges want as instructors can be trained in twelve to eighteen months of graduate study. Even allowing for greater articulation of undergraduate and graduate study, a one-year master's degree in history would represent a less demanding program than present master's training affords in many universities and colleges.

SUMMARY

The master's in history in a majority of institutions involves: (1) relatively undiscriminating admission of candidates; (2) a very low casualty rate during the first year of graduate study; (3) requirement of B-average grades; (4) 30 semester hours of study; (5) an academic year or its equivalent in formal residence requirement, but eighteen months in actual practice; (6) a thesis of 100 to 160 pages in length; (7) use of foreign languages in master's theses that treat foreign areas; (8) some study in disciplines closely related to history; and (9) a one-and-a-half- to two-hour oral examination by a committee of three faculty members covering fields and courses plus the thesis (if a thesis is required). Three percentage points make it impossible to say that this model of master's training in history involves an examination in a foreign language, for only about 47.5% of the respondents report this as a requirement.

Disagreement about the character and professional function of

[19] Our inquiries brought helpful responses from officials of the New England Association, the Middle States Association of Colleges and Secondary Schools, the Southern Association of Colleges and Secondary Schools, the North Central Association of Colleges and Secondary Schools, the Western College Association, and the Northwest Association of Secondary and Higher Schools.

master's training is deeply rooted in the development of education in America. Only the metaphor was new when a graduate dean recently described the master's degree as "a bit like a streetwalker—all things to all men (and at different prices)."[20] Berelson has shown that as early as 1902 the Association of American Universities debated whether the master's was a terminal degree or a signpost en route to the Ph.D. In 1910 the AAU heard a report that the thesis requirement was far from universal; that the degree was partly cultural, partly research-oriented, and mainly of professional use to secondary teachers. Dissatisfaction through the years has produced several proposals that the degree be strengthened. But Berelson is probably right in his conclusion: the master's "carries its weight in the academic procession, but it cannot carry a great deal more."[21]

Whatever it has been in the past or may be in the future, the master's degree in history is now primarily a signpost en route to the doctorate. Whether viewed in this light or as a degree for secondary teachers, it appears that the period of study it requires in most institutions—the average period is eighteen months—is too long. If it is not to be used as a degree for college teachers, a way should be found to make it possible to complete the degree in twelve months without seriously lowering standards. This can be done if quality rather than quantity of work is the test of student excellence. Much more rigorous selection of students, careful and early screening of those who are admitted, and financial support for full-time study offer hopes for success.

Among the requirements for the degree the thesis is most often the cause of delayed progress. Two terms of seminar work should certainly be required of first-year graduate students, and many history departments accept satisfactory work in seminars in lieu of the thesis. Departments that continue to require it can restrict the scope and length of theses. More adequate faculty guidance at the beginning of graduate study can also help avoid unduly long master's programs.

[20] J. P. Elder as quoted by Berelson, *Graduate Education*, 185.
[21] *Ibid.*, 18, 30, 185–186, 190.

It is impossible to imagine the general adoption of a uniform program for the master's degree in history that would adequately prepare college teachers, though some departments might wish to award the master's to Ph.D. candidates when they pass the general examination for the doctorate.

In any case it is to be hoped that revised master's programs will not prolong doctoral studies. For the education of Ph.D.s is the most challenging task in graduate education and the one most in the interest of history instruction in the colleges during the 1960s.

Chapter 6
PH.D.-TRAINING INSTITUTIONS

The availability of fellowships will do much to determine the number of doctoral candidates in history and their choice of graduate schools.[1] But few doctoral candidates of real promise are drawn to a university that has only money to offer.[2] The reputation of the department (especially in the field of history in which the student wishes to specialize), library resources, the fame of a single professor, and the general prestige of the institution—all these are considered along with the lure of financial aid in determining the choice of a graduate school.[3]

How strong are the existing Ph.D. programs in history? Do they have sufficient capacity to expand to meet the increased needs of the 1960s for history Ph.D.s? Are new Ph.D. programs in history needed? What standards should new programs expect to meet? Directly or indirectly this chapter answers these questions.

[1] Sibley, *The Recruitment, Selection, and Training of Social Scientists*, 56 (table 15); the NORC study of 1959.

[2] See NORC study of 1959; Robert M. Lester, *A Review of Faculty Fellowships Granted by the Southern Fellowships Fund, 1955–1958* (Chapel Hill, 1958), especially table D; Gropper and Fitzpatrick, *Who Goes to Graduate School?*, 23; our own survey of the Ph.D.s of 1958.

[3] See also the conclusions reached by: Wilson, *The Academic Man*, 50; Berelson, *Graduate Education*, 143; Charles M. Grigg, "Who Wants to Go to Graduate School, and Why?" *Research Reports in Social Science of Florida State University*, II (February, 1959), 11.

WHICH INSTITUTIONS OFFER THE PH.D. IN HISTORY?

The 5 most productive universities in the nation awarded half the nation's annual supply of Ph.D.s (all fields) until the mid-1920s, but by the 1950s the top 5 awarded less than one-fourth. That is because new doctoral programs have sprung up, have struggled up, or have been stillborn in every decade since 1900.[4] History has followed the general trend. In the period 1893–1935, 6 universities awarded 54% of all the Ph.D.s in history in the nation. In the period 1948–1958 the output of the 11 most productive institutions had to be added up to account for 54% of national production. The increase in number of Ph.D. programs through World War II can be followed in Table 6-1, which also shows the size of the programs in terms of the average annual output of Ph.D.s in history. The number of institutions with relatively large history

TABLE 6-1

GROWTH OF DOCTORAL PROGRAMS IN HISTORY BY SELECTED FIVE-YEAR PERIODS, 1881–1945

Period	Approximate number of institutions *awarding* Ph.D. degrees in history	Approximate annual average Ph.D.s per institution
1881–1885	5	0.4
1891–1895	13	0.7
1901–1905	18	1.1
1911–1915	22	1.2
1921–1925	30	1.6
1931–1935	46	2.9
1941–1945	58	2.0
1955–1959	73	4.1

SOURCE: Data from William B. Hesseltine and Louis Kaplan, "Doctors of Philosophy in History: a Statistical Study," *American Historical Review*, XLVII (July, 1942), 772–773; Clarence S. Marsh (ed.), *American Universities and Colleges*, 4th ed. (Washington, 1940), 72–81, 90; and A. J. Bruembaugh (ed.), *American Universities and Colleges*, 5th ed. (Washington, 1948), tables 1–3.

[4] Berelson, *Graduate Education*, 93–94.

programs (at least 30 Ph.D.s in five years) rose from 1 in the period 1916–1920 to 7 in the years 1926–1930, and to 18 in the period 1955–1959.

At the outbreak of World War II, 60 institutions were *awarding* the Ph.D. in history; almost 80 were doing so by the late 1950s, and well over 80 were *offering* doctoral training. A little more than one-fourth of them first awarded Ph.D.s in the period 1876–1914. An equal proportion began awarding the Ph.D. only after 1945. Since World War II the South and West have added Ph.D. programs in history more rapidly than other regions; 43% of the programs in the South and 40% of those in the West have been inaugurated since 1945. By early 1960, 88 institutions were reported to be offering Ph.D. training in history—between 4 and 5% of all the institutions of higher learning in America.[5]

Why does the number of programs increase through the years? Explanations are to be found in the prospectus with which one history department inaugurated Ph.D. training in 1959–1960: "Even before the Department began to plan it, applications and inquiries came to it from masters of arts and other graduates. . . . Beyond the immediate need, however, there exists an urgent, nation-wide demand for doctors of philosophy in history. . . . Moreover, in order to teach the rapidly growing undergraduate classes efficiently and economically, the Department here must have graduate assistants and readers and must provide scholarly reasons to attract them." Letters of endorsement of the proposed Ph.D. program from distinguished historians were mimeographed and circulated to the graduate faculty in support of the program. One of these letters added yet another justification: "You will have great difficulty in keeping good men at _____ if you do not offer them the opportunity of giving graduate work."

These quotations will seem familiar to any member of a gradu-

[5] This survey of development is based on Hesseltine and Kaplan, "Doctors of Philosophy in History," 772–773 (for 1881–1935); Marsh (ed.), *American Universities and Colleges*, 4th ed., 72–81, 90; Brumbaugh (ed.), *American Universities and Colleges*, 5th ed., tables 1–3; Sibley, *Recruitment, Selection, and Training of Social Scientists*, 105–106.

ate faculty who has sat through discussions of new doctoral programs in recent years. To them might be added two other factors that are seldom put in the form of written arguments: the pressure of a university administration for initiating a Ph.D. program, and the fear that the School of Education may soon supply colleges with pseudo historians unless the Ph.D. in history is offered locally. The arguments in all their variety usually prove to be locally convincing and, in recent years, convincing off campus as well; the specific proposal noted above earned its institution a number of National Defense Fellowships for its first Ph.D. candidates in history.

There is no way for us to be certain that _____ University should *not* have inaugurated a Ph.D. program. The company it joins is already large and heterogeneous. Table 6-2 shows the 79 institutions that actually awarded Ph.D.s in the eleven-year period 1948–1958. To these should be added the following 9 institutions, 7 of which have inaugurated Ph.D. programs since 1958: Arizona, Delaware, Florida State, Idaho, Mississippi State, Mississippi, Occidental, Tennessee, and Wayne State.

The institutions involved vary tremendously in output of history Ph.D.s. One-third averaged fewer than one Ph.D. per year in the period 1948–1958. The 38 smallest producers altogether awarded fewer Ph.D.s than did Columbia (which awarded 9% of the national total). Harvard's production (with Radcliffe's, 12% of the national total) was greater than the combined production of the 42 smallest producers. Harvard (with Radcliffe) awarded 1 out of 8 of the history Ph.D.s in the nation; Columbia, which gave first place to Harvard in the period 1931–1935, awarded 1 out of 11. Together they awarded more Ph.D.s in history than all the institutions of the South; together they awarded more than all the universities of the West. But they are by no means the only very large programs. The 18 largest producers awarded two-thirds (67%) of all the Ph.D.s in the nation, 1948–1958; the 28 largest awarded four-fifths (81%) of the total. The paradox is apparent: while most of the Ph.D. programs in history are small, most history Ph.D.s are trained in very large ones.

TABLE 6-2

PRODUCTION OF 3,133 PH.D.S BY 79 UNIVERSITIES* AWARDING
THE DOCTORATE IN HISTORY, 1948–1958 (11 YEARS)

377	Harvard and Radcliffe	34	Colorado	9	Alabama
		34	Pittsburgh	9	Maryland
288	Columbia	33	Fordham	9	West Virginia
212	California (Berkeley and UCLA)	32	St. Louis	8	Dropsie
		31	Nebraska	8	South Carolina
161	Wisconsin	29	Missouri	7	Bryn Mawr
155	Chicago	29	Vanderbilt	7	Washington U. (Mo.)
100	Yale	26	Northwestern	6	Claremont
99	Pennsylvania	24	Boston U.	6	Kansas
91	Stanford	22	U. of Washington	5	George Washington
90	Texas	21	Kentucky	5	Michigan State
86	North Carolina	21	Oklahoma	5	Pennsylvania State
80	Michigan	21	Western Reserve	5	Rutgers
70	Minnesota	19	American	5	Utah
67	Illinois	18	Brown	4	Rice
61	Georgetown	18	Clark	4	Syracuse
58	Cornell	18	George Peabody	4	Washington State
57	Indiana	18	New Mexico	3	Lehigh
54	State U. of Iowa	16	Rochester	3	North Dakota
53	NYU	14	St. John's	3	Texas Technological
48	Catholic	13	Florida		
44	Duke	12	Louisiana State	2	Boston College
44	Southern California	12	U. of Notre Dame	2	Tufts
42	Ohio State	11	Emory	1	Arkansas
39	Johns Hopkins	11	Loyola (Ill.)	1	Buffalo
39	Princeton	11	Tulane	1	Cincinnati
37	Virginia	10	Oregon	1	Georgia

* The total is 78 if UCLA and Berkeley are counted as one institution, as they are in the source from which these statistics were taken. From reports to this Committee it appears that Berkeley accounted for 69% of the Ph.D.s in history offered by both institutions in the period 1955–1959. The 1948–1958 total can be divided, therefore, to show approximately 147 for Berkeley and 65 for UCLA.

SOURCE: The basic source for table 6-2 is Mary Irwin (ed.), *American Universities and Colleges*, 8th ed. (Washington, 1960), 1157–1159. Rutgers is credited in our table with 5 Ph.D.s (the number reported in our survey for the years 1955–1958), though Irwin reports only 1 Ph.D. for Rutgers. Irwin does not include Tufts, which awarded at least 2 Ph.D.s in history in the period 1955–1960 according to reports received by this committee. Cf. table 6-2, above, with table IV in Wellemeyer, "Survey of United States Historians, 1952," 346.

TABLE 6-3

41 Universities that Were First Choices for Graduate Study by 1 or More of 202 Woodrow Wilson Fellows in History, 1960, plus 15 Other Universities Chosen by Fellows in 1958 or 1959*

University	Fellows	University	Fellows
American	1	(Minnesota)	
Boston U	1	Missouri	1
Brandeis	1	New Mexico	1
Brown	3	North Carolina	3
(Bryn Mawr)		Northwestern	2
(Buffalo)		Notre Dame	1
California (Berkeley)	17	Ohio State	1
UCLA	2	(Oklahoma)	
Catholic U	1	Pennsylvania	3
Chicago	3	(Pittsburgh)	
Cincinnati	1	Princeton	14
Claremont	1	Rochester	2
Colorado	1	(Rutgers)	
Columbia	19	St. Louis	1
Cornell	2	(South Carolina)	
Duke	2	Stanford	6
(Emory)		(Syracuse)	
Fordham	1	Texas	3
Georgetown	1	Toronto	6
George Washington	1	Tufts	1
Harvard and Radcliffe	55	Tulane	1
Illinois	1	(Vanderbilt)	
Indiana	2	(Virginia)	
Iowa	1	(U. of Washington)	
Johns Hopkins	8	(Western Reserve)	
(Kansas)		Wisconsin	8
McGill	1	(Xavier)	
Michigan	1	Yale	21

* Institutions chosen in 1958 and 1959 are shown in parentheses.

SOURCE: Data compiled from Woodrow Wilson National Fellowship Foundation, *Report for 1959* (n. p. [Princeton], n. d. [1960]) 32–35, 58.

As Table 6-3 shows, the most promising students have tended to enroll in centers that are already large, or that have much prestige. Table 6-3 shows the 56 universities named as first choices for graduate study by Woodrow Wilson Fellows in history, 1958–1960. It might be compared with Table 6-2. An indication of the tendency of large programs to become larger may be seen in the fact that more than one-fourth of the 202 Woodrow Wilson Fellows in history in 1960 named Harvard (including Radcliffe) as first choice. Next most popular as first choices were Yale, Columbia, California, Princeton, Johns Hopkins, and Wisconsin. Six of these institutions appear among the top seven in the nation in prestige in a survey of opinion of Ph.D.-training history faculties, undertaken as part of this study in 1959. (Chicago was ranked among the top seven in that survey. Johns Hopkins was rated high, but not among the top seven.)

FACULTIES AND FIELDS

The institutions offering the Ph.D. in history vary greatly in faculty strength. The seven that are ranked highest in prestige by their peers report (1958–1959) an average (mean) history faculty of 39 persons, of whom 35 have the Ph.D., 31 have three or more years of teaching experience, and 29 actually teach graduate students. On the other hand, almost one-fourth (22%) of all the Ph.D.-training departments in the nation report fewer than 10 historians on their faculties; 5% only 4 to 5. Small departments are more common in the West and are next most common in the East: 42% in the West, 28% in the East, 15% in the South, and 11% in the Midwest in 1958–1959 had fewer than 10 history faculty members. The average number of faculty members per department in the East and Midwest is slightly larger than the national average, while the average in the South and West is slightly smaller (see Table 6-4). The average (mean) Ph.D.-training history faculty in the nation included 17 persons in 1958–1959, 15 with the Ph.D. and 13 with three or more years of teaching experience; 13 of the 17 were actually engaged in teaching graduate students.

The hypothetical average (mean) program in the nation in the period 1955–1959 awarded 4 history Ph.D.s per year. In the year 1958–1959 it had 24 Ph.D. (post-master's) candidates in residence

TABLE 6-4

SIZE OF HISTORY FACULTIES IN 80 INSTITUTIONS OFFERING
THE PH.D. IN HISTORY, 1958–1959

Group	% of faculty with B.A.	% of faculty with M.A.	% of faculty with Ph.D.	Average No. of history instructors			Average No. of history instructors with 3 years or more of experience	Average No. of history instructors teaching graduate students
				Total	Without Ph.D.	With Ph.D.		
Top 7 institutions in prestige.....	1	9	90	39	4	35	31	29
29 Eastern institutions........	3	15	82	19	4	15	14	14
20 Southern institutions........	5	13	82	15	3	12	12	11
19 Midwestern institutions....	0.3	6	91	18	2	16	15	15
12 Western institutions........	0.0	7	92	16	1	15	15	13
80 U.S. institutions....	2	11	86	17	2	15	13	13

and another 15 not on campus but working toward completion of the Ph.D. The "average" program also awarded 11 master's degrees (9.4 in 1956, 11.2 in 1958) per year and in 1958–1959 enrolled 41 master's candidates. The average program thus awarded a total of 14 graduate degrees per year per 65 students in residence, or 1 graduate degree for every 4.6 graduate students.

How large *should* a Ph.D. program be? It is almost impossible to speak in detail with any authority on this subject. Enough graduate students are needed to provide mutual stimulation and criticism and to challenge the best efforts of the faculty. But a small group of able students is better than a large group of mediocre ones. A program—small or large—is too large whenever a sizable proportion of its students is not capable of development into able Ph.D.s. A program is also too large when its faculty cannot provide graduate students with individual help and criticism in planning their programs, in their research, and in their writing. A survey of Woodrow Wilson Fellows has discovered that those in small departments report satisfaction with graduate training somewhat more often than those in the largest and middle-sized centers.[6] This may mean that instruction is better in the smaller places or—at least as likely—that competition is not as keen.

Should there be any minimum size for Ph.D.-training history faculties? The Ph.D.s of 1958 were asked this question. The variations in their answers were almost as numerous as the variations in size of the training faculties. Thus 38% reported that 9 to 12 historians were needed before a history faculty offered Ph.D. training; 34% thought no minimum number was necessary or named a number smaller than 9, and 28% said 13 or more historians were needed. Two-thirds or more of these Ph.D.s were products of large programs, yet 72% of them would be satisfied to see doctoral training offered by a history faculty no larger than 12 professors. Most historians with experience on graduate faculties probably would not wish to be involved in the education of history Ph.D.s in a department that included fewer than 8 well-trained historians, most of them experienced teachers and active scholars. (As was noted in Chapter 4, the average size of the history faculty in 126 better *colleges* in 1958–1959 was 8.8 instructors.)

Other characteristics of a faculty are more revealing of its capacity for doctoral training than size alone. Do faculty members hold the doctorate? Are their services best utilized by allowing them to teach in their specialized fields? Are they active contributors to research scholarship? Do those who teach the history of foreign areas obtain firsthand knowledge of these areas through travel and study?

The Ph.D. is almost a mandatory qualification for teaching in history departments that offer doctoral training; in 1958–1959, 6 out of 7 members of these departments held the Ph.D. (82% in the East and South, 91 to 92% in the Midwest and West). Only 4% of these departments anticipate a need in the future to appoint persons who lack the doctor's degree, notwithstanding expected

[6] Woodrow Wilson National Fellowship Foundation, *Report for 1959*, 9.

enrollment increases. Two-thirds say flatly that they do not. The remaining 29% expect to appoint persons who lack the Ph.D. or its equivalent "only as a temporary measure." Most departments will allow the new faculty members to teach in their fields of specialization: 53% report that "new" faculty members "always" teach in the fields of their graduate school specialization, and the remaining 47% report that they "usually" do so.

The research scholarship of the Ph.D.-training history faculties is impressive, measured in quantitative terms (see Table 6-5).

TABLE 6-5

SCHOLARLY PUBLICATION BY 1,121 MEMBERS OF PH.D.-TRAINING
HISTORY FACULTIES IN 77 INSTITUTIONS, 1958–1959

Type of publication	Nation	Top seven institutions	East	South	Midwest	West
% of total faculty having published	82	98	77	80	86	87
% of total faculty publishing within last five years	76	94	66	72	84	86
% of publishing faculty who have published on subject other than Ph.D. dissertation topic	82	92	79	79	83	92

More than four-fifths of the faculty members have published "books or articles in scholarly journals," and 76% have done so in the last five years. The seven most prestigious faculties publish more (98%; 94% in the last five years).

Members of Ph.D.-training faculties who teach the history of foreign areas are in every part of the nation a well-traveled group. Only 5% of them have never "traveled or studied in the area of their teaching specialty"; 14% were born in the area of specialty. In 1958–1959 two-thirds had traveled or studied in their major areas of interest within the last five years (see Table 6-6).

Table 6-6
Foreign Travel and Study of 674 Specialists in History of Foreign Areas, 77 Ph.D.-training Institutions, 1958–1959

Status	Nation		East		South		Midwest		West	
	No.	%	No.	%	No.	%	No.	%	No.	%
A. Per cent of total history faculty teaching history of foreign areas	674	49	259	48	118	40	192	57	105	54
B. Per cent of A abroad during last five years	458	68	166	64	83	70	133	69	76	72
C. Per cent of A never abroad	34	5	7	3	10	8	15	8	2	2
D. Per cent of A born in area of specialization	98	14.5	57	22	8	7	22	11	11	10

Should a history faculty have strength in only one field or in several fields of history before offering the doctorate? If in several, which fields? The 1958 Ph.D.s were asked to name any fields they thought *must* be covered in order to provide "minimum satisfactory Ph.D. training." Modern European and United States history were rated as "indispensable" by 88% and 85% of the Ph.D.s respectively. Coverage of the following fields was rated as "indispensable" or as "strongly desirable" (percentages of Ph.D.s answering for each field are shown in parentheses): (*a*) modern European (93%); (*b*) United States (92%); (*c*) English and British Commonwealth (78%); (*d*) medieval (78%); (*e*) Russian-East European (70%); (*f*) ancient (63%); (*g*) Far Eastern (61%); and (*h*) Latin-American (47%). Most graduate faculties would probably agree that a desirable faculty strength for doctoral training would include experienced and able faculty members in modern European and United States history plus at least three of the six other fields noted by the 1958 Ph.D.s.

A number of institutions award the doctorate only in United States history, and many others only in two or three fields of history. Tables 6-7 to 6-10 show the number of new Ph.D.s in

TABLE 6-7

PH.D.s IN VARIOUS FIELDS OF HISTORY AWARDED BY 29 INSTITUTIONS IN THE EAST, 1955–1959 (5 YEARS)

Institution	U.S.	Modern European	English-Br. Com.*	Latin American	Ancient	Medieval	Russian-East European*	Asian	Other
American.......	4	2	..	1	..	..	..	2	1
Boston College..	3	..	..	..	..	..	..	..	..
Boston U.......	8	2	..	..	..	..	..	..	..
Brown.........	9	1	1	..	..	1	..	..	..
Bryn Mawr.....	..	5	1	..	..	..	..	..	..
Buffalo........	..	..	..	..	..	..	..	..	..
Catholic........	11	10	..	3	..	7	..	..	..
Clark..........	3	3	2	..	..	..	..	..	..
Columbia.......	54	34	8	3	2	4	..	5	10
Cornell.........	5	3	3	..	..	..	3	1	2
Fordham.......	12	6	1	..	..	6	..	..	..
Georgetown....	15	11	..	..	..	2	3	1	..
George Washington..	1	1	..	1	..	..	..	..	..
Harvard-Radcliffe.....	45	56	8	5	2	9	..	8	1
Johns Hopkins..	10	4	2	..	..	5	..	1	1
Lehigh.........	1	..	1	..	..	..	..	..	..
Maryland.......	3	..	..	..	..	..	..	..	..
NYU...........	22	6	2	..	..	..	..	..	..
Penn. State.....	3	..	..	..	..	..	..	..	..
Pennsylvania....	19	15	2	2	1	6	..	1	..
Pittsburgh......	8	..	4	1	..	1	..	..	..
Princeton.......	5	6	..	..	..	9	..	1	..
Rochester......	15	..	..	..	..	..	..	..	..
Rutgers........	5	..	..	..	..	..	..	..	..
St. John's......	10	9	..	..	..	..	..	..	..
Syracuse........	3	..	1	..	..	..	1	..	..
Tufts...........	1	..	..	..	..	..	..	..	1
West Virginia...	4	..	..	..	..	..	..	..	..
Yale...........	6	10	7	..	..	3	..	4	1
History field totals†.....	285	184	43	16	5	53	7	24	17

* Some institutions reported Ph.D.s in English history and in Russian history as modern European history.

† The total number of history doctorates awarded, the sum of the field totals on this line, was 634.

TABLE 6-8

Ph.D.s in Various Fields of History Awarded by 17 Institutions in the South, 1955–1959 (5 Years)

Institution	U.S.	Modern European	English-Br. Com.*	Latin American	Ancient	Medieval	Russian-East European*	Asian	Other
Alabama	3	1	..	5	..	..	..	..	..
Duke	13	8	5	..	..	..	..	..	..
Emory	11	2	..	..	..	..	..	..	..
Florida	5	..	..	4	..	..	..	..	..
George Peabody	8	1	..	..	..	..	..	..	..
Georgia	1	..	..	..	..	..	..	..	..
Kentucky	7	1	..	..	..	..	..	..	..
Louisiana State	4	..	..	1	..	..	..	..	..
North Carolina	30	6	..	1	..	2	..	..	..
Oklahoma	7	1	..	2	..	..	..	..	..
Rice	2	1	..	..	..	..	..	..	..
South Carolina	5	..	..	..	..	..	..	..	..
Texas Tech	3	..	..	..	..	..	..	..	..
Texas	26	8	1	15	..	..	..	..	..
Tulane	2	..	..	2	..	..	..	..	..
Vanderbilt	12	..	..	..	..	..	..	..	..
Virginia	16	1	2	1	..	..	..	..	..
History field totals†	155	30	8	31	0	2	0	0	0

* Some institutions may have reported Ph.D.s in English history and in Russian history as modern European history.

† The total number of history doctorates awarded, the sum of the field totals on this line, was 226.

each of the major geographical fields in the period 1955–1959. These statistics are not complete indices of the fields of history in which Ph.D. training is *offered* by the various universities but they suggest the degree of activity in each of the major geographical fields. These tables are based upon reports on 1,458 Ph.D.s, 96% of all the history Ph.D.s awarded in the nation during the five-year period 1955–1959. Tables 6-7 to 6-10 show clearly the relativity of size in Ph.D. programs. A department that trains two Ph.D.s

TABLE 6-9

PH.D.s IN VARIOUS FIELDS OF HISTORY AWARDED BY 17 INSTITUTIONS IN THE MIDWEST, 1955–1959 (5 YEARS)

Institution	U.S.	Modern European	English-Br. Com.*	Latin American	Ancient	Medieval	Russian-East European*	Asian	Other
Chicago	19	8	12	3	1	1	..	3	..
Illinois	19	14	2	3	1	..	1	..	..
Indiana	23	6	1	..	..	1	..	..	..
Iowa	5	4	1	..	..	1	..	..	..
Kansas	3	3	..	..	..	..	..	..	..
Loyola (Ill.)	4	1	3	1	..	..	..	..	..
Michigan State	2	..	1	..	..	..	..	..	..
Michigan	10	10	5	..	2	1	..	7	..
Minnesota	23	15	8	..	1	..	..	..	..
Missouri	9	1	..	..	..	..	..	..	..
Nebraska	11	4	2	1	..	1	..	..	..
Northwestern	13	4	2	1	..	..	..	..	..
Notre Dame	4	4	..	..	..	..	..	..	..
Ohio State	16	6	1	1	..	1	..	..	..
St. Louis	9	3	..	..	..	..	..	..	..
Western Reserve	5	2	1	..	..	..	..	..	..
Wisconsin	36	18	12	..	..	5	..	1	5
History field totals†	211	103	51	10	5	11	1	11	5

* Some institutions reported Ph.D.s in English history or in Russian history as modern European history.

† The total number of history doctorates awarded, the sum of the field totals on this line, was 408.

a year in United States history is not a large program, but the producer of two Ph.D.s a year in modern European history is among the 11 largest producers in the nation; and not even the largest programs award as many as two Ph.D.s a year in medieval or Asian history.

The fields recent Ph.D.s think must be covered are the ones most often actually taught in the history departments that offer doctoral training, as Table 6-11 shows. These fields are most often

TABLE 6-10

PH.D.s IN VARIOUS FIELDS OF HISTORY AWARDED BY 11 INSTITUTIONS
IN THE WEST, 1955–1959 (5 YEARS)

Institution	U.S.	Modern European	English-Br. Com.*	Latin American	Ancient	Medieval	Russian-East European*	Asian	Other
California (B)...	22	6	..	4	..	..	2	7	..
UCLA.........	12	3	7	1	1	2	..	..	..
Colorado.......	6	2	..	1	..	3	..	1	..
New Mexico....	4	..	..	1	..	1	..	..	..
North Dakota..	1	..	..	..	..	..	..	..	..
Oregon.........	5	2	..	..	..	1	..	..	..
Southern California....	17	3	5	1	..	1	..	2	..
Stanford........	16	17	1	3	..	..	..	7	..
Utah...........	2	..	..	..	..	..	..	..	..
Washington State.........	3	..	..	..	..	..	..	..	..
U. of Washington..	9	1	..	..	..	3	..	4	..
History field totals†.....	97	34	13	11	1	11	2	21	0

* Some institutions may have reported Ph.D.s in English history or in Russian history as modern European history.

† The total number of history doctorates awarded, the sum of the field totals on this line, was 190.

taught as "advanced" courses, open to both upper-division undergraduates and graduate students. Courses most often taught exclusively for graduate students include United States, modern European, and English-British Commonwealth history; historiography; methodology; medieval, Latin-American, and diplomatic history.

Expansion since 1948 has been accomplished chiefly in fields already well developed. Table 6-12 shows the types of courses departments most often report as additions or deletions since 1948. It may be supplemented by Table 6-13. (These tables might be compared with college data presented in Chapter 4.) The increases

TABLE 6-11

PERCENTAGES OF 77 PH.D.-TRAINING INSTITUTIONS OFFERING
COURSES IN VARIOUS FIELDS OF HISTORY AT 3 LEVELS

Field of history	% offering at introductory level	% offering at advanced level	% offering exclusively for grad. students
United States	87	90	83
Western civilization	68	8	0
English-British Commonwealth	58	90	60
Modern European	57	92	74
Ancient	55	70	27
Medieval	53	91	47
Latin-American	38	77	44
Far Eastern	31	71	27
State	23	38	14
Russian-East European	22	82	27
General education course	21	4	1
World	18	6	5
Interdisciplinary course	13	25	19
Economic	9	57	19
Religious	9	30	10
Cultural-intellectual	8	79	26
Constitutional	6	64	18
Near Eastern (incl. Indian)	6	39	8
Diplomatic	4	69	39
Historiography	4	40	66
Military	4	21	5
History of science	4	30	6
Social	4	62	22
Methodology	3	21	53
Philosophies of history	3	16	17
African	1	13	3

reported in the top two or three fields are in large part accounted for by expansion of existing courses in the ten-year period. Expansion in several other fields reflects the development of new courses and programs, especially in Asian, Russian, and cultural-

TABLE 6-12

TYPES OF COURSES REPORTED AT LEAST 3 TIMES AS ADDED OR DROPPED, 1948–1958, IN 77 PH.D.-TRAINING HISTORY DEPARTMENTS

Type of history course	No. of times reported added	No. of times reported dropped
United States	45	7
Asian	33	0
Cultural-intellectual	30	0
Modern European	19	5
Russian-East European	18	0
Social	10	0
Economic	8	1
Latin-American	7	2
History of science	6	0
English-British Commonwealth	6	1
World history or Western civilization	6	0
Medieval	5	1
Recent	5	0
Historiography	4	0
Methodology	3	0
Diplomatic	3	0

intellectual history and the history of science. The expansion that is contemplated in the decade after 1960 parallels rather closely the expansion that has actually been accomplished in the past decade.

UNDERGRADUATE EDUCATION

Some features of the undergraduate programs of institutions that offer the doctorate in history are noteworthy. One is particularly striking: five-sixths of the departments report that all their faculty members teach undergraduates as well as graduate students. *Only 4 to 5% of the entire faculty of the nation's Ph.D.-training history departments are reported to be teaching graduate students exclusively.* Here is an important corollary to the fact that two-fifths of the history teachers in the better colleges teach graduate students as well as undergraduates. Clearly history instructors who

TABLE 6-13

NOTABLE ENROLLMENT INCREASES AND DECREASES, 1948–1958, IN VARIOUS TYPES OF COURSES IN 77 PH.D.-TRAINING HISTORY DEPARTMENTS

Type of history course	No. of times reported more than 20% larger in 1958 than in 1948	No. of times reported more than 20% smaller in 1958 than in 1948
Specialized, United States	29	25
Specialized, modern European	23	11
Russian-East European	21	2
United States survey	21	5
European survey or Western civilization	16	8
Ancient	15	5
All history courses	14	0
Asian	11	1
Medieval	10	9
Seminars or methodology	6	0
Historiography or philosophies of history	5	0
English-British Commonwealth	5	30
Latin-American	3	11
Topical	3	0
Graduate-level generally	3	1
Urban	1	0

find positions in departments that offer doctoral training should be prepared to be successful teachers of undergraduate students.

The second feature of the undergraduate program of these departments that is of special relevance here is that certain courses are commonly required of all undergraduates or of large groups of them. In some institutions more than one history course is reported as a requirement. Thus 34% report a requirement of Western civilization, world history, or modern European history, and 26% report a requirement of United States history. In some Ph.D. programs students specializing in United States history have especially benefited from the post-1945 trend toward requiring United States history or American civilization for graduation, since doctoral candidates often help defray the expenses of graduate education by teaching such survey courses. The over-all amount of history required for graduation in 1958–1959 was about the same as ten years earlier; 15% of the departments report "more" and 11% say less.

The Ph.D.-training departments are only about 4% of the institutions of higher learning in the nation, but they accounted for more than one-fourth of all the history majors graduated in 1958. As was noted in Chapter 4, half the better colleges reported that 10% or more of their bachelor's graduates of 1958 were history majors; more than half (58%) the Ph.D.-training history departments claim such percentages (see Table 6-14). It appears, therefore, that undergraduate teaching of history may be in even stronger condition in these institutions than in the better colleges.

TABLE 6-14

HISTORY MAJORS, 1956 AND 1958, IN 71 INSTITUTIONS OFFERING PH.D. TRAINING IN HISTORY

Region	Graduating majors, 1956	Graduating majors, 1958	No. of departments in 1958 graduating few and many majors		Increase, 1958 over 1956, in No. of majors	Average No. of graduating majors per department, 1958	% of institutions in which history rates among top 3 disciplines in number of majors, 1956–1958
			Under 30	Over 70			
East.......	1,010	1,097	10 (42%)	4 (17%)	9%	46	74
South......	440	593	11 (61%)	2 (11%)	35%	33	80
Midwest...	637	734	4 (24%)	3 (18%)	15%	43	69
West.......	680	803	5 (42%)	5 (42%)	18%	67	70
Nation.....	2,767	3,227	30 (42%)	14 (20%)	17%	45	74

Another feature of undergraduate programs in Ph.D.-training history departments that must be noted here is the tremendous variation in size of the enrollments in history courses. In every region a number of departments were much smaller and much larger than the average. The following are the smallest and largest enrollments reported by single departments for the first term of 1958–1959: East: 120 and 3,120; South: 444 and 3,256; Midwest: 659 and 4,541; and West: 579 and 4,148. With an enrollment of about 1,700 students in 1958–1959 (1,500 in 1956–1957) the average history faculty offering doctoral training is giving much of its time and thought to the education of undergraduate students. It is obvious that with such variations in enrollment the circumstances of instruction must vary widely from campus to campus.

TEACHING CONDITIONS

The most common form of instruction in the Ph.D.-training history departments is the lecture, as might be expected. The freshman survey courses in these departments very often have large enrollments. In these cases large sections are commonly divided into discussion sections for one meeting each week, with graduate students leading some or all of the discussion sections. In the nation as a whole, half the departments report that one course or more is given by these combined forms of instruction. The only region in which this is rare is the South. Other forms of instruction are shown in Table 6-15. They are provided chiefly for graduate students and undergraduate history majors (cf. Chapter 4).

TABLE 6-15

VARIOUS FORMS OF HISTORY INSTRUCTION OFFERED BY 77 PH.D.-TRAINING INSTITUTIONS, 1958–1959

Form of instruction	% of institutions reporting
Seminars	95
Directed Readings	76
Honors Work	44
Instruction to Individual Student	40
Tutorial Work	21

In appointing new instructors the Ph.D.-training history departments understandably are more concerned about their potentialities for scholarly research than are the college departments. Asked to list the most important criteria in making appointments to their faculties, all the departments mentioned scholarly publication or potentialities for it. But these departments also look for good teachers. Thus 88% of them list teaching experience or promise of successful teaching among their criteria in making appointments and 43% list personality, character, or general intelligence, all of which contribute to good teaching.

Evaluations of the teaching ability of new Ph.D.s by the departments that trained them have been found to be "very valuable" by almost half the Ph.D.-training departments, but "not especially helpful" by 30%.

Many of the departments more or less systematically take steps to ascertain for themselves the success of new appointees as teachers of history. While 42% of the departments directly observe the new teacher in his classes (at least in some cases), 44% report that they do not (many explicitly oppose this). Enrollment trends admittedly are viewed as at least a partial index of successful teaching by 43% of the departments. Formal or informal student comments are acknowledged by four-fifths to be a partial element in the evaluation of the success of a new teacher; and three-fifths report that they "size up" the new man in conversation, departmental meetings, or committee work. Some 88% of the departments report that through conversation (sometimes formal but more usually informal) older faculty members seek to help new instructors become more successful teachers. Three institutions report orientation programs for new teachers. In a number of institutions—including Pennsylvania, North Carolina, Wisconsin, Oklahoma, and Oregon—special awards are offered for excellence in teaching. Teaching of a high quality is generally expected in the departments of history that offer doctoral training.

The faculty member in these departments has obligations to graduate students and to research scholarship that are not easily measured in terms of hours of teaching, the number of separate courses requiring preparation, and the number of students enrolled in formal courses. Half the departments report that each faculty sponsor in the two-year period 1956–1958 usually directed the studies of 3 to 6 Ph.D. candidates; 38% say the normal load was 1 to 2 Ph.D. candidates, and 12% say it was more than 6. The highest numbers reported being directed by single sponsors were 21 in the East, 19 in the South, 12 in the Midwest, and 10 in the West.

The average (mean) member of a Ph.D.-training history department in the period 1955–1959 was supervising the work of 3 Ph.D. candidates each year (1.9 in residence and 1.2 off campus) and turning out 1 finished Ph.D. every three years. In addition, he was faculty sponsor or supervisor for 3 master's candidates in residence each year, and was turning out about 3 master's graduates every four years. One authority has recommended that the graduate faculty member should direct no more than 4 or 5 resident students at work on Ph.D. dissertations, and that reduced teaching loads be provided for the professor who directs that many Ph.D. candidates.[7] Yet 62% of the departments make no reduction in the number of formal teaching hours of faculty members who direct master's and Ph.D. candidates.

In view of their special obligations, the formal teaching loads in most of these departments are high, though the hours of teaching tend to be lower than in the colleges. Table 6-16 shows the teaching loads that 77 departments reported for 1,121 faculty members in the first term of 1958–1959. The average load was 8.8 hours per faculty member. Only 2 out of 5 faculty members taught no more than 8 hours; but 72% of those in the top seven Ph.D. programs in prestige (where there are most doctoral candidates to add to the

[7] Hayward Keniston, *Graduate Study and Research in the Arts and Sciences at the University of Pennsylvania* (Philadelphia, 1959), 70. Dimock and Hawley (eds.), in *Goals for Political Science*, 265, report that political scientists believe that "not more than 5 or 6 students can be given adequate supervision by even the best of teachers."

TABLE 6-16

TEACHING LOADS OF 1,121 MEMBERS OF HISTORY FACULTIES
IN 77 PH.D.-TRAINING UNIVERSITIES, FIRST TERM, 1958-1959

Hours of teaching per week	% of faculty members teaching various loads					
	Nation	Top seven	East	South	Midwest	West
Some but under 6 hr	10	13	15	8	8	6
6-8 hr	31	59	34	11	37	41
9-10 hr	29	20	24	31	36	28
11-12 hr	27	7	24	45	16	25
13-15 hr	3	0.4	3	4	3	0.6
More than 15 hr	0.2	0	0.2	0.4	0	0

faculty load) taught no more than 8 hours. In the South only one-fifth of the faculty in Ph.D.-training departments taught 8 hours per week or less. It should be noted that 13% of all 1,121 teaching loads represent reductions for administrative services.

Should there be a maximum teaching load for professors who direct master's theses and doctoral dissertations in history? If so, how heavy should it be? The Ph.D.s of 1958 were asked these questions. Two-thirds of them would set the teaching load of an active member of a Ph.D.-training faculty at less than 9 hours a week. Half the 1958 Ph.D.s suggest that faculty sponsors of master's and doctoral candidates should teach no more than 60 students per term (undergraduates and graduates), and nine-tenths say no more than 100 students per term. In actuality, the average (mean) member of a Ph.D.-training department in the first term of 1958-1959 taught 99 students. Thus, without considering the extra burden of attention to individual graduate students, the student load of graduate faculty members is about the same as that of college instructors, and higher than the load that a majority of recent Ph.D. graduates believe should be maximal. Undergraduate classes on the average are much larger than in the colleges (see Chapter 4). Table 6-17 shows the variations in class size that were

TABLE 6-17

AVERAGE SIZES OF HISTORY CLASSES AT VARIOUS LEVELS IN 77 PH.D.-TRAINING INSTITUTIONS, 1956-1957 AND 1958-1959

Type of history course	Average No. of students per class								
	Nation		East		South		Midwest		West
	1956	1958	1956	1958	1956	1958	1956	1958	1956	1958
Introductory, U.S...	67	71	47	58	41	45	89	89	97	98
Introductory, other	57	70	35	50	44	53	61	77	98	107
Advanced undergraduate, U.S....	38	41	30	42	23	23	51	60	48	43
Advanced undergraduate, other...	27	31	26	32	20	21	33	42	29	32
Advanced undergraduate and graduate.........	25	25	19	22	19	19	31	32	32	29
Exclusively for graduate students	9	9	9	10	8	7	10	11	11	7

reported in this study. Classes at all levels tend to be smallest in the South. Classes at all levels increased in size between the fall of 1956 and the fall of 1958.

Service on committees is another demand that weighs heavily on faculty members in Ph.D.-training history departments. This survey solicited no data on committee service, but a number of departments reported that it handicaps both the teaching and the scholarly research of faculty members. On many campuses the number of standing committees or their membership can be reduced without damaging the principle or the practice of representative faculty government. And members of committees often can save time by making certain that they concern themselves with policy matters, leaving clerical routine and implementation of policy to others. The central question involved in this matter is: "How can the faculty participate most effectively in activities without either excessively diverting themselves from their basic duties or unwisely infringing on the proper and essential role and responsibilities of administration and management?"[8]

RESEARCH AND TEACHING

A major function of the history faculty in a university is contribution to research scholarship. Graduate history faculties generally agree that the obligation of a university to promote original scholarship is equal or almost equal to its obligation to educate undergraduates and to train future historians. If the universities do not foster historical writing it will not be allowed to languish, for it is too important for that; it will be done by individuals or institutions less able to guarantee its scholarly integrity. The university is obligated not only to support research scholarship but to make certain that it is of the highest quality obtainable.

The insistence on publication in quantity in some universities and the insignificance of some research have inspired many criticisms of overemphasis on research publication.[9] Caplow and McGee write that "in the faculties of major universities . . . the evaluation of performance is based almost exclusively on publication of scholarly books or articles in professional journals as evidence of research activity."[10] The anxiety about overemphasis on publication marks a great change since 1927, when Marcus W. Jernegan criticized graduate faculties for failing to give graduate students adequate instruction in the methods of research, and for being "unproductive."[11]

To what extent are the current complaints about overemphasis on publication justified by practices in the institutions that offer the doctorate in history? Ph.D.-training departments were asked: "Is some scholarly publication required for promotion?" At one

[8] Newburn, "Faculty Personnel Policies in State Universities," 141.
[9] See, e.g., Barzun, *The House of Intellect,* 191 and *passim.*
[10] Caplow and McGee, *The Academic Marketplace,* 83. See also *ibid.,* 81, 82, 164, 221, 231 and *passim.*
[11] Jernegan, "Productivity of Doctors of Philosophy in History," 18.

level of rank or another, say 93% of the departments, publication usually is required. There are only slight regional variations in the response. The variations appear rather in the rank levels at which it is usually necessary to publish in order to be promoted. Only 6 departments specifically report that publications are necessary for promotion to assistant professor, but 20 say they are needed for the raise to associate professor; and 33 merely say that publications are expected, not specifying the rank levels at which the expectation becomes operative. Since 12 departments specify the full professorial level, they probably promote a faculty member up to the associate professorship even if he has not published.

Does research, as is so commonly stated, interfere with teaching in the Ph.D.-training departments? The departmental chairmen who completed questionnaires for this study usually report that it does not. Only 11% of the departments say "yes" in response to this question; 84% say "no." Rather, say the "no" respondents, research scholarship contributes to the quality of teaching done by history instructors at all levels. They often report that the amount of teaching is so great that "the development of history teachers as research scholars is retarded." Two-fifths (39%) report this to be the case.

The Ph.D.s of 1958 were asked whether as graduate students they at any time received insufficient professional attention from their graduate faculties and if so, why. Almost half (46%) of the recent Ph.D.s "sometimes," "frequently," or "always" felt neglected by the graduate faculty. As they saw the situation, the chief causes were the preoccupation of faculty members with their own research or with administrative duties. Table 6-18 shows the frequency with which these and other causes of faculty neglect of doctoral candidates were reported by the recent Ph.D.s. It should be noted that 54% of the recent Ph.D.s report no sense of neglect by their graduate faculties, one more evidence of the variation in conditions within training institutions. Caplow and McGee suggest that graduate students, as recruits to the profession, are less often neglected than are undergraduates.[12]

[12] Caplow and McGee, *The Academic Marketplace*, 231–232.

TABLE 6-18

FACTORS REPORTED BY HISTORY PH.D.s OF 1958 AS CAUSES
OF NEGLECT OF PH.D. CANDIDATES BY GRADUATE FACULTY

Factor believed to be cause of neglect	% of total times all factors were mentioned
Preoccupation of faculty members with their own scholarship	25
Preoccupation of faculty members with administrative duties	17
Too many graduate students	15
Belief by faculty that graduate students should work on their own	15
Demands of undergraduate teaching	13
Community or national service	10
Other factors	5

Alternating periods of concentration on research and concentration on teaching improve the quality of instruction while encouraging scholarly publication. Sabbaticals and grants for research leaves in summer or during the regular academic year are reported by 90% of the departments. A number of others report that they help secure off-campus grants for individual faculty members. Though these are available in an abundance never before known to American scholarship, they are still inadequate. In one way or another about 8% of the faculty in Ph.D.-training history departments managed to be on leave during the first term of 1958–1959. At this rate each faculty member would be given a year's leave every twelve years, or half a year's leave every six years. Fortunately there are other types of support for research scholarship. Over half (55%) of these departments report that teaching loads are reduced to support faculty research; and 45% provide clerical help or research assistants. In addition, 1 out of 7 reports special funds for research travel and 1 out of 9 provides partial or complete subsidies for research publications. Two-fifths (39%) report that research materials are purchased, usually to be deposited in the university library. But with American universities in 1957–1958 spending 2600% more for research than in 1939–1940, history departments lag far behind others in research opportunities.[13]

LIBRARY RESOURCES

The strength of libraries in the Ph.D.-training departments conditions the quality of graduate training no less than the quality and quantity of faculty research. A university's own library is usually inadequate as the only base for Ph.D. dissertations. "Are dissertation subjects chosen which can be completely worked up on the spot?" In response to this question 11% of the departments say "never," 36% say "seldom," 29% say "sometimes," and 25% say "often"; none says "always." In acknowledgment of library inadequacies, some Ph.D. programs provide financial assistance for doctoral candidates who must travel to complete their dissertations. At least one-sixth of the 1958 Ph.D.s got some financial support from their graduate schools for dissertation travel; and 54% of the departments report that grants are sometimes provided Ph.D. candidates when "considerable" dissertation travel is made necessary by "significant gaps in library holdings." (Cf. page 47.)

How strong should library resources be before an institution offers doctoral training in history? Certainly they should provide a basis for intensive seminar research as well as for extensive reading in secondary sources. One director of graduate study has realistically estimated that a new Ph.D. program in modern European history should expect to spend "between $10,000 and $25,000 annually for several years" for library materials and that an established program should require "upwards of $4,000 per year" to sustain itself.[14] According to a recent report a Ph.D. program in Russian

---

[13] The problem of publishing studies that have been completed is still bothersome but it is not of as serious proportions as is usually believed, according to Rush Welter, *Problems of Scholarly Publication in the Humanities and Social Sciences* (New York, 1959), 66–68 and *passim*. Nathan D. Pusey in an address at the University of North Carolina, October 12, 1960, cited the increase of 2600%.

[14] George V. Taylor in Snell (ed.), *European History in the South*, 23.

area studies "should have Russian language holdings of not fewer than 20,000 volumes, and an annual budget of not less than $10,000 for the purchase of Russian language books." [15] The minimum library costs of a Ph.D. program in United States history may be less prohibitive, but even in this field a Ph.D. program is expensive. One index of library strength in Ph.D. programs in history is to be found in the over-all size of institutional libraries. They have changed drastically since Ph.D. training was begun. In 1890 only 5 college or university libraries in the nation possessed more than 100,000 volumes. In 1959 no less than 277 reported collections that large, and 19 institutions reported libraries with more than 1,000,-000 volumes.[16] There are great discrepancies in library resources among the institutions that offer the Ph.D. in history. In terms of smallest and largest library holdings, the following extremes are to be found: East: 165,000 and 6,617,243 volumes; South: 202,300 and 1,400,000; Midwest: 327,403 and 3,200,000; and West: 150,-000 and 2,397,117.[17]

Library strengths are shown by regions and by prestige of Ph.D.-training programs in history in Table 6-19. The ratings of the Ph.D. programs that were used in compiling Table 6-19 were synthesized from evaluations made in 1959 for this study by Ph.D.-training history departments. It is apparent that the prestige rankings by historians closely parallel the actual library strength of the institutions. In average total volumes, volumes added in 1958–1959, and average budgets for 1958–1959, the seven universities that have most recently added Ph.D. programs are markedly weaker than even the third-rated older programs. It is especially disheartening that the newcomers, though building from smaller holdings, had budgets in 1958–1959 little more than half as large as the annual budgets in the 36 lower-ranked institutions.

[15] Black and Thompson (eds.), *American Teaching about Russia*, 101.
[16] Irwin (ed.), *American Universities and Colleges*, 8th ed., 40. (In 1901, 105 years after the founding of the University of North Carolina, its library held fewer than 45,000 volumes; it was adding that many each year by 1959–1960, according to Louis R. Wilson, *The Library of the First State University* [Chapel Hill, 1960], 29.)
[17] *Ibid.*, 153–1126 for statistics above.

TABLE 6-19

STRENGTH OF LIBRARY RESOURCES OF 85 UNIVERSITIES
OFFERING PH.D. TRAINING IN HISTORY, 1960

Universities	% of all 85 universities	% of total volumes of all 85 universities	Average (mean) total volumes per university, 1959	Average (mean) budget for books and periodicals, per university, 1958–1959	Average (mean) No. of volumes added per university, 1958–1959
21 universities rated in first rank as centers of Ph.D. training in history	24.7	55.7	2,077,836	$338,569	66,727
21 universities rated in second rank as centers of Ph.D. training in history	24.7	19.6	732,561	$164,854	31,921
36 universities rated in third rank as centers of Ph.D. training in history	42.3	22.3	487,398	$121,361	22,167
7 universities that have inaugurated Ph.D. training in history since 1958	8.2	2.7	275,628	$ 68,286	14,389
30 universities in East	35.3	39.4	1,029,935	$156,371	29,981
21 universities in South	24.7	17.9	669,618	$177,562	31,192
19 universities in Midwest	22.3	28.7	1,185,097	$263,525	46,201
15 universities in West	17.6	13.9	724,988	$145,313	31,599
Total sample of 85	100	100	902,409	$185,693	34,743

SOURCE: Library strengths are from Mary Irwin (ed.), *American Universities and Colleges*, 8th ed. (Washington, 1960), 153–1126. Ratings of Ph.D. programs were made from evaluations made for this study in 1959 by Ph.D.-training history departments.

SUMMARY

Library potentialities, like other features of the nation's Ph.D.-training programs in history, reflect the tremendous gains that have been made in the twentieth century. The variety of conditions continues to illustrate Logan Wilson's generalization of almost two decades ago: "the weakest institutions struggle to keep alive, the average ones to maintain themselves or to improve their status, and the best to stay at the forefront." [18]

Berelson has concluded that "the range in quality of doctoral work from the worst to the best institutions is probably less, and considerably less, than the range in the colleges or the secondary schools." [19] This survey of the situation in a single discipline raises a good many doubts about this generalization. Berelson himself has recommended that *"over the visible future, the national load of doctoral study should be carried mainly by the presently established institutions of top and middle-level prestige."* [20]

There are, however, no reliable systems of accreditation for Ph.D. programs already operating, much less watchdog committees to prevent the development of new ones. The Association of American Universities has shied away from the suggestion that it publish a list of universities qualified to offer the Ph.D.[21] Regional accrediting associations find evaluation of doctoral programs "one of the leading problems" confronting them.[22] Each Ph.D. program is largely left to make its own way, and each tends to believe that it is stronger than it is usually considered to be by other Ph.D. programs.[23]

---

[18] Wilson, *The Academic Man*, 157.

[19] Berelson, *Graduate Education*, 232.

[20] *Ibid.*, 252; italics in original.

[21] Hollis, *Toward Improving Ph.D. Programs*, 23, 25.

[22] Jennings B. Sanders in Lloyd E. Blauch (ed.), *Accreditation in Higher Education* (Washington, 1959), 12–13.

[23] Caplow and McGee, in *The Academic Marketplace*, 45 and *passim*, confirm our own findings.

In general, minimum assets for offering the Ph.D. in any field of history probably should be: (1) a history faculty of at least ten members in at least five broad fields of history, most of whom are experienced teachers whose scholarly contributions are recognized by fellow specialists; (2) financial resources for the assistance of graduate students and the support of faculty research; and (3) library resources upon which research seminars and the general education of history Ph.D.s can be based; this would seem to demand library assets stronger than most of the seven newest Ph.D. programs possess (see Table 6-19).

Two-thirds or more of the recent Ph.D.s seem satisfied with the doctoral training they received, and most Ph.D. candidates will continue to find institutions of appropriate sizes and levels of prestige at which to pursue their professional training. If one-third of the total sample of 1958 Ph.D.s have doubts about whether they would seek doctoral training over again at the same place, it is not always because they took Ph.D. training in weak departments; for one-fourth of the Ph.D.s from the top seven institutions in prestige express the same doubts.

Certainly there are advantages in attending large institutions. Logan Wilson has written that their training is "superior to that afforded by lesser universities where student competition sets a slower pace and research facilities are more limited." [24] On the other hand, the situation to which Elbridge Sibley pointed a dozen years ago continues to exist: "Statistics would add nothing significant to our common knowledge of the present extreme degree of overcrowding in many graduate departments, especially in those of the leading universities." [25]

Expected increases in numbers of graduate students do not make the inauguration of new Ph.D. programs necessary.[26] The increased

[24] Wilson, *The Academic Man*, 29.
[25] Sibley, *The Recruitment, Selection, and Training of Social Scientists*, 53.
[26] A survey conducted in 1959–1960 by the U.S. Office of Education brought reports from 139 universities on capacity for expansion of doctoral programs. The sample presumably included almost all universities offering the Ph.D. in history. (The 139 universities accounted for 94% of all earned doctorates in

numbers of applicants will enable the largest Ph.D. programs to raise admission standards and will make for better seminars in institutions that now have strong faculties and libraries but relatively small groups of graduate students.

A fundamental and challenging problem for all Ph.D. programs—new and old, large and small—will be the continued need to educate hundreds of undergraduate students while maintaining high standards in doctoral programs.

---

the arts and sciences, 1957–1958.) Among programs in history, 73 reported that they could accommodate an additional 772 doctoral candidates "with present faculty and facilities." (Compare this with our own reports of 1,955 Ph.D. candidates in residence in history in 1958–1959.) Chase, *Doctoral Study*, 26.

Chapter 7

DOCTORAL STUDY IN HISTORY

A majority of history departments training Ph.D.s agree that the aim of doctoral training should be the education of "scholar-teachers." But, while 7% "put more emphasis upon teaching," one-fifth avowedly "put more emphasis upon research." Thus the quality most demanded in doctoral candidates is "research skill and zeal." This is mentioned as a top quality twice as often as any other. "Interest in teaching" and "general intellectual curiosity" are tied as the second most desired qualities, and these are closely followed by "skill in teaching."

These variations in the aims of doctoral education are manifested in the detailed provisions of Ph.D. programs. This chapter shows how history faculties are currently training Ph.D. candidates. It describes the scope of Ph.D. study through a review of "field" requirements, surveys the forms of study, shows how student performance is tested in various examinations, and points to changes that are being contemplated.

WHAT IS STUDIED: FIELD REQUIREMENTS

Ph.D. candidates are usually expected to enroll in at least three academic years of graduate study ("residence") and it is common to specify that one academic year "in residence" must be spent at the institution awarding the doctorate. In actuality, however, it is a rare student who completes Ph.D. training in three years of study. The usual "full course load" for first- and second-year graduate students in Ph.D.-training departments varies from 12 hours—i.e., four courses (reported by 58% of the departments)—up to 15 hours (one-third of the departments) and down to 9 hours (one-tenth of the departments). Just how much study is expected in terms of credit hours the history faculties are reluctant to state explicitly, for in doctoral studies evidence of qualitative scholarship is considered the goal and quantitative efforts only means toward the desired end. Two-fifths of the departments report that they "require" or "recommend" that doctoral candidates take 60 or more semester hours of graduate study, and almost two-thirds (62%) report 48 semester hours or more. The largest requirement reported—90 semester hours—was cited by one of the least well-known departments. Only a small minority expect more than 70 hours of course work.

The basic intellectual dilemma now involved in planning units of study for doctoral candidates was well stated in the early nineteenth century by Leopold von Ranke: to understand universal history one must first know the specific events of history; but to know the specific one must first understand the universal. The accumulation of knowledge since Ranke's time has made the problem enormously more difficult than it was in his day. One cannot master all of history. Deciding how much mastery Ph.D. candidates should demonstrate is complicated by practical considerations. First, the able Ph.D. candidate should earn the doctorate in no more than four years of full-time graduate study. Second, as a potential research scholar and teacher of advanced college students, he needs depth—the mastery of facts and materials in a specialized field of history. The units of historical study must be relatively small if this mastery is to be achieved. But, third, as a man, as a citizen, and as a teacher giving instruction in broad survey courses —and also as a scholar doing research and writing—the Ph.D. candidate needs breadth. This can be acquired most readily in the study of broad units of history.

Large or small, the units of study in Ph.D. programs are usually called "fields." A number of very good Ph.D. programs define these fields broadly and have students study two fields. Some departments require Ph.D. candidates to show some degree of mastery in three, four, five, or even six fields of history, each broadly defined (e.g., all of United States history as one field). Most departments, unwilling to accept the superficial acquaintance with fields so broadly defined, divide history into several relatively small units of study. The divisions sometimes are (or may be) topical as well as geographical or chronological. Through the study of several relatively small fields in differing cultural areas and different periods of time, it is hoped that the Ph.D. candidate will acquire a sense of the universal in history. At the same time he is able to achieve considerable mastery in the field of his specialization, which is also restricted in size.

Definitions of the fields of history and the number to be required of Ph.D. candidates have never been uniform. By the late 1930s the number of history fields required in various institutions ranged from 1 to 6, and most institutions also required 1 or 2 fields in cognate disciplines.[1] Striking variations currently exist in field requirements. Data from the history Ph.D.s of 1958 show that when only 2 fields are required history departments usually define fields broadly (e.g., all of United States history as 1 field; all of modern history as 1 or 2 fields). Departments requiring 3 fields of history tend to define fields of medium scope (e.g., United States history as 2 fields; modern European history as 2 or 3 fields). In departments that require 4 fields the fields are likely to be small (United States history is usually treated as 2 fields but frequently as 3; modern European history is more often treated as 3 than 2). History faculties that require 5 or 6 fields of history restrict the fields even more; they tend to divide United States history into 3 fields and modern European history into 3 or 4.

A survey of the 1959–1960 graduate school bulletins of 49 Ph.D.-training universities shows that 57% require 5 fields or more; 38% require 3 to 4 fields, and only 2 require only 2 fields (these numbers include fields in related disciplines when they are

[1] Hesseltine and Kaplan, "Doctors of Philosophy in History," 769–770.

specifically required). Only one-fifth (18%) of the 49 institutions define fields broadly (e.g., all of modern European history as one field). While less than half (21) of the 49 Ph.D. programs in history require as few as 2 to 4 fields, all but 1 of the top-prestige programs require 2 to 4 fields. Since the top-prestige programs train the largest numbers of Ph.D.s, it is not surprising that two-thirds (64%) of the 1958 Ph.D.s took 2 to 4 fields of history.

Usually history faculties demand that Ph.D. candidates achieve greater mastery in one field than in others. This is known variously as the "field of concentration," the "first field," or the "major field." Less concentrated work is expected in other fields ("minor," "first minor," or "second field"; and thus followed by "third field," "fourth field," etc.). When graduate study in another discipline is required it is sometimes described as a "minor," but also often as an "outside field." The bulletins of more than half the institutions (57%) explicitly require one outside field. Two-thirds of the Ph.D.s of 1958 were "required" (58%) or "encouraged" (8%) to study at least one outside field, and another 14% took such work on their own volition. While 5% more took work in two outside fields on their own volition, 6% were "discouraged by the faculty" from studying any outside field.

Two surveys of recent Ph.D.s in history show that political science is the most popular cognate field. All other cognate fields are reported much less frequently. They include English, American, or other literature; economics; religion; philosophy; Education; sociology; and anthropology.[2] In the combined samples of 325 recent Ph.D.s in history, none reported any graduate-level study of psychology, a field in which historians might profitably seek insights.[3] In general, like history majors and master's candidates, Ph.D. candidates have tended to study cognate fields that call for relatively little intellectual reaching out on their part.

[2] Prepublication data on 143 Ph.D.s from a study by the Southern Regional Education Board, 1958–1960; our own data on 182 Ph.D.s of 1958.

[3] See the American Historical Association presidential address by William L. Langer, "The Next Assignment," *American Historical Review*, LXIII (January, 1958), 283–304; and the similar recommendation by Wilhelm Dilthey in the late nineteenth century.

FORMS OF STUDY

The program of study for the Ph.D. in history typically involves a combination of different types of instruction. Departments offering doctoral training generally agree that lecture courses should constitute no more than half the "full course load" of graduate students, and less during the second than during the first year of graduate study. In an introductory "methods course" [4] or in research seminars the student becomes acquainted with the tools and techniques of critical historical research and develops his capacity for writing history. Students, it is generally agreed, should be enrolled in research seminars during the first and second years of graduate study. One or more courses in historiography or the philosophies of history provide an awareness of the development, theories, potentialities, and limits of historical scholarship. Nine-tenths of the 1958 Ph.D.s believe a course in historiography or philosophies of history should be required of all doctoral candidates.

With usually a minimum of guidance and supervision from a faculty member, Ph.D. candidates in directed reading courses—especially in the second year of graduate study—expand their acquaintance with historical literature and sharpen their ability to judge it critically. Many Ph.D. candidates are introduced to college teaching through participation in survey courses of the department in which they are studying for the doctorate. In some departments their part-time instruction is critically supervised, and at least 11 departments offer either a course, a noncredit seminar, or an informal student-faculty colloquium on college teaching.

Meanwhile, the Ph.D. candidate begins and carries out an intensive research project, presenting the results in a substantial treatise—the Ph.D. "thesis" or "dissertation." There is, too, always a great amount of independent reading required of him in preparation for the various examinations that stand between the candi-

---

[4] A survey of a related discipline in 1951 recommended that a course in scope and method during the first year of graduate study should be "an inflexible requirement of all graduate institutions." (From Dimock and Hawley [eds.], *Goals for Political Science*, 266.)

date and the Ph.D. degree. Departments tend to agree that "individual reading" or "directed research" should constitute less than half of the Ph.D. candidate's program during the first and second years of graduate study, but more than half during the third year. In practice, lecture courses frequently make up half or more than half the course loads of first- and second-year graduate students. At their best, these lecture courses are given exclusively for graduate students and have relatively small enrollments. Three-fifths of the Ph.D.s of 1958 as graduate students took no courses in which over 50 students were enrolled, and the overwhelming majority of those who did take them agree that they were not as valuable as classes in which fewer than 30 students were enrolled. Asked to rate nine types of work in terms of their value as "preparation for college teaching," the recent Ph.D.s rated lecture courses enrolling only graduate students seventh while lecture courses enrolling graduate students and advanced undergraduates were rated eighth. Only research seminars enrolling 11 or more students were rated lower than lecture courses.

The Ph.D.s of 1958 emphasized the central importance of research seminars, however, by giving *first* rating to research seminars enrolling fewer than 11 students. In this strong preference for small seminars the recent Ph.D.s are in general agreement with the training faculties: the overwhelming majority (about four-fifths) of the departments state that a seminar should have no fewer than 3 students but no more than 12. As Robert G. Albion put it in the May, 1960, issue of the *History Department Newsletter* of Harvard University, "the ninth or tenth student joining a seminar does something to damage its effective intimacy." Nine-tenths of the departments report that their research seminars *usually* enroll no more than 10 students, but large numbers of students and limited faculties cause frequent exceptions to be made. Half the departments report giving at least one seminar in the period 1956–1959 with 13 or more students enrolled.

A majority (55%) of the Ph.D.s of 1958 took at least four semesters (or equivalent quarters) of research seminars for credit; 25% took two semesters and 14% took three semesters. Three-fifths (61%) of the 1958 Ph.D.s took research seminars in two or more fields of history, and three-fourths (75%) state that all candidates should be required to take research seminars in at least two fields. (But in many programs United States history, e.g., is two or even three fields.) Half the 1958 Ph.D.s who took fewer than four semesters of research seminars report that "Ph.D. candidates should be required to take *more* terms of research seminars than I took."

The Ph.D.s of 1958 were asked to describe the characteristics of a seminar that they found "most useful." Their comments suggest that in an outstanding seminar some or all of the following factors are present. The instructor is provocative, demanding, critical, and yet encouraging. He is himself engaged in research and is informed about the history of the period and topic of the seminar. Introducing students to the bibliographical aids, key sources, and major depositories of his field, the instructor somehow manages to convey to them the intellectual challenge and excitement that he himself finds in his work. He encourages a balance between initiative and aggressive competition on the one hand and, on the other, caution, humility, and a strong sense of responsibility toward past and present. By seeing that papers are prepared by deadlines and within specified space limitations, he develops disciplined work habits. He requires bibliographical and progress reports and, usually, one substantial research paper of each student. The instructor makes certain that each student's paper is criticized by all students in gentlemanly but vigorous and straightforward fashion, and adds his own critique. Comprehensiveness of research, critical use of evidence, logical inferences, technical competence, and literary style are thoroughly evaluated and improved.

The 1958 Ph.D.s acknowledge that the success of a research seminar depends upon the students as well as upon the professor. The qualities needed in students if a seminar is to be outstanding are enviable ones. Among them are: superior intelligence; vigorous interest in the subject area; capacity for hard work under general supervision; a creative, imaginative, inventive turn of mind, tempered by critical faculties; initiative in finding sources and facts;

courage to make decisions coupled with caution against making them prematurely and without necessary qualifications; systematic habits in organizing research and collecting data; competence in the use of foreign languages if the seminar treats the history of a foreign area; and ability to write lucid and vigorous prose concisely and in a well-organized pattern. All these qualities are needed as the research project is developed and the paper is prepared. Ability to perceive and accept correction, and sufficient resilience to capitalize upon self-disillusionment—these additional qualities are useful when the student's paper is exposed to criticism.

These qualities in instructor and students can make a research seminar one of the most rewarding of all educational experiences, an apprenticeship that forms the very core of the education of historians. In seminars Ph.D. candidates come to know the excitement as well as the drudgery of scholarly research, the fun as well as the effort of historical writing. But too many or inadequate students and a slow-witted or uninterested professor can make the experience a dreary travesty of scholarship.

Directed reading courses for small groups are rated the third most valuable form of formal instruction by the Ph.D.s of 1958— the first being small seminars and the second, "individual study or research under faculty supervision." As noted in Chapter 6, three-fourths of the Ph.D.-training departments offer directed reading courses. Whether in reading courses or independently, most Ph.D. candidates do much reading. Two-fifths (41%) of the 1958 Ph.D.s estimate that they were expected to read more than 60 books in their first field "apart from dissertation research." But one-third (37%) estimate that they were expected to read less than 40 books in their first field. In each field that is added somewhat less reading is done, as is shown by Table 7-1. Most reading is done in English-language material: 58% of the 1958 Ph.D.s read fewer than 2 books in foreign languages while in graduate school. On the other hand, 25% read more than 10.

The Ph.D.s of 1958 rate the doctoral dissertation as the fourth most valuable phase of training *for college teaching*. Four-fifths of the 1958 Ph.D.s (82%) strongly believe that the dissertation

TABLE 7-1

NUMBER OF BOOKS RECENT HISTORY PH.D.s BELIEVE THEY WERE
EXPECTED TO READ IN VARIOUS FIELDS OF HISTORY

Field	No. of Ph.D.s reporting for each field	% of total Ph.D.s taking each field and reading—			
		0–20 books	21–40 books	41–60 books	More than 60 books
First	153	10	27	22	41
Second	153	25	37	17	21
Third	126	36	36	17	10
Fourth	104	40	37	14	8
Fifth	63	43	41	11	5
Sixth	28	57	36	7	0

should be a part of the training of "college" teachers of history, and there is no disagreement about this between the group teaching in colleges and the group teaching in universities. But members of graduate faculties may be surprised to learn that only one-fifth (22%) of the recent Ph.D.s in history describe the dissertation as an "indispensable" part of the training of "college" teachers. The percentages would probably have been different if the recent Ph.D.s had simply been asked to rate the value of their training experiences without regard to the value of these as preparation for teaching. Putting the question that way, Berelson found that the recent recipients of the Ph.D. even more often than graduate faculty members—and three-fourths or more of both—regard the dissertation as the most valuable of all the facets of Ph.D. training.[5]

The dissertation is a major part of Ph.D. training. Graduate history faculties generally agree that it should represent twelve to eighteen months of full-time work at research and writing. Dissertations often require more effort than this, and some faculty members strongly believe that they should require more. But a majority of graduate faculty members agree that doctoral disserta-

[5] Berelson, *Graduate Education*, 176.

tions usually should be no longer than 300 typed pages in length (i.e., about 75,000 words); and although there is abundant opposition to setting an arbitrary limit on the length of dissertations, a number of high-prestige Ph.D. programs have set 300 typed pages as the maximum acceptable length. The average (median) history dissertation of 1957-1958 seems to have been about 350 pages in length, longer than those in most other disciplines. The shortest history dissertation of 1957-1958 was 145 pages long; the longest was over 1,000 pages in length. History dissertations of 2,000 pages, while mercifully rare, have been approved by graduate faculties. Faculties training doctoral candidates generally agree, however, that dissertations should be evaluated according to qualitative rather than quantitative standards (see Table 7-2).[6]

TABLE 7-2

AVERAGE LENGTHS OF DOCTORAL DISSERTATIONS OF 1957-1958 IN VARIOUS DISCIPLINES

Discipline	Length in pages
Political science	357
History	352
English	317
Anthropology	311
Economics	260
Sociology	248
Philosophy	242
Zoology	124
Psychology	106
Mathematics	71

SOURCE: Adapted from Bernard Berelson, *Graduate Education in the United States* (New York, McGraw-Hill Book Co., Inc., 1960), 181.

What, then, is the dissertation supposed to be? It is, in the opinion of the training departments, at once a training experience

[6] The reader may readily form an impression of the scope of doctoral dissertations in history and current trends by consulting the lists published periodically by the American Historical Association. See, e.g., *List of Doctoral Dissertations in History in Progress or Completed at Colleges and Universities in the United States since 1955* (Washington, 1958).

and evidence of scholarly attainment in research, critical analysis, and writing. Two-thirds of the departments require students to explore original topics. A majority expect the dissertation also to be a contribution to knowledge, but only one-fourth demand the use of unpublished sources in dissertation research. Dissertations usually are detailed descriptive narratives. A few of the departments encourage works of synthesis (10%); a few encourage critical editing or translation (11%); but one-third (34%) of the departments state that works of synthesis are "not permitted" and at least half do not accept critical editing or translations as fulfillment of the dissertation requirement.

A few graduate faculty members believe that the dissertation should be a publishable book. A larger number (but still a minority) think it should be a work of publishable quality though it need not be published. About 1 out of 3 believes that the dissertation should be considerably reduced in scope and length and frankly viewed as a training exercise. It is worth noting, however, that the recent recipients of the Ph.D. surveyed by Berelson were less willing to regard the dissertation primarily as a training exercise than the graduate deans or members of graduate faculties; about half the members of all three groups favored less ambitious dissertations.[7] A majority of graduate faculty members in history favor somewhat reducing the scope and length of dissertations while continuing to demand that they be substantial scholarly contributions.

Most members of Ph.D.-training history faculties believe students should start work on dissertation research fairly early in their graduate study. Most are willing for students to work on aspects of the dissertation in seminars or in doing the master's thesis, and a majority encourage this. For almost one-third (31%) of the Ph.D.s of 1958, the dissertation was, in fact, an outgrowth of the master's thesis; and two-thirds (64%) developed dissertations out of seminar research. Special dissertation-writing seminars exist at Princeton, Notre Dame, the University of Washington, and perhaps at a few other institutions. Two or three faculty

[7] Berelson, *Graduate Education*, 174.

members participate in the thesis writers' seminar at Princeton, in which chapters of dissertations are presented and constructively criticized. In most Ph.D. programs, however, the student works almost exclusively under the guidance of a single faculty member (his "sponsor" or "director") in preparing a draft of the dissertation. A faculty committee supervises the completion of the dissertation and is ultimately responsible for its acceptance or rejection.

The doctoral dissertation, net product of student and faculty labor, is fairly often the only substantial work of research scholarship in which the history Ph.D. engages in a lifetime. The dissertation is rarely a historical masterpiece but it is sometimes the beginning of one. In preparing the dissertation all Ph.D. candidates test, refine, and make sustained application of the principles of historical craftsmanship that they have been taught in research seminars. Since this process yields insight into history and historical writing that enriches college-level teaching, the dissertation stands with the research seminars at the very core of the training of historians. The student who completes one with adequate but restrained faculty help has achieved considerable maturity as a scholar.

EXAMINATIONS

Coming at intervals during the other work for the doctorate in history are a series of formal examinations that, by their nature, contribute to the training of Ph.D. candidates.

Foreign language examinations constitute major obstacles on the way to the Ph.D. for many candidates. Though only about 14% of all high school students in the nation (1958) study even one foreign language,[8] most Ph.D. programs require candidates to pass

---

[8] Report by William R. Parker in Byrnes (ed.), *The Non-Western Areas in Undergraduate Education in Indiana,* 56. James Bryant Conant's observation during an intensive study of American high school education needs to be repeated here: "Almost without exception, I found a deplorable state of affairs in regard to foreign languages." (From *The American High School Today: A First*

reading knowledge examinations in two foreign languages. French and German are usually those preferred, but most Ph.D. programs allow the candidate who has good reasons for doing so to substitute another language (e.g., Russian) for French or German. Very often it is specified that the languages must be from different language groups (thus ruling out a combination of French and Spanish, two Romance languages). At least one institution requires one ancient and one modern language. In a few institutions, including some excellent ones, members of the history faculty give the foreign language examinations, and in a few cases they are administered by a graduate school committee. More generally, however, the examinations are given by the respective foreign language departments. In many universities they are based upon historical literature. Quite commonly students are allowed to use dictionaries for part or all of these examinations.

Several departments have tried to ease the burden of the requirement without eliminating one of the languages. At Harvard, where formerly Ph.D. candidates were given only "pass" or "fail" on their examinations, letter grades of A to E are now assigned; it is possible for a candidate whose dissertation demands little or no use of foreign languages to pass the examinations with low grades. Still other institutions have made it possible for some or all students to complete the Ph.D. with a reading knowledge of only one foreign language. At Chicago and Northwestern only one foreign language is required. A few other institutions allow the substitution of other types of graduate training for one foreign language examination. Thus at Stanford the candidate may substitute cognate courses for one of the foreign language examinations: "the proposed courses must form a coherent group and contribute more toward the candidate's proficiency in history than would a second foreign language." Still other Ph.D. programs,

---

Report to Interested Citizens [New York, 1959], 69.) In 1958 only 44% of the public high schools of the United States offered foreign language instruction. By contrast, every secondary school child in the U.S.S.R. received instruction in one foreign language for six years, beginning in the fifth year of schooling. U.S. Office of Education, *Soviet Commitment to Education*, 10.

instead of reducing the language requirement, have demanded early demonstration of competence in foreign languages. Cornell and, more recently, the University of California (Berkeley) require students to pass one language examination before taking history courses for graduate credit. At least three other Ph.D. programs require that two foreign language examinations be passed before the student begins a second year (or the thirty-first credit hour) of graduate study.[9]

Because of the foreign language requirement, some students do not go beyond the master's degree; for others the master's examination is the first insuperable obstacle. Three-fourths of the doctoral programs report that by the end of one year of graduate study or upon completion of the master's degree they formally discourage students who appear to lack promise of completing the Ph.D. degree. One-fourth of the programs seem to wait until the major Ph.D. comprehensive examination to offer formal discouragement to unpromising students. Some graduate history faculties might well ask themselves, therefore, if they are screening students as early, as continuously, as systematically, and as rigorously as they should. Faculty time and institutional funds as well as the student's investment are lost when a Ph.D. candidate, after three or more years of graduate study, fails to pass the major examination for the Ph.D. The loss is especially serious when the place the failing student has filled might have been occupied by a successful Ph.D. candidate.

To avoid this loss, some 22 departments have established a special examination to screen candidates, test their progress, and discover shortcomings while there is time to remedy them. It is sometimes given early in master's training, but more often it is interposed between the master's and the major Ph.D. examination. In some departments this examination is especially designed for new students who have completed the master's degree in other institutions.

[9] It may be worth noting that a committee of the American Political Science Association in 1951 recommended that "if there is any validity" in the foreign language requirement "it should be rigidly enforced, and at the very beginning of graduate study." (From Dimock and Hawley [eds.], *Goals for Political Science*, 274.)

It is usually relatively brief and sometimes informal, but in one institution it consists of an all-day written test plus a two-hour oral test. At Chicago this examination is written; it can simultaneously serve as an examination for the master's degree and (if passed at a sufficiently high level) pass the doctoral candidate in two of the five fields required for the Ph.D. This examination is known variously as the "validating," "qualifying," or "preliminary" examination.

The terms "preliminary" and "qualifying" are more commonly reserved for a more advanced examination, often also known as the "general" or "comprehensive" examination for the Ph.D. This is the major examination for the doctoral degree. A third of the Ph.D.s of 1958 know it as the "preliminary" examination, though the somewhat less common but second most prevalent term, "general," is more accurately descriptive of the usual scope of the examination. It is taken after two or more years of graduate study, normally after all course and foreign language requirements have been met, but before the dissertation has been completed. Usually the student is officially "admitted to candidacy" for the Ph.D. only after this examination has been passed; it is "preliminary" to admission to candidacy.

In most Ph.D. programs the general examination (as it will be called here) is given in two parts, written and oral. But there are variations. In five institutions the student's faculty committee can decide to make the test oral only, written only, or both; in a number of other institutions it is always one or the other, not both. The examinations, written and oral alike, test the candidate's knowledge and understanding of *fields* of history, not simply of history courses that have been taken. Princeton and perhaps a few other universities move the candidate from a written examination over several fields to an oral examination covering only the major field of history. A few other universities partly accomplish the same result—narrowing the scope of the oral examination—by giving a written examination over some of the fields and orally examining the candidate over the other fields (cf. the Chicago practice, cited above). Several universities waive both the written and oral examination in one or more (but never all) of the required fields of study (Brown, Clark, Iowa, Michigan, North Carolina, Princeton, Tufts, and Tulane).

But for some reason, when both a written and an oral test are required as parts of the general examination, the oral usually covers more fields than the written examination. This can be illustrated from the experience of the Ph.D.s of 1958. Only one-third of those who were required to take work in 5 to 6 fields report that they took a written examination over that many fields; but half (47%) of them had to stand oral examination over 5 to 6 fields.

Though it tends to cover more fields, the oral examination (usually lasting about two hours) is almost always briefer than the written examination. It appears that the written examinations always last at least four to five hours; in a number of departments they amount to twenty-five or more hours of work, sometimes distributed in two, three, four, or five parts. The written examination typically includes broad questions designed to elicit long interpretative and comparative essays in which generalizations are supported by precisely stated factual information. Both written and oral tests usually seek bibliographical as well as factual knowledge.

The number of professors present at the oral examination varies from one institution to another (three, four, five, six, or more). What the oral examination in history is like has been well summarized in the description George Lyman Kittredge once gave of the examination in English literature: "Questions test . . . the candidate's reading and thinking; . . . his ability to give a good oral account of himself and of what he knows and thinks. Questions are very varied; some are minute, some general, some specific, some vague. Some call for learning, some for nimbleness, some for thought." [10] The character of the oral examination helps to explain why the Ph.D.s of 1958 rate preparation for it above lecture courses as a valuable part of Ph.D. training.

In short, the general examination is demanding. Ph.D. candidates fear it, learn from preparation for it, and complain about it.

---

[10] Quoted by Wilson, *The Academic Man*, 47.

The complaints most often heard are those Marcus W. Jernegan voiced in 1927: that the general examination often covers "more ground than should be expected of the candidate, and more minute memory-knowledge, in particular portions of the subject of history, than should be exacted."[11] Student fears of the examination are often exaggerated. Usually the examination can be taken a second time if it is failed on the first attempt. An initial failure somewhat delays the progress of the candidate toward the degree, but students who have survived several years of graduate study are not often permanently barred from access to the doctorate by one failure in the general examination. And it should be reassuring to Ph.D. candidates to know that 93% of the 1958 Ph.D.s passed the general examination in only one attempt.

When the general examination is out of the way and the dissertation has been completed, in the classical pattern of doctoral training the candidate must "defend his thesis." Today this usually is done prosaically and in detail, chapter by chapter, as the dissertation is written. Thus some departments believe that the final examination for the Ph.D. has become a superfluous formality. At Harvard and at Michigan the candidate's faculty committee can waive the final examination if the student's capacity has been proven in a satisfactory fashion. At Brown the final examination is not required. But in at least 60 Ph.D.-training departments (and probably more) an oral final examination follows completion of the dissertation. In 50 of the departments it normally covers only the dissertation or the field of the dissertation. But in 10 departments it covers two or more fields; and one department at this point even adds a field over which the candidate has not previously been examined.

Several years may elapse between the passing of the general examination and the passing of the final examination, for the dissertation is often slowly completed by Ph.D. candidates who teach full time in colleges with high teaching loads and inadequate library resources. In the fall of 1958, when Ph.D.-training departments reported 1,955 Ph.D. candidates (post-master's students)

[11] Jernegan, "Productivity of Doctors of Philosophy in History," 15.

as "enrolled and on campus," they reported 1,210 others as not on campus but working toward completion of the Ph.D. In the fall of 1959 the U.S. Office of Education asked departments offering doctoral training to estimate the number of Ph.D. candidates who had completed all requirements except the dissertation "at least 3 years ago" and whom they would be willing to recommend for a one-year fellowship "to enable them to finish the dissertation." History departments (58) reported 315 such persons, more than in any other discipline except Education and English-and-dramatic-arts.[12] Financial support for these people would enable many college teachers to complete the degree and thus raise their own morale along with the degree qualifications of the faculties on which they serve.

SUMMARY

Research seminars and the dissertation constitute the core of Ph.D. training in history. A majority of history Ph.D. candidates take at least four semesters of research seminars and a large majority of the recent Ph.D.s would supplement these with a course in historiography or philosophies of history for all doctoral candidates.

The dissertation continues to be an original and a substantial study in which the Ph.D. candidate proves his capacity for critical research and literary craftsmanship. But there is a growing conviction in this as in other matters involved in graduate education that emphasis must be placed on quality of performance rather than on quantity of effort.

Most history Ph.D.s now study several fields of history of medium or small scope, but only about one-third study more than four fields of history. About five-sixths study at least one cognate field. Research seminars are often taken in at least two fields. Lecture courses play a major part in doctoral training but are not popular among recent Ph.D.s.

Most Ph.D. programs continue to require candidates to demonstrate reading knowledge of two modern foreign languages. But

[12] Chase, *Doctoral Study*, 31.

two different types of modifications have been made in this requirement in recent years: (1) a few Ph.D. programs have required examination in one foreign language for admission to graduate study in history, or have set early deadlines by which an examination must be passed; but (2) a few other Ph.D. programs have reduced the requirement to one foreign language. It appears that few doctoral candidates offering United States history as a major field read foreign language material as part of their doctoral training, and interviews reveal that few use foreign languages in postdoctoral research.

Most Ph.D. programs try to discourage students who show in master's training that they lack ability to do satisfactory work for the Ph.D. But some Ph.D. programs need to screen students earlier and more rigorously than they do.

The general examination continues to be a serious trial for history doctoral candidates, though more than nine-tenths of all those who actually earn the Ph.D. degree pass it in only one attempt. What follows—completing the dissertation—is the obstacle in doctoral studies that most prolongs the process of earning a Ph.D. Financial aid that will enable Ph.D. candidates to complete the dissertation *before* accepting regular teaching appointments is the only real solution to this basic problem, though somewhat less ambitious dissertation topics can sometimes help.

Candidates who complete satisfactory dissertations seldom—it appears—fail the final examination for the Ph.D.; its partial or complete abolition has been accomplished by at least three Ph.D. programs and is being considered by others.

Until a few years ago direct efforts at teacher training had no part in Ph.D. programs in history, but many departments now make some attempt to prepare candidates as teachers of history (see Chapter 9). There is a widespread belief that more should do so, as the next chapter shows.

Chapter 8
MAJOR CRITICISMS OF PH.D. TRAINING

Some dissatisfaction with graduate study in history is endemic. One can expect to find up to 15% of the participants in graduate education unhappy about either present circumstances or future prospects.[1] On the other hand, a majority of the graduate faculty as a group—not just the history faculty—is conservative. It tends to cling to all the elements of training with which it has been familiar. Complacency with established training procedures is more commonly encountered than carping criticism. The one significant addition to Ph.D. programs for which graduate faculties generally show favor is training in teaching: this is supported by about 2 out of 5 members of arts and science graduate faculties.[2] Graduate faculties in economics, political science, sociology, and English tend to be slightly more critical of graduate education

---

[1] A complaint is judged worth noting when it is voiced by 15% of the respondents, says J. P. Elder in *A Criticism of the Graduate School of Arts and Sciences in Harvard University and Radcliffe College from Those Who Took the Ph.D. at These Institutions between 1950 and 1954* (n.p. [Cambridge?], n.d. [1958?]), 13. Berelson has estimated that dissatisfaction "of the order of 20%–25%" is normal and *should* exist in so complex an enterprise (in *Graduate Education*, 217). The *major* criticisms reviewed in this chapter are voiced directly or indirectly by more than 25% of the respondents.

[2] Berelson, *Graduate Education*, 206.

MAJOR CRITICISMS OF PH.D. TRAINING 161

than history faculties. Faculties in all the humanistic disciplines are more dissatisfied than are those in the natural sciences.[3]

Against this perspective we can evaluate criticisms of doctoral training in history, criticisms reported by Ph.D.-training faculties, graduate students, recent Ph.D.s, departmental chairmen and executives in the colleges, and editors who read the scholarly contributions of recent as well as older Ph.D.s. Each group that was questioned tends to reflect its own position in its major criticisms of graduate study. The colleges most often want Ph.D.s to be better prepared as college teachers. Graduate students also want more teacher training. Recent Ph.D.s call for more faculty guidance and greater breadth of training. The editors want more successful preparation for research scholarship and for effective writing.

But each group voices several criticisms that overlap. Thus in these groups there is major concern about (1) the preparation of Ph.D.s as teachers of history,[4] (2) breadth in Ph.D. training, and (3) protracted Ph.D. programs. There is somewhat less general but noteworthy concern about (4) the quality of history Ph.D.s as scholars. These are the areas of criticism that will be reviewed in this chapter.

PREPARATION FOR COLLEGE TEACHING

In 1956 Dexter Perkins reminded fellow historians that they tended "to exalt the written over the spoken word." He suggested, however, that the "best chance of making some impact on others will come through the influence we can exert in the classroom, through the enthusiasms we kindle, through the interests we arouse, through the wisdom that history teaches and that we can strive to disseminate."[5]

Widespread approval of the Perkins address suggested that graduate history faculties should give more attention to teacher

---

[3] *Ibid.*, 205. Since the scientists have fewer financial worries, one may guess that this conditions their outlook on graduate education.

[4] The editors were asked only about qualities of scholarship.

[5] Dexter Perkins, "We Shall Gladly Teach," 293.

preparation in training doctoral candidates. This survey has verified the existence of a large demand for more direct efforts at teacher training in the graduate schools. This is, by a large margin, the number-one criticism offered by history graduate students, as Table 8-1 shows. Three-fifths of the graduate students in history

TABLE 8-1

CRITICISMS OF GRADUATE SCHOOLS BY ABOUT 2,780 GRADUATE STUDENTS, 1958–1959

Criticisms rated as "valid" or "somewhat valid" by one-fourth or more of the respondents	% of history graduate students (about 300)	% of all graduate student respondents (about 2,780)
1. Not enough training for teaching....	60	49
2. Too many formal "hurdles"........	46	51
3. Encourages overspecialization.......	45	44
4. Stifles creativity of students.........	36	37
5. Accepts and encourages more students than it can place in desirable jobs	32	23
6. Training has little to do with jobs students will get.................	29	27
7. Faculty members tend to build research empires...................	29	33
8. Admission standards too low........	28	26
9. Not enough training for research....	28	26
10. Rewards conformity and punishes individualism....................	25	28

SOURCE: Data provided by the National Opinion Research Center.

regret the lack of training for teaching. Two-fifths of the recent Ph.D.s who hold full-time college teaching positions are less than enthusiastic about their doctoral training as preparation for college teaching (see Table 8-2). Improved training of doctoral candidates for teaching was, next to better faculty guidance and greater breadth, the third most common recommendation they would make to the history departments in which they took Ph.D. training.

It is important to note in this connection that half (52%) of

Table 8-2

Evaluations by 152 History Ph.D.s of 1958 of Their Doctoral Training as Preparation for College Teaching

Rating	% of 152 Ph.D.s holding college teaching positions
More than adequate	25
Very well suited	34
Fairly well suited	24
Just adequate	6
Somewhat less than adequate	9
Very inadequate	3

the 1958 Ph.D.s report that examples set by their graduate schools made them feel that good teaching was not as important as research and writing. Only 10% were made to feel that good teaching was *more* important than research and writing. Yet, two-thirds to three-fourths of the 1958 Ph.D.s undertook graduate study in history chiefly to prepare for careers in college teaching (see Table 8-3).

Table 8-3

Reasons Why 182 History Ph.D.s of 1958 Undertook Graduate Study

Reason cited	% of Ph.D.s citing each reason
1. Chiefly to prepare for a career in college teaching	66
2. To prepare for a career in college teaching and to learn more about the history of one country or area or topic (each in about equal degree)	12
3. Chiefly because of a desire to learn more about the history of one country or area or topic	9
4. To prepare for a career in research and writing	2
5. To prepare for government work	1
6. Other reasons	10

College employers of new Ph.D.s agree emphatically about the need to improve teacher training: this is the most common criticism of doctoral training from departmental chairmen in the colleges.

About half of all the recommendations offered by junior colleges (54%), selected four-year colleges (48%), and other four-year colleges (44%) call for more systematic efforts to train doctoral candidates as teachers (see also Table 8-4). College presidents,

TABLE 8-4

FREQUENCY OF RECOMMENDATIONS FOR MORE SPECIFIC TEACHER TRAINING FROM 126 SELECTED FOUR-YEAR COLLEGES

Type of college	Percentages, departments recommending more teacher training	
	% of those returning questionnaires	% of those making recommendations of any kind
Teachers' colleges	44	80
General colleges*	35	62
Professional colleges	30	75
Catholic colleges	33	50
Total sample	33	62

* Public, private, or sectarian liberal arts colleges.

even more unanimously than departmental chairmen, call for improved teacher preparation in Ph.D. training. Large numbers of historians on Ph.D.-training faculties in 1959 readily admitted in interviews that more systematic efforts to prepare and check on doctoral candidates as teachers are needed. And while the chairmen of the training departments offered few recommendations at the end of a long questionnaire, the few who did so called more often for deliberate teacher preparation than for any other measure to improve "graduate training for college teachers of history."

It is important to note the nature of the teacher preparation called for by the historian-critics. More than anything else they want what Hayward Keniston has called "a new attitude of respect for the dignity of the teaching career." [6] The president of a noted

[6] Keniston, *Graduate Study and Research in the Arts and Sciences at the University of Pennsylvania*, 100–101.

liberal arts college warns that the attitudes of graduate school faculties are of crucial importance: "If they are willing to convey a real enthusiasm about the central importance of teaching, their students will take it seriously. If they convey the idea that it is quite secondary . . . no amount of 'teacher training' will help us." Professor Perkins sounded the same advice for the training of future teachers in his American Historical Association address: "If our work is central to us, it will become central to them." [7]

Two other points about the recommendations for teacher training must be made most emphatically. First, they are *not* aimed at making Ph.D.s into "pitchmen," mental manipulators who know all the tricks that can "sell" their subject to students who are reluctant to buy. The aim, it is generally believed, is to instill in Ph.D. candidates some of the qualities of great teachers of history that were noted earlier in this study (see Chapter 4). The Committee of Fifteen in 1955 briefly summarized the kind of teacher that is portrayed as desirable in the recommendations gathered by this study: "a person who can stimulate his students to think critically, to understand deeply, and to solve problems successfully." [8] Second, the recommendations leave no doubt that professional educators (those whose field is Education) should have no part in the deliberate efforts to prepare Ph.D. candidates in history as college teachers. What is desired is a twofold program conducted by *the history faculties* and offering (1) supervised teaching experience and (2) formal or informal orientation in the professional methods, functions, and mores of a college teacher of history.

The demand for teaching experience for Ph.D. candidates is vigorously raised by the college employers of history Ph.D.s. Three-fifths (57%) of the specific recommendations for improved teacher preparation from college history departments call for practice teaching. Actual conduct of lecture courses is the experience that is most desired, and very many respondents specify that the practice teaching should be supervised by one or more members of the

[7] Dexter Perkins, "We Shall Gladly Teach," 297.
[8] Strothmann and others, *The Graduate School Today and Tomorrow*, 12.

history faculty.⁹ The conduct of discussion or "quiz" sections is regarded as supplementary to the more desirable experience of regular classroom teaching.

Independent teaching under supervision is also the chief recommendation made by executives of 134 four-year colleges. The college presidents persuasively reason that Ph.D. candidates need the experience to find out if they like teaching, to gain a measure of confidence, and to develop teaching techniques. They also argue that the Ph.D.-training departments themselves need supervised student teaching to discover the specific strengths and weaknesses of the candidates, both in order to advise them wisely and to be able to write reliable letters of recommendation about them. At least 30% of the college executives make it clear that practice teaching should be a part of Ph.D. training, and about half of these explicitly recommend that it be supervised.

Recent Ph.D.s also call for practice teaching. Half of those who recommended more attention to teacher preparation in Ph.D. programs think it should be accomplished through supervised teaching. And interviews with some 230 members of graduate history faculties in 1959 showed an overwhelming majority in favor of supervised part-time teaching or teaching assistantships as the best means of preparing Ph.D. candidates as teachers.

Many Ph.D. programs cannot provide teaching experience in their undergraduate colleges. Some respondents suggest that they might find neighboring colleges willing to do so on an internship basis. It may be noted in this connection that the Committee of Fifteen in 1955 urgently called upon universities to "recognize the need of internships and take steps to establish them." [10] Most Ph.D. programs that can provide teacher preparation on their own campuses will probably prefer this to internship systems, but it should be possible to overcome the difficulties in arranging for internships

[9] This reiterates a demand long heard among proponents of teacher preparation in Ph.D. programs. See, e.g., the 1950 report by Blegen and Cooper (eds.), *The Preparation of College Teachers*, 127–129.

[10] Strothmann and others, *The Graduate School Today and Tomorrow*, 22; 33–34.

MAJOR CRITICISMS OF PH.D. TRAINING 167

if they are thought to be desirable. The Council on Medical Education and Hospitals of the American Medical Association somehow annually manages to evaluate and approve 1,093 internship programs in 867 hospitals with positions for 12,325 interns.[11]

Second only to the demand for practice teaching among proponents of teacher preparation is the recommendation that Ph.D. candidates be offered formal or informal instruction in college teaching. Two-fifths (43%) of the specific recommendations of teacher preparation from the college departments call specifically for this; the recommendation is made by 63 departments.

What this instruction should include is a matter of disagreement. Some proponents believe with a California state college respondent that it ought to train Ph.D. candidates "to construct a curriculum, a course, a lecture, a reading list or syllabus, and a test,—also how to order intelligently for a library." Others say with Dexter Perkins that there are elementary things that can be taught candidates about classroom teaching: "To speak slowly, and so that you can be heard; to make the big facts stand out from the subordinate ones . . . ; to avoid ponderosity and flippancy alike; to talk, not to read; to present a subject as a related whole."[12] Still others suggest that Ph.D. candidates should be introduced to the history and conflicting philosophies of higher education, others that they should study the values, standards, and accepted ethics of the profession.[13] Many supporters of an orientation course would have it touch on all these matters. Realizing that it would take many months to present so much in a lecture course, some respondents would make the course a reading and discussion pro-

[11] Irwin (ed.), *American Universities and Colleges*, 8th ed., 112. These figures are averages for the years 1957–1959. For literature on teaching internships see Eells (ed.), *College Teachers and College Teaching*, 59.

[12] Perkins, "We Shall Gladly Teach," 297. For literature on college teaching methods see Eells (ed.), *College Teachers and College Teaching*, 169–219.

[13] It may be noted in passing that every Ph.D. candidate might profitably be required to read and ponder the statement of ethics drafted by the American Association of University Professors in 1937 and reprinted in Wilson, *The Academic Man*, 231–235.

gram. Several suggest that it should be an informal, noncredit colloquium lasting only about half a semester.

This idea of a formal or informal course on college teaching finds numerous and diverse supporters. Two-fifths of the 1958 Ph.D.s state that such a course should be required of all Ph.D.s in history, and it may surprise many readers that one-fifth of them report having had "a course in problems of college teaching." Members of graduate faculties who were interviewed in 1959 were divided on the desirability of a required course on teaching. Those who opposed it were numerous in most of the departments that were visited, and they were usually very rigorous in their opposition. But many members of the graduate faculties—about one-third of them—agree that Ph.D. candidates should be required to take a course on college teaching, "taught by the history department and lasting no more than one semester and perhaps less."

If such a course is to be offered in Ph.D. programs, careful attention to its content and conduct is needed, of course. This is underscored by the variety of sentiments toward such courses among those 32 Ph.D.s of 1958 who report having taken them. Almost one-third of them describe the course as "valuable" or "very valuable." Almost one-third more say it was "not very valuable" or that they would "eliminate it from Ph.D. program." And somewhat more than one-third say that the course was "not as valuable as part-time teaching." One thing is clear: whether by supervised teaching, through a course, or through a combination of both, Ph.D.-training departments need to give most serious consideration to the responsibility that goes with their near-monopoly over the supply of teachers of history in American higher education.

BREADTH AND SPECIALIZATION

Critics of both the teaching and the writing of new Ph.D.s in history have agreed in the past—and still agree—that they demonstrate insufficient breadth of learning, notwithstanding the impressively broad field requirements that were reviewed in Chapter 7. From a study of 1945 comes the lament of a college president:

"... we ask a man with a Ph.D. in history if he will take a class in American history since 1850 and he will hope to be excused since his advanced work made him a specialist in 'the Constitution'." [14] Ten years later a historian member of the Committee of Fifteen complains: "We don't turn out historians any more; or even American historians; and sometimes not even American diplomatic historians." [15] Something is radically wrong, Jacques Barzun has written, "in a 'philosophy' which says that the college student should receive a general and liberal education, and which makes its teachers a living refutation of that ideal." [16]

While one-sixth of the recent history Ph.D.s wish their Ph.D. programs had provided more work in their specialized fields of history, complaints against overspecialization are heard everywhere. The third most common criticism of their graduate schools by graduate students in history in 1958–1959 was that they demanded overspecialization (see Table 8-1). A large majority of recent Ph.D.s are satisfied with the breadth of their doctoral programs, but the demand for broader training in history and related disciplines is the second most numerous criticism encountered among their suggestions. It is raised by almost one-fourth (23%) of the Ph.D.s of 1958. Among the comments of presidents and departmental chairmen in the colleges the cry for greater breadth is second in intensity and frequency only to the demand for teacher preparation.

"How in the world," Barnaby Keeney has asked, "is a student who has concerned himself for a year or two with a barren, worthless, and unstimulating subject going to bring inspiration and interest into his classes?" [17] The college respondents call for broader programs of study as well as for less narrow dissertations. All in all, 29% of the recommendations received from departments in all types of colleges would broaden doctoral training. Many college respondents would like all Ph.D. candidates in history to study in

[14] Quoted by Hollis, *Toward Improving Ph.D. Programs*, 132.
[15] Strothmann and others, *The Graduate School Today and Tomorrow*, 23.
[16] Barzun, *The House of Intellect*, 118.
[17] Barnaby C. Keeney, "A Dead Horse Flogged Again," *Speculum*, XXX (October, 1955), 607.

at least one related discipline. Graduate faculty members for the most part agree that one outside field is desirable. But the number of graduate faculty members favoring the requirement of "as much or more breadth in history as now" is almost exactly the same as the number favoring "fewer fields of history or heavier concentration than now in the major field."

To the colleges greater breadth in doctoral programs means better teachers. So far as the colleges are concerned, therefore, the recommendation for more deliberate teacher training and the recommendation for greater breadth add up to only one demand, a demand for better teachers of history. Looked at this way, three-fourths (74%) of all recommendations from the 376 four-year colleges say "prepare Ph.D. candidates more successfully for college teaching." The recommendations from the 126 selected four-year colleges provide even more impressive evidence of this: five-sixths (85%) of those making recommendations call either for more deliberate teacher training or for greater breadth.

But Ph.D. programs that provide for greater breadth will heed more than the recommendations of the colleges, and they will improve more than teacher training. As scholars no less than as teachers, historians need to "interpret the past broadly, in the spirit of a man to whom nothing human is alien." [18] The strongest reminders of the need for greater breadth in historical training come not only from teachers in the colleges but also from research scholars in related fields. Thus an American political scientist observed in 1958 that: "History, the political scientist's 'laboratory,' cannot be fully exploited because its guardians, the historians, have been interested mainly in demonstrating the uniqueness of historical events instead of developing generalizations." [19] Criticism of overspecialized training comes also from editors who daily read manuscripts produced by Ph.D.s in history. From one of them comes the opinion that the "greatest need" in doctoral training is

[18] Dexter Perkins, "We Shall Gladly Teach," 309.
[19] Henry L. Mason, *Toynbee's Approach to World Politics*, vol. V in *Tulane Studies in Political Science* (New Orleans, 1958), 101.

to help Ph.D. candidates "relate their specific research topics to matters of broader historical significance."

TRAINING FOR RESEARCH SCHOLARSHIP

Historians on graduate faculties made many helpful comments about training in research and writing when the author of this study interviewed them in the spring of 1959. These comments harmonize so perfectly with what we learned about these matters from the editors of six historical journals and four university presses that only the editorial opinions need be summarized here (see Appendix K).

The editors' comments suggest that the scholarly writings of new Ph.D.s usually reflect sound reasoning and adequate use of critical research method. They also show a proper balance of boldness and caution in reconstructing historical developments from limited or controversial material. But a notable number of dissertations fail to reflect adequate acquaintance with older or more recent literature on the subject treated. The research contributions of new Ph.D.s reveal too little breadth. Little knowledge of history outside the subject area, little awareness of the philosophies of history, lack of familiarity with other disciplines in the humanities and social sciences, and failure to relate the specific topic to matters of broader historical significance—these are faults that all or most of the editors notice in the manuscripts of new Ph.D.s.

Fairly often the prose submitted for publication by new Ph.D.s is not as clear and grammatical as it should be. More typically the prose of new Ph.D.s is competently written, but, as one editor comments, it is "seldom lively; it does not delight one." Many manuscripts could be "better organized and more vigorous and succinct" (to use the words of one of the press editors). Historical writing often is "over-long, diffuse, lacking a clear theme or argument." Two journal editors report the acceptance for publication of only 1 of 10 manuscripts submitted in the period 1956–1958, and this limited acceptance was dictated by more than space limitation. One editor writes that, "some papers are submitted to me that are totally unfit for publication." In the opinion of 4 of the 10 editors the graduate schools are "overly encouraging" publication by their Ph.D. graduates, and only 1 says publication is being "insufficiently" encouraged.

More than the methods of training doctoral candidates is involved in the weaknesses of historical writing. The editors of historical magazines a generation ago were already "dubious about the quality of pieces of research offered for publication," and more than one of them believed that "the emphasis on 'production' for promotion" probably stimulated the preparation of "too many unimportant and mediocre research works." [20] One of the press directors suggested the outlines of another explanation when he wrote the following in the fall of 1958: "The introduction of 'scientific' techniques has deluded scholars into teaching their students that there is no art to historical writing." More recently Allan Nevins has also cited "the sweeping transfer of history into scientific channels" to explain why historical writing since the nineteenth century has become "more original, but more confusing; more expert, but grayer and grimmer." [21]

In the eighteenth century, when much less history was published than now, one-fourth of the books in private libraries in France were histories.[22] Can history in America today hope for so large a measure of acceptance? A rediscovery of literary art and a renewal of the capacity for generalization can make history a more vital cultural force than it has been in this century; the admonitions of the last decade allow one to hope that both are underway. The graduate schools can play a decisive role in this development by preserving scholarly values while training students to write prose

[20] Jernegan, "Productivity of Doctors of Philosophy in History," 14.

[21] Allan Nevins, "Not Capulets, Not Montagues," *American Historical Review*, LXV (January, 1960), 257.

[22] H. Butterfield, "The History of the Writing of History," in Comité International des Sciences Historiques, XI Congrès International des Sciences Historiques, *Rapports*, 5 vols. (Göteborg, Stockholm, Uppsala, 1960), I, 27.

MAJOR CRITICISMS OF PH.D. TRAINING 173

that is distinguished for its clarity, vigor, and grace of expression no less than for its relevance to the broad and vital concerns of a busy people.

Clearly the rate of publication is less important than its quality. It is well to examine, nevertheless, the complaint that graduate schools are overly encouraging publication. Jernegan estimated in 1927 that "less than twenty-five per cent of the doctors of philosophy in history are consistent producers," but Hesseltine and Kaplan stated that more than half the new history Ph.D.s of 1926–1935 by 1936 "had publications to their credit and gave promise of continued productivity." [23] Today fewer graduate schools require the publication of doctoral dissertations, and by 1959 only one-fifth of the history dissertations of 1947–1948 had been published. Only one-third (34%) of the history Ph.D.s of 1947–1948 had published one or more titles by 1959; only one-fifth (19%) had published beyond the dissertation.[24] Thus, while more historians are publishing than in the past, the percentage of historians who publish seems to have declined since the 1930s.

A second step in deciding whether young historians now publish too much is to compare their output with that of Ph.D.s in other disciplines. Berelson has done this for the Ph.D.s of 1947–1948, and his study shows that history, with 34% of its Ph.D.s publishing one title or more, is much the least productive—by titles—of nine disciplines (e.g., chemistry, 89%; philosophy, 63%; English, 61%). This situation undoubtedly helps to explain why only one-fifth of graduate faculty members (19%) as well as of recent Ph.D.s in history (20%) view the present state of their discipline as a whole as "very satisfactory," whereas three-fifths of the physicists and almost half the chemists think of their disciplines with that degree of confidence.[25] Production comparisons between history Ph.D.s and chemistry Ph.D.s are not revealing, because 96% of the publications of the historians are single-author works, while

---

[23] Jernegan, "The Productivity of Doctors of Philosophy in History," 1–2; Hesseltine and Kaplan, "Doctors of Philosophy in History," 798–799.

[24] Berelson, *Graduate Education*, 55, 177.

[25] *Ibid.*, 55, 212.

only 17% of the publications of the chemists are. Historical publications are also longer than those in the sciences. Although the writing of history commonly requires more research than do studies in English and philosophy, scholarly publication in these disciplines is approximately comparable, for as in history it usually involves single-author projects. At a time when three-fifths of the Ph.D.s in English, almost two-thirds of those in philosophy, and only one-third of those in history are publishing, it seems unreasonable to conclude that too many history Ph.D.s are writing for publication.

It is possible, however, that some Ph.D.s in history are prematurely submitting their contributions to managing editors of journals and presses. In the fall of 1959 no less than 17% of the Ph.D.s of 1958 (16.9% of those from the seven top-prestige programs) reported having had one book or more accepted for publication since the award of the Ph.D.; and more than one-third (36%) of the responding Ph.D.s of 1958 reported having at least one article accepted for publication. But almost one-fourth (22%; 26% from the seven top-prestige programs) reported having one article manuscript or more than one rejected, and at least one-sixth (16%) reported having had a book manuscript rejected. Some of those who are unready would develop their research science and their literary art if postdoctoral study in history —rare as compared with practice in other disciplines—were expanded. Both the quality and quantity of the publications of young Ph.D.s in history would undoubtedly be improved if more postdoctoral grants were available to enable them to rethink and rewrite the results of their doctoral research or to begin new studies arising from it.[26]

Professional historical associations also can and do foster scholarly excellence in graduate study. Prizes of the American Historical Association (AHA), the Pacific Coast Branch of the AHA, the

[26] On postdoctoral study see *ibid.*, 190–196. If ignorance of available funds partly explains why historians do not get more postdoctoral grants, it can still be substantially dispelled by consulting Louise Carroll Wade, "Assistance Available for Post-Doctoral Historical Research and Publication," *American Historical Review*, LXII (April, 1957), 570–593.

Mississippi Valley Historical Association, and the Southern Historical Association frequently go to recent Ph.D.s for dissertations or for books that are begun as dissertations. One prize-winning book in recent years was actually written as a master's thesis. Sometimes, while still Ph.D. candidates, young historians are invited to appear on the convention programs of the associations. Articles by Ph.D. candidates—often developed as seminar papers —appear from time to time in *The Historian, Journal of Modern History, American Slavic and East European Review*,[26a] *Journal of Central European Affairs, Journal of Southern History, Pacific Historical Review, Southwestern Social Science Quarterly, Mississippi Valley Historical Review*, state and other historical journals, and even in the *American Historical Review*. The European History Section of the Southern Historical Association in 1960 inaugurated an annual prize for the best seminar paper in European history by a graduate student in a Southern university.

More steps of this kind might be taken to stimulate excellence in research and writing among graduate students. It has been suggested, for example, that a special annual program in which many advanced Ph.D. candidates would present very short papers (ten minutes each) might be scheduled as part of the annual meeting of the AHA. Incidentally, this would allow would-be employers to see and hear at least some of the young talent in the nation in professional action. In more scholarly terms, this could influence Ph.D. training in a desirable way by emphasizing the need for Ph.D. candidates to think through their dissertation research and succinctly state their major contributions, to present their conclusions stripped of all but the most essential detail.

In these and other ways, perhaps more than the present 2 out of 5 Ph.D.s in history can be brought to find a publisher for part or all of their dissertations. With no more than 40% now doing so it is impossible to conclude that the Ph.D. programs are doing a job of educating historians that should cause complacency. Yet it would be deplorable if any reforms of graduate education should add to the length of time currently required for the overall Ph.D.

[26a] Published in 1961 and after under the title *Slavic Review*.

program. On the contrary, ways need to be found to improve teacher preparation, to keep field requirements broad, and to improve training for research and writing while simultaneously reducing the time commonly required for the Ph.D. in history.

PROTRACTED PH.D. STUDY

There is abundant opinion and some evidence that Benjamin Wright's "tentative conclusion" of 1957 is valid: that "the lengthening of the process has made the doctorate somewhat easier for those whom we call capable routineers, while discouraging a good many young people who would be much more stimulating teachers." [27] Berelson has shown quite clearly that members of graduate faculties who took a shorter time to complete the Ph.D. are more productive as scholars than those who took longer. To Berelson this does not mean that protracted doctoral programs burn out scholarly interests; he believes it simply means that "the better people tend to finish sooner and the better people are more productive." [28] The opinion of experienced sponsors of Ph.D. candidates in history coincides closely with this judgment.

In 1861, when Yale granted its first Ph.D., the degree was based upon 2 years of study.[29] How long should doctoral studies last today? It is a rare member of a graduate faculty in history who believes 3 academic years—or even 3 calendar years—is a realistic estimate of the time required for most students, even if they can devote full time to their studies.[30] But there is widespread agree-

[27] Benjamin F. Wright, "The Ph.D. Stretch-Out and the Scholar-Teacher," in Arthur E. Traxler (ed.), *Vital Issues in Education* (Washington, 1957), 144.
[28] Berelson, *Graduate Education*, 166.
[29] Keniston, *Graduate Study and Research in the Arts and Sciences at the University of Pennsylvania*, 13.
[30] The report of the four graduate deans in 1957 argued that three years of residence should be sufficient, and briefly suggested ways in which training might be completed in that period. This report by J. Barzun and others appears in the Association of Graduate Schools, Association of American Universities, *Journal of Proceedings and Addresses*, 58th Annual Conference. See also Keniston, *Graduate Study and Research in the Arts and Sciences at the University of Pennsylvania*, 31.

ment among historians on graduate faculties that 4 years of full-time study—including the master's training if it is taken—should be sufficient for Ph.D. candidates who are capable of earning the degree unless exceptional problems are involved (e.g., learning a language not commonly taught in the colleges).

In actuality, however, Ph.D. candidates in history rarely complete the degree within 4 years after beginning graduate study. *Only 8% of the history Ph.D.s of 1958 were awarded the degree within 4 years after beginning graduate study in history; 71% required 7 years or more* (see Table 8-5). *Only one-fourth of the*

TABLE 8-5

TIME LAPSE BETWEEN START OF GRADUATE STUDY AND AWARD OF DEGREE TO 182 PH.D.s IN HISTORY OF 1958

Award of degree within—	Cumulative No. of Ph.D.s	Cumulative % of total
3 years	4	2
4 years	15	8
5 years	31	17
6 years	53	29
7 years	78	43
8 years	97	53
9 years	112	62
10 years	134	74
11 years or more	182	100

Ph.D.s were under 30 when the degree was awarded; 35% were 36 or older (see Table 8-6). The Ph.D.s of 1958 who started graduate study young tended to take shorter periods to earn the degree; those who started later took longer. Ph.D.s in the West and Midwest finished considerably faster than those in the East and South. Ph.D.s from the South were notably older than those from other regions (almost half—48%—were 36 or more) and Ph.D.s from the Midwest were notably younger (27% were 36 or more).

Separate studies confirm the fact that only a minority of Ph.D.s in history obtain the degree in less than 6 or 7 years. These studies

TABLE 8-6

AGES OF 181 PH.D.s OF 1958 UPON AWARD OF THE DEGREE

Age	Cumulative No. of Ph.D.s	Cumulative % of Ph.D.s
25 or less	2	1
27 or less	23	13
29 or less	44	24
31 or less	72	40
33 or less	96	53
35 or less	117	65
37 or less	139	77
39 or less	150	83
40 or more	31	17

also show that the Ph.D. in history commonly is more protracted than doctorates in most other disciplines. Sibley showed in 1948 that the time required in history from bachelor's to Ph.D. was 7.8 years and that only political science in a group of 11 social and natural sciences required more.[31] More than half (54%) of all the history Ph.D.s at Columbia, 1940–1956, spent 8 years or more getting the degree. The average length of time required for the Columbia Ph.D.s in history, 9.5 years, was the longest for all but 3 of 13 disciplines; and the average time required to achieve a Harvard Ph.D. (8.1 years for the history Ph.D.s of 1954) is almost as protracted as for Columbia.[32]

But it is a rare Ph.D. faculty that can criticize the protracted Ph.D.s of Columbia and Harvard without illustrating the tendency to "reform some other guy" instead of tackling one's own problems. Thus a study of 143 recent Ph.D.s in history from universities in the South shows a mean time lapse of 9.7 years from the beginning of graduate study to award of the doctorate (the median was 8.0). This study shows that only in foreign languages

[31] Sibley, *The Recruitment, Selection, and Training of Social Scientists*, 87.

[32] Rosenhaupt, *Graduate Students: Experience at Columbia University, 1940–1956*, 73, 79, 124.

and English does the Ph.D. take longer. (The time reported in economics, political science, and sociology averages from 6 to 18 months less than in history.)[33] The mean time lapse *from bachelor's degree* to Ph.D. for 95 history Ph.D.s of 1957 in Berelson's sample was 10.1 years.[34] This is very much in harmony with the data reported above, for the mean time lapse from bachelor's to Ph.D. is 18 to 24 months more than the lapse from start of graduate study to Ph.D.

In the decisive opinion of graduate faculties in history, Ph.D. programs are overly protracted, and just as decisively they believe the cause to be part-time or full-time work by graduate students, made necessary by inadequate fellowship aid. Chapter 3 has already demonstrated that great numbers of history Ph.D. candidates do engage in part-time or full-time work between the beginning of graduate study and award of the Ph.D. It also suggested that part-time work while in residence does not cause serious delays in progress toward the Ph.D. Thus, one-third (33%) of the 57 Ph.D.s of 1958 who devoted full time to studies while in graduate school completed the degree within 6 years, but so did 29% of the entire sample of 182. Three-fourths (75%) of the whole sample were thirty or more upon award of the Ph.D., and so were three-fourths (75%) of the Ph.D.s who devoted full time to study while in residence. Part-time work in graduate school somewhat delays the Ph.D. candidates who engage in it, but the main problem lies elsewhere.

A comparison of time actually spent in residence with the total time from start of graduate study to Ph.D. strengthens the argument that the main problem of candidates is lack of funds. Two-fifths (42%) of the 1958 Ph.D.s completed their residence in graduate school in 3 years or less and three-fourths (73%) completed their residence within 4 years (cf. Table 8-5). For 143 recent Ph.D.s in history in the South the mean length of time in graduate study in all institutions was exactly 4 calendar years

[33] Prepublication data made available by the Southern Regional Education Board.
[34] Bernard Berelson generously provided a separate IBM tabulation for the history group in his sample of recent (1957) Ph.D.s.

(median, 3.8); somewhat longer averages are reported in most other disciplines, including the natural sciences.³⁵ Berelson's respondents in the social sciences estimated that the Ph.D. required 3.7 years (median) of actual work—as nearly as they could translate protracted activity into equivalent full-time work. Berelson reports that it takes the same length of time "in the top places and the others." ³⁶

Obviously programs of 8, 9, or 10 years (and sometimes more) usually are not caused by time in residence but by delays in completing dissertations after residence is completed and while candidates hold full-time jobs. Why do candidates plunge (or sink) into full-time work before completing dissertations? The cause which has been pointed out and which seems obvious is the financial need of Ph.D. candidates.

But it is possible that a different kind of financial problem than the need for fellowships is involved. Rosenhaupt has noted that Columbia candidates in fields that offered high post-Ph.D. salaries finished the degree rapidly.³⁷ In a report released in 1960 the National Opinion Research Center points to low post-Ph.D. salaries and reluctance to go from a graduate school to a college teaching position as the major reasons why Ph.D. candidates in the humanities have such protracted Ph.D. programs. There is insufficient incentive to finish in three to four years.³⁸

If, indeed, the Ph.D. "stretch-out" in history is caused in part by insufficient financial reward for completing the degree, the graduate schools are left with four basic devices to speed the training process. One way is to obtain more fellowship funds. The second is closely related to the first: graduate faculties can recruit better students. The need for both of these measures has been reviewed in Chapter 3. A third way is to encourage the students

---

³ Data provided by the Southern Regional Education Board.

³⁶ Berelson, *Graduate Education*, 159–160.

³⁷ Rosenhaupt, *Graduate Students: Experience at Columbia University, 1940–1956*, 75.

³⁸ Davis and others, "The Financial Situation of American Arts and Science Graduate Students," 261.

to do all their graduate work in a single institution. Changing graduate schools after a year or so of study is a stimulating and broadening experience, but it contributes to the Ph.D. stretch-out.[39] A fourth way is to tighten the training process. Tighter training is the one way to shorten programs that is directly and immediately open to all graduate faculties in history. One may hope that tighter training will attract larger numbers of superior students; one may also hope that it might convince the sources of fellowship aid that more funds should be entrusted to history faculties. However this may be, these moves might well be tried, for they are desirable in their own right.

What, then, can be tightened? Recent Ph.D.s in history and graduate faculty members generally are in agreement about the steps that might be taken. The Ph.D.s of 1958 recommend them in this order:

1. Provide better orientation and guidance of graduate students, especially in work on the dissertation
2. Set deadlines for various stages of progress
3. Put less emphasis on formal courses, especially lecture courses
4. Restrict the dissertation somewhat in scope of topic, amount of research expected, or length
5. Raise general standards for admission; require fulfillment of the language requirement for admission
6. Encourage Ph.D. candidates to bypass the master's degree; waive the requirement of a master's thesis
7. Eliminate the final oral examination for the Ph.D.
8. Relax or eliminate the foreign language requirement
9. Reduce the number or size of the fields that are covered on the general examination for the Ph.D.

Large numbers of historians on graduate faculties during interviews in 1959 recommended points 1 to 5. A good many of the members of graduate faculties also favored points 6 to 9, though these are more controversial. Points 5 to 7 and point 9 have already

[39] Only about half the social science Ph.D.s covered in the Sibley report of 1948 had done all their graduate work in a single institution. Sibley, *The Recruitment, Selection, and Training of Social Scientists*, 60.

been discussed in other contexts in this study (see Chapters 3, 5, 7). It seems especially relevant to this discussion to comment on points 1 to 4, 8, and 9.

Graduate students support the demand of recent Ph.D.s for better faculty guidance to history graduate students. The reports of some 300 history students in 25 universities indicate that they are somewhat less satisfied with advice from their professors than are students in other disciplines. Table 8-7 shows the frequency

TABLE 8-7

COMPARISON OF FACULTY GUIDANCE RECEIVED BY GRADUATE STUDENTS IN HISTORY AND OTHER DISCIPLINES
(SAMPLE OF 2,764 STUDENTS), 1958–1959

Type of advice	% of students advised by at least one faculty member	
	History students	Total sample
Definitely strive for the Ph.D.	43	47
Apply for a fellowship or scholarship.	35	41
You have a flair for research.	28	32
You were best student in a class.	25	27
You have a flair for teaching.	20	26
You are one of the best students in the department.	16	23
You are taking too long to get the degree	7	9
Consider transferring to another university.	6	4
Modify a few personality traits.	3	8
You should not plan on Ph.D.	2	3
Research would not be best for you.	2	2
Teaching would not be best for you.	1	2
You might do better in a different department.	1	2

SOURCE: Statistics provided by the National Opinion Research Center.

with which they report receiving advice of various types. The amount of guidance students receive varies greatly from one Ph.D. program to another, largely depending upon the student-teacher ratio. Thus one-fourth of all the Ph.D.s of 1958 state that too many students beyond the master's degree were in residence in their universities for adequate faculty attention, and almost half (46%) of the group from the seven top-prestige programs register this complaint (three-fourths—74%—of the 19 Ph.D.s from one of the seven).

Improved guidance at initial registration is needed in many departments. In most of them the new student confers with only one faculty member. With about equal frequency this is: (1) the departmental chairman; (2) the department's graduate adviser; or (3) any appropriate faculty member. In 22% of the Ph.D.-training departments the student confers with more than one faculty member. An informal discussion of previous training and the development of a program for the first year of graduate study between the new student and two or three faculty members can be especially helpful at this stage—to students and faculty members alike. If a master's thesis is to be written, time can be saved by the appointment on the spot of a faculty sponsor or a committee to spur and aid the student in the choice of a subject.

A second stage at which better guidance is very much needed comes at the end of the first year of graduate study. Whether or not the student is seeking the master's degree, he should then be definitely encouraged to go on to the Ph.D.—or just as vigorously discouraged. The student who seems no better than a risky prospect for the doctorate at the end of one year of graduate study is likely to be in the end no better than a risky prospect. And he will not be made much better than risky if he is kept in the Ph.D. program for eight years or more.

Guidance toward the end of the Ph.D. program can also be improved. Students need faculty help in selecting dissertation topics. Much time can be saved if topics can be selected early and developed in seminars and in the master's thesis, if one is written. Students are sometimes delayed because chapters of dissertations are read slowly, or by changes in faculty personnel, or by disagreements among faculty members who read their dissertations. In one department visited in this study it is not uncommon for the student to wait *two months or more* after taking the general written examination before being told whether he has passed or failed. While this does not happen in most Ph.D. programs, it is difficult to justify its happening at all.

Guidance alone will not drastically shorten the time required for the Ph.D., and some faculty members are prepared to try more radical reforms. Members of graduate faculties almost unanimously agree that Ph.D. programs are protracted by the requirement of reading knowledge in foreign languages. A small minority are willing to waive the requirement completely. Large numbers are in favor of requiring Ph.D. candidates to stand examination in only one language on the condition that greater mastery be demonstrated than is now commonly required by language examinations. But an almost exactly equal number would prefer to continue requiring examination in two languages. On the other hand, all but a small minority of the graduate faculty members favor setting a deadline for the passing of one foreign language examination by new graduate students. A good many would require this before the initial registration for graduate courses in history; the majority would demand it before the beginning of a second year of graduate study.

The graduate faculty members agree almost without dissent that the general examination causes delays in Ph.D. programs. None of those interviewed in this study want to make this examination less rigorous, but many faculty members would reduce the scope or number of fields covered on the examination, and this is thought by some to be especially appropriate in the case of candidates whose specialty requires competence in three or four foreign languages. A large majority are in favor of setting a deadline by which Ph.D. candidates must take the general examination. And there is a widespread conviction that students should prepare for the general examination more independently than is usually the case, that they should not be required to accumulate large amounts of course credit.

The doctoral dissertation in history has long been the target of criticism. In 1927 J. Franklin Jameson, convinced that "most universities make too formidable a job" of it, suggested that the student could "learn those arts of continuous research and methodical construction and composition, which it is of course necessary for him to learn, quite as well by producing a monograph of a hundred pages as by producing one of six or seven hundred." [40] Admonitions by Jameson and others have not resulted in shorter dissertations, and the time invested in Ph.D. dissertations is a large element in the arithmetic of prolonged programs. Data provided by 1,869 recent Ph.D.s from universities in the South, including 139 in history, show that the average (mean and median) time lapse between approval of topics and submission of complete dissertations is longer in history than in any of 15 disciplines. The mean time lapse in history of 2.8 years may be compared with 2.1 in political science, and 1.9 in the physical sciences.[41]

A few historians on graduate faculties today are ready to settle for dissertations of 100 to 150 pages in length. But most agree that 300 pages is the *maximum* desirable length, and most believe that one calendar year of full-time work should be sufficient for dissertation research and writing. In considering this as well as other proposals for tightening doctoral training the following comment by Hayward Keniston is worth the serious attention of graduate faculties in history: "In a word, we must give up the idea that the graduate student should emerge from his studies a fully formed scholar; the most that we can hope is that he has gained a fairly broad vision of his field, its problems and limitations, and that he has learned how to carry on independent research, and, above all, that he enters on his career with undiminished zest in the great adventure of learning." [42]

[40] Quoted by Jernegan, "Productivity of Doctors of Philosophy in History," 17–18n.
[41] Data provided by the Southern Regional Education Board.
[42] Keniston, *Graduate Study and Research in the Arts and Sciences at the University of Pennsylvania*, 32.

SUMMARY

Criticism is the subject and the substance of this chapter. As a result, a word of caution and qualification is in order, for as Merle Curti has noted, "American and European scholars alike" have often been "misled by the tendency of American scholars to be self-critical."[43] Solid accomplishments should not be lost from sight as the hopes of greater accomplishments are passed in review. In the opinion of many graduate faculty members in American universities in 1959, graduate study in this country is "better" than it was in the 1930s, and better than its counterpart in France, West Germany, and the U.S.S.R.[44]

The criticisms solicited in this study serve most of all to emphasize the supreme importance of attracting superior students to graduate study in history. If the students are first-rate, the Ph.D. graduates can be capable teachers of breadth, effective contributors to scholarly publications, and young enough upon the award of the Ph.D. to cause less concern than there is now about protracted doctoral programs. But there is widespread agreement that repairs are overdue in the training system if Ph.D.s in history are to be educated more efficiently as teachers and as scholars. The repairs are recommended whether or not larger numbers of Ph.D.s are to be trained.

Foremost among the suggested changes in doctoral training is the more deliberate preparation of Ph.D. candidates as teachers. History graduate students, recent Ph.D.s, and the colleges that provide positions for so many of these all want improved teacher training. Many members of graduate faculties concur in this desire, and a number of history Ph.D. programs have already made provision for better teacher preparation (see Chapter 9).

Closely related to the demand for more deliberate teacher training is the demand—also strongly expressed—for greater breadth of training. There is widespread opinion that overspecializa-

[43] Curti (ed.), *American Scholarship in the Twentieth Century*, 16–17.
[44] Berelson, *Graduate Education*, 209–210.

tion produces both teachers and research scholars ill-equipped to meet the broad demands of historical scholarship. The instilling of a broader historical approach and more attention to the literary skills are the major recommendations editors have to offer Ph.D. programs in history.

Finally, this chapter shows how protracted Ph.D. programs in history have become. It suggests ways in which they might be tightened, and Chapter 9 will suggest others. Statistics proving that the Ph.D. in history requires an average of eight years to achieve should summon up realistic determination and inventiveness on the part of every graduate faculty in the nation in attempting to reduce the Ph.D. "stretch-out." And determination should not be sapped by talk of producing "half-baked" Ph.D.s as a result of the tightened program. Half-baked bread is no good, but medium-rare steaks are a different matter. It is generally agreed that Ph.D. candidates in history have commonly been left too long over a slow fire.[45]

[45] Readers may be interested in comparing this chapter with the mimeographed report prepared by G. W. Pierson (August, 1961) on criticisms of Ph.D. training at Yale University offered by former graduate students at Yale.

Chapter 9

EXPERIMENTS WITH TEACHER TRAINING AND TIGHTENED PROGRAMS

The most realistic formula for training Ph.D.s who are first-rate scholar-teachers is, in the opinion of many members of graduate faculties, one of five parts: (1) get first-rate students; (2) provide them with adequate financial support for full-time or nearly full-time study; (3) inspire and require them to work very hard; (4) make them feel that teaching is important and orient them in the qualities of good teaching; and (5) turn them loose after three or four years, judging them by the quality of their work more than by its quantity and acknowledging that Ph.D. training is a beginning, not a culmination, of scholarly development. Since better salaries for history Ph.D.s are needed if the first-rate students are to be attracted to doctoral training, it is believed that they are a precondition for the success of this or any other training formula—and that what the student can expect to earn at forty or sixty is more important than what he is offered upon completing the degree.

Explicit efforts at teacher preparation and deliberate attempts to tighten the training program are direct expressions of the last three parts of this five-part formula.

TEACHER PREPARATION

A great many Ph.D. programs provide graduate students with experience as leaders of discussion groups, and some add instruction in college teaching. The instruction may be given informally by the course director during staff meetings—as at Harvard—or it may be put on a more formal basis—as at Wisconsin. Still other institutions appoint graduate students to part-time instructorships, giving them full control over their classes and, typically, providing no faculty supervision and criticism. Since these types of preparation are well known, they will not be reviewed here. Instead, a number of more experimental attempts to meet the need for teacher preparation will be summarized.

Princeton's program since 1950 has included a seminar on "Teaching History at the College Level." It is required of all second-year graduate students and lasts the better part of one semester. In the first part of the course a faculty member lectures on the ways students learn and on the attributes and techniques of teaching that encourage or discourage learning. Students then prepare outline plans for the conduct of parts of a freshman survey course, showing the central aim of each session; they also provide illustrative material, questions for discussion, and a fifteen-minute test based on assigned reading, and indicate the way a single session would be summarized at the beginning of the next session of the course. Each student's plan is critically discussed by the whole group. Some attention is also given in this course to the role of history in relation to other parts of a college curriculum.

In the "laboratory" part of the course each graduate student gives (to the seminar and its director) a fifty-minute lecture of the sort that would normally be presented in an undergraduate course. Each performance is followed by vigorous criticism of content, style, and delivery by students and the director of the course. This experience is thought to be especially valuable, for it may be the last time in a teaching career when the lecturer is "told what is wrong with his teaching with complete, if rather brutal, candor."

This experience enables the faculty to write "honest and informed" recommendations about the students when they apply for teaching positions. It is also believed that this course strengthens the motivations of the students for teaching and helps develop among them a professional approach to their whole graduate program.[1]

The University of Rochester, like Princeton, a decade ago searched for a way to provide teacher preparation to graduate students without assigning them to teach undergraduate courses. The doctoral candidate who is accepted at Rochester as a "graduate associate" manages two or three discussion sections of the survey course during his first and second years. During his second year he also prepares 10 lectures to be given in undergraduate courses of differing sizes and at differing levels. Each lecture is prepared in consultation with the instructor in whose course the student will give it. The instructor then listens to the lecture and subsequently criticizes it. The graduate associates also receive practice—under faculty supervision—as advisers to undergraduate majors. The Rochester experience illustrates one way in which a Ph.D. program can provide a limited amount of supervised teaching of varied types to doctoral candidates even if it is unwilling or unable to assign them full responsibility for undergraduate classes.

Duke University's approach to teacher preparation of Ph.D. candidates in history combines some of the instructional features of the Princeton program with the supervised practice features of the Rochester system. Since 1952 a seminar in "The Teaching of History in College" has been required of doctoral candidates in their last year of required residence. It is conducted by two members of the history faculty with the close collaboration of other members of the department. In the first part of the year-long seminar each student is assigned to observe the teaching of an instructor in an undergraduate course during a period of about six class meetings covering a unit of the course and, if possible,

[1] See Gordon A. Craig, "College Teaching: Theory and Practice," *Princeton Alumni Weekly*, LIX (January 30, 1959), 9–12; Craig, "New Needs and Old Values," paper presented to the annual convention of the American Historical Association, December, 1959.

ending with a test. During this period the student confers with the instructor about his objectives and methods. Each student prepares a detailed written report on the goals and methods of instruction and testing that he has observed. These reports are then discussed in evening meetings of the seminar, held every two weeks in the homes of the seminar directors.

In the second semester each member of the seminar prepares a detailed plan of instruction for a unit of three class meetings of the course he observed during the fall term. This plan must show general objectives, objectives for each class meeting, approaches to be used, illustrations to be used, reading assignments, plans for student participation, a twenty-minute test, and a fifty-minute test. The student then teaches the class in a three-meeting period, following which he revises his teaching plans, writes a report on his experience, and presents this report to the seminar. Besides reviewing teaching experiences the seminar members discuss matters of broad professional concern on the basis of readings assigned by the professors in charge. These treat such topics as: (1) academic freedom and responsibility; (2) the relationship of teaching and research; (3) professional societies; (4) administrative and committee work of faculty members; (5) ethics and etiquette of the profession; (6) getting a job; and (7) responsibilities of faculty members toward the library. The Duke program thus moves first from observation of good teaching to actual teaching and then to consideration of professional matters.

Indiana University in 1958–1959 inaugurated a course in "The Teaching of College History" somewhat like that at Duke, offering it to second- and third-year graduate students. At Indiana as at Duke the students prepare outlines of courses and lectures and give practice lectures. Plans were being made in 1959–1960 for tape recording the conduct of discussion sections and trial lectures, and for making five-minute films of parts of each student's lectures. In this way the student could actually hear and see his own teaching and thus identify—with the help of other members of the seminar and the instructor—the qualities needing improvement. At Indiana as at Duke the course in 1958–1959 involved discussion of the seven matters of professional concern enumerated in the above paragraph.

The program at Tulane University to prepare history students for college teaching includes a one-semester seminar, required of all doctoral candidates. This is conducted by the chairman of the department, who also serves as adviser to graduate students. The seminar gives considerable attention to the history of higher education in the United States and to the professional matters discussed in the Duke and Indiana seminars. The Tulane program differs from the others here reviewed chiefly in that it includes the independent teaching of a section—occasionally two sections—of the freshman survey courses for an entire academic year by each doctoral candidate. Ideally this is done during the student's third year of graduate study, and the seminar on college teaching is taken during the first term in which the student is actually teaching. Each member of the seminar observes the teaching of every other member and prepares a written critique on it. Thus at the end of the seminar there are 5 to 10 critiques on each student's teaching. In a conference with each student-instructor the department chairman reviews the critiques of his work, making suggestions for the improvement of shortcomings that were noted by the student-critics. Meanwhile, each student's major professor also observes his classroom performance and offers constructive criticism.

Some supervised teaching is also provided in the Intercollegiate Program of Graduate Studies operated by the Claremont Graduate School, Occidental College, the University of Redlands, and Whittier College. This program, in fact, "aims primarily at improved preparation for college teaching." Believing broad understanding of the liberal arts to be the way to good teaching in the colleges, this program features interdisciplinary seminars in which three professors direct and try to interrelate extensive reading by 6 to 15 students in their various fields (e.g., history, philosophy, and art). Two of these interdisciplinary seminars are normally completed by each doctoral candidate.

Yet another approach to teacher preparation was inaugurated

at Stanford University in 1959–1960. In this experiment each professor sponsoring Ph.D. candidates undertook to give them a course on methods and problems of teaching. Because of the burden on professors with many graduate students, the department at the end of the year was considering the possibility of having one faculty member conduct a unified course on teaching.

REDUCING THE PH.D. "STRETCH-OUT"

Many doctoral programs in history have taken steps in recent years to make Ph.D. programs less protracted. The change in foreign language examinations and the waiving of the final doctoral examination in some cases at Harvard have already been cited (see Chapter 7). Several other Ph.D. programs have made even more comprehensive attempts to reduce the Ph.D. "stretch-out."

The basic step in some programs is (as it is at Harvard) the careful scrutiny of applicants for admission to graduate school: thus Yale in 1959 admitted 1 of 4 applicants, and Princeton 1 of 6. While the obligations of state universities may make it impossible for them to turn away such a high proportion of applicants as do Princeton, Yale, and other private universities, the University of California in 1958–1959 inaugurated a new foreign language requirement that also has the effect of screening applicants more carefully than was earlier the case: each applicant is required to pass an examination in one foreign language before he can enroll in graduate courses in history.

The guidance a student is given when he first arrives at a graduate school and during his first year of study can do much to prolong or shorten his period of study. At Berkeley, as a result of the reforms that went into effect in 1958–1959, each entering student is informed that the department expects students with sound undergraduate training and a reading knowledge of two foreign languages to complete the general examination for the Ph.D. after two years of full-time graduate study. Students who have not taken the Ph.D. examination by the beginning of the third year of graduate study must petition the department for an extension.

The department thus no longer allows the students to set their own pace. "They must plan their program to get to the qualifying [general] examination in two years or explain why they are delaying." [2] To enable the students to prepare for the examination by the end of the second year of graduate study, field requirements were altered. Adequate undergraduate preparation can now satisfy the previous requirement of a fourth (minor) field. Examination over the major field is separated from examination over two minor fields of history, underscoring the subordinate character of the latter. In addition, students are encouraged to enroll in two 3-hour reading courses in order to prepare for examination in the whole field of the major. These reading courses are directed by a specifically designated adviser from the major field of study, and the contact this affords makes possible more adequate guidance in the planning and development of a total Ph.D. program than was previously afforded Ph.D. candidates at Berkeley.

The history department at Stanford University in 1959–1960 also moved to screen graduate students more systematically than it had previously, and to speed their progress toward the Ph.D. Students are told that they should pass an examination in one foreign language during the first year of graduate study at Stanford, and in a second language during the second year; that failure to pass on schedule will result in suspension of their candidacy for the doctorate. After four quarters (or soon after one quarter for students who have received the master's degree elsewhere) each student is evaluated by a faculty review committee. This committee gives in effect a qualifying examination, scrutinizes seminar papers, considers the student's plans for Ph.D. study, and generally assesses the student's ability and readiness to perform as a doctoral candidate. Admission to candidacy for the Ph.D. or termination of the student's study at Stanford follows the review of this "washout" committee.

Each entering student at Stanford is told that "except in the

[2] Hunter Dupree, "The State University Graduate School and the Deluge," paper read at the annual convention of the American Historical Association, December, 1959.

most unusual cases, the Department expects completion of the requirements for the doctorate in not more than three academic years of residence"; that "at the end of his second year the candidate should take his general examinations and by the end of his third year he should have completed his dissertation." To this end the department has changed the number of fields required in history from six narrow fields to three broader ones (e.g., Europe since 1700). It also authorizes the student and his adviser to "delimit a particular area of study" within the secondary fields for major consideration during the general examination. A minor in another discipline (or in a combination of disciplines) may be substituted for one of the secondary history fields. The general examination is divided into two parts. A written examination covers two secondary fields and, if this is satisfactory, the oral examination may be limited to the major field. Finally, the student at Stanford is told that the doctoral dissertation—"except in the most unusual of cases"—should not be longer than "250 typewritten pages" and that the subject should be "sufficiently delimited to admit of completion within one year." A committee of three faculty members, including one from outside the history department, supervises and approves the dissertation. No final examination is required.

The history faculty at Yale tightened its Ph.D. program in 1958–1959. Early screening is an important element in the speed-up. In an all-day meeting at the end of the spring semester the faculty decides which students are to be allowed to continue into their second or third years of study and which are to go beyond the master's degree. Students unable to pass an examination in either French or German cannot matriculate in history. The passing of the second language is urged at entrance, or no later than the beginning of the second year. Fellowship aid is normally not given to those who have not satisfied both language requirements before the end of their third term of residence. Another feature of the Yale reforms of 1958–1959 is a special provision for independent study. Henceforth second-year students will drop one of the four courses they were previously expected to take in order to use the released time for independent study in preparation for the general (oral) examination. This is scheduled for the end of the second year. By the middle of the third year each student is expected to have a doctoral dissertation underway, and a length limitation of 300 typed pages on the dissertation is enforced.

Early and systematic faculty screening of graduate students is also a feature of attempts to tighten the Ph.D. program in history at Tulane University. There a faculty "reception committee" of three or four instructors and the department chairman meets each new graduate student in an interview lasting about thirty minutes. This involves an informal review of the student's previous study, an attempt to ascertain his professional objectives and his central interests in history, the tentative planning of a full year of courses and seminars, and the designation of a faculty committee to advise the new student during his first semester in the choice of a topic for the master's thesis. At the end of the first and second semesters the department chairman receives an evaluation form on all new students from each professor with whom they are studying. Thus the coordination of faculty evaluations of student performances is made possible. Intellectual growth, prospects for attainment of the Ph.D., readiness for part-time teaching, and qualification for fellowship aid are all noted in the evaluation check-sheets. This affords a more careful and earlier screening of graduate students than was previously practiced.

The University of Michigan in 1959 sought in different ways to accelerate the progress of doctoral candidates. One slight change was made in field requirements. Ph.D. candidates will be required to offer five fields of history plus one cognate field as before. From now on, however, Ph.D. candidates may omit the examination over one of these fields. This may be the cognate field or any field of history except the field of concentration. Course work satisfies the requirement for this field. As another means of reducing the Ph.D. stretch-out, Michigan requires that a committee meeting be held to discuss each candidate's work when he is about one-third of the way through with the dissertation. It is hoped—but no rule is adopted to cover this—that each Ph.D. dissertation will be no more than 300 pages in type. Michigan has also agreed to waive the final examination on the Ph.D. dissertation when it shows exceptional ability.

One of the suggestions most often made for shortening the period of study for the doctorate is to reduce the number of courses— especially lecture courses—required of Ph.D. candidates. The history department at the University of Texas in 1958 revised its Ph.D. program to eliminate the traditional lecture courses taken by both graduate and undergraduate students. Henceforth graduate students are to take sequences of "seminars" and "research seminars." The former, given in the fall, introduce students to a field of history, its major themes, problems, conflicting interpretations, and primary and secondary sources. The "research seminar" in the second term involves the student in supervised research and writing. A drastic reduction in credit hours was part of the Texas reform. A minimum of 36 credit hours for the Ph.D. is now set, 24 hours in the major area (three limited fields) and 12 in the minor area (two limited fields). These reforms look toward "a two-year course program for the doctorate."

A somewhat similar approach to revising the character of graduate courses was adopted at Emory University in 1959–1960. In three quarters during the academic year students are now moved in sequence within each field from lectures about content to emphasis on literature and then to full-time research and writing. It is hoped that this will culminate in the completion of a master's thesis within one academic year, thus accelerating progress toward the Ph.D. degree.

To some extent both the Texas and Emory approaches to courses resemble the approach that has been used for some time at the University of Washington (Seattle). There the courses taken by graduate students directly point toward field preparation in restricted areas of history, usually covering periods of twenty-five to fifty years. In two hours of formal class meetings each week the professor discusses the scholarly problems, varying interpretations, and literature of the field. Students are thus guided in wide and intensive reading, and since each course carries five hours of credit, only two of which are spent in class each week, there is time for independent study. These "field" courses are supplemented by research seminars and a course in historiography. The over-all emphasis is, therefore, upon achieving competence in fields rather than upon the accumulation of large numbers of hour-credits.

This is also the aim of graduate courses at Princeton, which pioneered in several of the techniques for tightening doctoral programs that have been reviewed here. The major tactical moves in the Princeton campaign against the Ph.D. stretch-out have been:

1. Careful selection of students, with admission of doctoral candidates only
2. Careful guidance and close screening of first-year students
3. Elimination of lecture courses for graduate students
4. Early selection of topics for doctoral dissertations and their development in seminars—especially in a "Thesis Writers' Seminar" that all students are expected to take during the second semester of their second year of graduate study and during their third year of graduate study
5. Restriction of the number and scope of fields to be covered on the general examination (three fields; one additional field in history and one outside field to be satisfied by "successful completion of advanced work")
6. Reduction of courses during the spring term of the second year of graduate study to allow for supervised independent study in the major field
7. Requirement that students take the general examination at the end of the second year of graduate study
8. Limitation of the scope and length of dissertations, which are not to exceed 75,000 words (or about 300 typed pages)

SUMMARY

All the experiments in teacher preparation that have been reviewed here have one feature and one result in common: they focus the thought of both students and faculty on teaching as a central concern of doctoral training in history. The doctoral candidate who goes through programs like those summarized above can be expected to emerge with an awareness of the importance of good teaching, familiarity with the various forms it can take and the problems it involves, and some actual experience in it. The students know more about themselves as a result of the experience; and the faculty is better able to be specific about the capacity for teaching of the Ph.D. candidates it recommends for academic positions.

The attempts to tighten Ph.D. programs in history have taken many forms. Some have involved a realistic elimination of certain requirements; some have been more specific about the timing of traditional requirements. All are based upon two guiding assumptions. One is that some quantitative aspects of previous practices can be sacrificed without damaging the quality of doctoral training; that the central concern of Ph.D.-training faculties should be with the student's demonstration of scholarly purpose and growth and with the *quality* of the student's performance. A second assumption is that the faculty must itself assume responsibility for pacing the doctoral candidate's progress toward the Ph.D.

Other experiments are being undertaken; those reviewed in this chapter are only representative. It is too early to say with certainty whether all the features of the experiments noted here will in the long run prove to be desirable. It is indicative, however, that the Princeton and Rochester faculties are convinced of the importance of deliberate teacher preparation after more than a decade of their efforts to achieve it. And it is encouraging to learn that the results of the increased speed of training are thought to be salutary where it has been effected. One year's experience, in the opinion of one member of the graduate faculty at the University of California, has been sufficient to allay the fear that a "watered-down Ph.D." would be the necessary result of acceleration. On the contrary, the experience at California suggests that "acceleration is the path to higher and more precise standards and a better level of performance on the part of the student." [3]

[3] *Ibid.*

Chapter 10
RECOMMENDATIONS

The Committee on Graduate Education in History has been guided by two major convictions in drafting recommendations for the profession. First, it believes that graduate education as it has developed and is now conducted in the United States needs improvement, not replacement. Second, its recommendations are offered not as absolutes but as the product of thought by historians who have responsibly sought (after a study of current practice and professional opinion through interviews, correspondence, and questionnaires) to arrive at decisions about complicated and controversial matters.

ATTRACTING AND ADMITTING GRADUATE STUDENTS

Considerably more Ph.D.s in history will be needed annually during the 1960s than have been annually trained in the 1950s. Shortages of Ph.D.s in some fields of history do not now exist, but shortages in all fields of history will appear by 1964–1965 unless special measures such as the following are taken to increase the number of serious and capable Ph.D. candidates in the country:

1. More fellowships and scholarships should be made available for first-year graduate study and especially for a year of dissertation research and writing. The committee believes that loans are necessary and helpful but that they should not be viewed as the major

means of financing graduate study. Fellowships and scholarships are more desirable and realistic forms of assistance. In the past, prospective history students have been offered fewer and smaller stipends than students in other fields, along with prospects of relatively low post-Ph.D. salaries. Only through increased financial support can the profession attract graduate students of outstanding ability in sufficient numbers to meet the needs of the next decade.

2. The American Historical Association should publish and circulate a short booklet (of 4 to 20 pages) designed for promising undergraduates, discussing the opportunities and procedures of graduate study in history.[1]

3. Teachers of history at all levels should make able students aware of the possibilities of graduate study in history and careers as teachers of history.

4. A few well-prepared departments that do not now offer doctoral training might wish to do so; but the needs of the 1960s are not sufficiently acute to warrant the creation of a special doctorate for teachers, inferior to the Ph.D., nor do they make it necessary for departments with inadequate faculty strength and library resources to offer Ph.D. training. Several Ph.D. programs in history that rank among the top twenty or thirty in the nation have faculty and facilities for educating larger numbers of Ph.D.s than they are now producing.

5. Three conditions should be met by history departments that offer Ph.D. training: (*a*) the department should have faculty members in at least three broad fields of history, the majority of whom must be experienced teachers whose scholarly research contributions are recognized by fellow historians in the nation; (*b*) doctoral training being an expensive undertaking, the history department should be able to command financial resources for the assistance of graduate students, allocation of faculty time, and development of faculty members as scholars; and (*c*) the institution should have library resources adequate for training in research

[1] *History as a Career: To Undergraduates Choosing a Profession*, basically prepared by Professor Snell, was published in 1961 and copies are available at nominal cost from the American Historical Association, Washington 3, D.C.

seminars and for preparation for the general examination. Experience suggests that institutions that command respect as centers of doctoral training have libraries with general collections of several hundred thousands of volumes, or outstanding collections in special areas of history, or both.

6. A more personal evaluation of applicants for admission to graduate school is needed. It should be possible to identify some students whose abilities may be greater than undergraduate grades suggest. It should also be possible to avoid the waste of time and money that results when students are admitted who lack the qualities required for successful graduate study. More critical letters of recommendation about applicants and more frequent interviews with them can assist in a more personal evaluation. The inclusion of an essay section in the Graduate Record Examination would also make for more satisfactory selection of applicants for graduate study.

UNDERGRADUATE PREPARATION

The specific talent of the historian is fed by direct and vicarious experience. A historian should have a wide knowledge of human activity. An undergraduate student who wishes to prepare for graduate study in history should study foreign languages and (depending upon previous education) introductory or advanced courses in literature, philosophy, the social sciences, and the natural sciences. Study in history should include a number of courses broad in scope and courses in at least two broad fields of history. Undergraduate study in history should usually range between 24 and 36 semester hours of credit. Quality of mind and breadth of historical knowledge are even more important than specialization and depth of historical knowledge. Instruction, however varied in character, should develop the student's capacity for written and oral expression. Superior students should be encouraged to acquire training in the mechanics of research and historiography through honors study, which will usually demand an honors paper and a comprehensive examination.

THE MASTER'S DEGREE

The master's degree serves several purposes. The degree with a thesis of 70 to 80 pages or substantial research papers in two seminars is desirable for secondary teachers and persons who aspire to governmental positions. Work for this degree usually should not require more than one calendar year of study. Many institutions award a one- or two-year master's degree in course of study for the Ph.D. Institutions should also exercise the right to award the master's degree to Ph.D. candidates upon the completion of all requirements for the doctorate except the dissertation. A master's degree in history representing less than two to three years of graduate study would not meet the desired requirements for even temporary teachers of history at the college level.

SHORTENING PH.D. TRAINING

The committee notes with great concern that for 71% of the 1958 Ph.D.s in history seven or more years elapsed between the beginning of graduate study and award of the Ph.D.; and that 35% of the 1958 Ph.D.s were thirty-six years of age or older when the degree was awarded. Measures to shorten the period of training are clearly needed. Promotions in rank and salary increases are very often delayed, even in meritorious cases, until the Ph.D. degree is awarded. Even more serious is the damage to scholarship; many vital teachers and productive scholars can complete the degree in relatively shorter periods of graduate study and their fully trained abilities and services are needed now and in the decade ahead.

1. The committee believes that the Ph.D. in history should require no more than four academic years for most full-time Ph.D. candidates, including study for the master's degree and the completion of the Ph.D. dissertation. Infrequent exceptions should be made for students in fields that require the acquisition of special skills.

2. The major cause of delayed progress toward the Ph.D. is most often the financial inability of students to undertake full-time study. Both to recruit able students and to avoid prolonging their training the committee urgently recommends that more nonduty fellowships and scholarships be made available for graduate study in history. At this time they are especially needed for the period of dissertation research and writing.

3. Many students are delayed by difficulty in passing foreign language examinations. It is highly desirable that students early achieve competence in foreign languages in schools and colleges. If graduate students are to be required to take examinations in foreign languages, each department should have autonomy in determining the method and number of examinations, and students should be required to demonstrate actual working knowledge early, preferably before or upon admission to graduate study. (Students unprepared in languages who otherwise show very great promise may be treated as exceptional cases.) If examinations are to be required, they should be seriously given and seriously graded, proving the student's ability to use foreign languages as tools in courses and research seminars. Students should ideally be required to pass an examination in one foreign language before being admitted to graduate study, but in any case before being admitted to doctoral studies (i.e., by the beginning of the second year of graduate study). If an examination in a second foreign language is to be required, students should ideally pass it by the beginning of the second year of graduate study but in any case by the beginning of the third year of graduate study.

4. Ph.D. candidates should be constantly engaged in either historiographical or research seminars during two full academic years (four semesters or six quarters of seminar work), but other course requirements should be minimal.

5. Programs should be adjusted to each candidate's academic needs. Doctoral training is an arduous undertaking, and students who lack the qualities for success should early be channeled into other activities. For those who prove their capacity for Ph.D.-level training, the accumulation of course credits in Ph.D. programs

should be de-emphasized. No uniform total number of credit hours should be required of all candidates, and independent study by Ph.D. candidates should be encouraged.

6. The committee believes that a deadline should be explicitly established in each department for the major Ph.D. examination (the "general," "comprehensive," "qualifying," or "preliminary" examination). In discussion and in writing about Ph.D. programs time could be saved if a common name could be given this examination, most appropriately, perhaps, the "general" examination. Students should take this examination at the end of the second year of graduate study and no later than the middle of the third year of graduate study.

7. Departments should explicitly establish the number of fields on which Ph.D. candidates are to be questioned during the general examination. The scope of these fields should be clearly defined with the deadline for the general examination in mind.

8. The final Ph.D. examination, if required, should cover only the Ph.D. dissertation.

9. In recent years the Ph.D. dissertation has become a serious cause of delay in Ph.D. programs. The subject should usually be sufficiently restricted to enable a successful Ph.D. candidate to complete the research and writing within one calendar year of intensive full-time work. The dissertation should be a substantial monograph, representing a high level of scholarly and literary quality in the opinion of the history faculty. To give evidence of this quality, dissertations usually need not be longer than 300 typed pages (double-spaced typing) or 75,000 words.

STRIKING A BALANCE

The quality of teaching by historians in colleges and universities is generally considered to be high. Where it is less than satisfactory a complaint often heard is that the instructor has been trained in too narrow a field of specialization.

It is essential that the historian acquire breadth of knowledge in his own and related disciplines. Much of this breadth must be acquired during the undergraduate years, for graduate study is primarily a time for specialization. But even in Ph.D. programs some provision must be made to develop breadth of mind in the student, especially during the first year of graduate study. Each department must find its own way to achieve the proper balance between breadth and specialization in its Ph.D. program. The following guiding principles may be useful:

1. Careful faculty guidance of Ph.D. candidates is essential as they plan their programs of study at all levels of graduate study.
2. Ph.D. training should involve the following:
   a. Specialization in one broad field of history (e.g., United States, medieval, or Far Eastern history), and more intensive specialization in one aspect or period of this broad field.
   b. Acquaintance with the history of certain other restricted chronological periods and geographical areas (this often can be accomplished during the first year of graduate study as work toward the master's degree).
   c. Acquaintance with the classics of historical writing and with the possibilities, limits, theories, and values of the historian's craft.
3. Thorough training and practice in research and writing is of major importance. At least four semesters of work in research seminars should usually be performed by each Ph.D. candidate. When a special seminar in historical method is offered, it may be counted as one of the four semesters (or six quarters) of research seminars. To assure a proper balance between specialization and breadth, one of the four semesters (or at least one of six quarters) of seminar work should be in a field of history other than the special field of the Ph.D. candidate.
4. All graduate students in courses that teach the history of non-English areas—not just in research seminars—should read foreign language materials.
5. Wide reading should be a constant part of graduate study in history. It is desirable that reading tutorials for graduate students supplement such lecture courses as they may take, and

that departments offer at regular intervals directed reading courses in which Ph.D. candidates become broadly acquainted with periodical, monographic, and synthesizing literature in the major fields of history.

6. Ph.D. candidates should write dissertations on significant subjects, even though they may explore in detail only one aspect or a few aspects of a large topic. They should be asked to show the relationship of their research to previous research and to relate their subjects to the general fields of history in which they lie.

7. Broadening of interest, knowledge, and outlook can be accomplished through informal daily contacts among graduate students, but this is lost if all Ph.D. candidates in a department are specialists in a single field of history. Study by foreign students in American graduate departments of history can contribute to the balancing of breadth and specialization among Ph.D. candidates.

8. To integrate and broaden knowledge and fill in gaps, departments that each year give the major examination to several Ph.D. candidates representing various fields of specialization might consider the desirability of offering a preparatory reading course-colloquium to them as a group, aiming at comparative discussion of the literature in the major fields of history.

9. Neither the goal of breadth nor the goal of specialization should be allowed to prolong Ph.D. programs beyond a reasonable period of training (about four years of full-time graduate study or its equivalent). As one way to assure breadth without undue delay and without interfering undesirably with specialization, some departments may wish to require training in fields of history for which the candidate will not be formally held responsible in the general examination for the Ph.D. That examination should cover at least the broad field of specialization (e.g., ancient, Russian, or English history).

PREPARATION FOR TEACHING

While we strongly believe that Ph.D. training should continue to emphasize research scholarship, we are aware of the fact that most of those who receive Ph.D.s in history will devote more of their time to scholarly teaching than to research scholarship. Ph.D. programs should give much greater recognition than most of them have previously given to the problems that confront new Ph.D.s in their careers as college teachers.

1. Lecturing under occasional supervision and guidance by Ph.D. candidates is highly desirable. Some departments can provide candidates with experience as regular classroom teachers, either in the Ph.D.-training department or through internship arrangements with other institutions. Departments that cannot do this are urged to provide other opportunities for supervised practice lecturing by each Ph.D. candidate. The experience will prove helpful even to those candidates who do not become teachers. Tape recorders and film may be used to enable Ph.D. candidates to discover their own strengths and weaknesses.

2. Practice in leading discussion groups is also desirable. This alone is not likely to prepare the Ph.D. candidate for teaching by the lecture method. But the teacher needs to develop the capacity for leading discussion as well as lecturing. In the development of this ability skillful coaching may be even more helpful than in the development of lecturing skills.

3. In conjunction with practice lecturing and leading discussions, an informal and brief seminar or colloquium on college teaching and professional matters should be offered by the history department and perhaps required, though not necessarily for course credit. This might profitably provide Ph.D. candidates with experience in the preparation of course outlines, reading lists, and examinations.

DISCOVERING TEACHING CAPACITY

Most Ph.D.s in history become teachers of history in colleges or universities. Ph.D. programs can only begin their training as teachers. It is especially important, therefore, that ways be found early in their professional careers to discover and help them develop their capacities as teachers. The prerequisite for the discovery of capacity for teaching is that an appointing department know what specific qualities of teaching it seeks. Its definition of these qualities will acknowledge the variety of forms of good teaching.

No single technique is adequate to discover teaching capacity. But one or more of the following suggestions may be usefully adopted:

1. Appointing departments should ask specific questions about the teaching capacity of Ph.D. candidates in letters or telephone calls to the graduate departments. The graduate departments should be prepared to give specific information and give it candidly.
2. An interview is indispensable. On-campus interviews with colleagues and administrators are highly desirable.
3. When possible, candidates for faculty positions should be invited to lecture or lead discussions before classes or informal groups (e.g., the history club) before appointments are made.
4. Direct observation of the newly appointed instructor's work is desirable during the period of probationary appointment.
    a. Where jointly conducted courses are taught, senior colleagues can appraise the teaching capacity of new appointees.
    b. Where such courses are not offered, it is usually possible and always desirable from the beginning to have new instructors participate in oral examinations of graduate or undergraduate students.
    c. New teachers can be asked to contribute to departmental or interdepartmental faculty seminars.
    d. Contributions to programs of professional associations can

be observed, and scholarly publications and unpublished scholarship can be critically evaluated.

e. In addition, without restricting the inexperienced teacher's right to develop his own ideas, departments might encourage him to discuss his course outlines, reading lists, and examinations with senior colleagues.

f. Senior colleagues may visit the classes of an inexperienced appointee during his probationary appointment. The purpose must be to help young historians improve their teaching, not to restrict their freedom of expression. Thus, visits should not be numerous; visits by more than one colleague are desirable; and they should be tactfully arranged with the knowledge of the new instructor.

FOSTERING AND REWARDING GOOD TEACHING

Historians devote more of their time to teaching than do colleagues in most other academic disciplines. They also reach more students in their classrooms than do teachers in many other disciplines. This situation should be acknowledged by the administrative policies of their institutions in the interest of promoting good instruction.

As in the discovery of teaching capacity, no one method can ever suffice to foster good teaching; the reward for good teaching must take several forms. The following suggestions seem to this committee to be generally useful:

1. A capacity for research scholarship is a very important quality of a good teacher of history. But quantity of publication should not be the only index of capacity for scholarship. Teaching based on scholarship and unpublished research scholarship of high quality as well as published works should be rewarded in policies governing tenure appointments, promotion, and compensation. Both successful teaching and evidence of research scholarship should be expected of history teachers and both should be fostered by colleges and universities. But superlative performance in either

of these activities should be rewarded by promotions and salary increases.

2. In so far as they are able, appointing departments should name to the history faculty persons who have completed the Ph.D. Much of the preparation of graduate students as teachers is accomplished in the last phases of Ph.D. programs, and graduate departments can appraise the capacity of a fully trained Ph.D. much more accurately than they can estimate the promise of a Ph.D. candidate or the holder of a master's degree.

3. The new instructor can informally be given encouragement and advice—often in the form of tactful hints—by his colleagues.

4. In so far as possible, the new instructor should be freed of chores such as committee work that contribute little or nothing to his growth as a scholar-teacher during the first year or so of his service.

5. Both the new and the older instructor should be given an opportunity to teach courses in the field of his specialization (e.g., United States, Latin-American, or English history).

6. Classes should be scheduled in ways that will foster the development of the faculty member as teacher and as scholar. Even a heavy teaching load can often be scheduled to leave whole days free of classroom teaching.

7. The teaching load of a college instructor is determined not only by the number of hours of classroom teaching but also by the number of different preparations he must make and the number of students he teaches in a given term. In the interest of satisfactory teaching as well as satisfactory research scholarship, college teachers of history should teach no more than 12 hours per week and have no more than three separate preparations. It is highly desirable that they teach no more than 9 hours per week. In Ph.D.-training departments the faculty member has a number of additional obligations that are not easily measured in terms of hours of teaching and number of separate courses. Instructors in these departments should teach no more than 9 hours per week; and the usual load should not exceed 6 hours with no more than two separate courses or seminars.

8. The provision of research and secretarial assistance is needed if scholarly teaching and the research scholarship of teachers are to be fostered. Typing services can be especially helpful. Tape recorders for office use can save faculty time and secretarial expense.

9. Attendance at professional meetings is essential if college and university instructors are to grow as scholars and teachers. It should be subsidized by their institutions.

10. For those who teach the history of foreign areas, travel abroad at intervals is necessary if the teachers are to make vital contributions in the classroom and in research. Travel is already subsidized to some extent by foundation and governmental grants. It should also be subsidized by the colleges and universities.

11. Leaves of absence to study a new field at a university that is strong in the field of new interest (e.g., in Asian history) should be granted, especially when the instructor is expected to teach in a field in which he needs additional training.

12. Colleges as well as universities should foster the growth of the scholar-teacher by supporting research scholarship. Sabbaticals or leaves with full salary for research, the purchase of research tools (e.g., microfilm readers), support for building library holdings of sources, and free interlibrary loan services are desirable means of fostering the development of scholarly teaching.

13. Colleges and universities should give recognition to superlative teaching through public honors and reward it by promotions and salary increases. These may be desirably supplemented by special annual prizes and cash awards for excellence in teaching.

14. Professional associations should elect outstanding teachers of history to their high offices. In this and other ways they may recognize and reward scholarly teaching of history, thus fostering it in the colleges and universities.

15. The Ph.D.-training departments have a special responsibility to foster and reward excellent teaching, for they do much to set the tone that prevails in the colleges. Attitudes and policies in these institutions must be made to convey to Ph.D. candidates the conviction that excellent teaching is a primary responsibility of the historian who joins a college or university faculty.

APPENDIXES

APPENDIX A

In November, 1958, a 12-page questionnaire was mailed to 203 history faculties in colleges that were selected as better-than-average representatives of various types of institutions. None of these was offering the Ph.D. in history in 1958. It should be emphasized that many excellent four-year colleges were not included. Some institutions listed in Appendix B are academically superior to some in this sample. When the term "better colleges" has been used in the text it describes the sample as a whole in comparison with the random sample noted in Appendix B as a whole. Used in this way, the term can be convincingly defended.

Response to our questionnaire to the "better" colleges was good. Two-thirds (62% or 126) of the questionnaires were returned. They usually were completed by the departmental chairmen, though many chairmen consulted other members of the history faculty in formulating answers to our questions.

This questionnaire was designed to discover chiefly: (1) the qualifications and strength of history faculties; (2) conditions of teaching history and expected changes; and (3) degree of satisfaction or dissatisfaction with new Ph.D.s in history and suggestions for the improvement of graduate training.

Departments in the following institutions, listed by states within a region, completed this questionnaire:

EAST (38)

Connecticut: Connecticut College; Wesleyan University. *Delaware:* University of Delaware. *District of Columbia:* District of Columbia Teachers College; Howard University. *Maine:* Bowdoin College; University of Maine. *Maryland:* Goucher College; Maryland State Teachers College; U.S. Naval Academy; Washington College. *Massachusetts:* Amherst College; Mount Holyoke College; Wellesley College; Williams College. *New Hampshire:* Dartmouth College. *New Jersey:* New Jersey State Teachers College (Jersey City). *New York:* Brooklyn College; City College of the City of New York; Columbia University (Columbia College and School of General Studies); Hofstra College; Hunter College of the City of New York; Queens College; Rensselaer Polytechnic Institute; St. Bonaventure University; College for Teachers (Albany); Teachers College (New Paltz); U.S. Military Academy; Vassar College. *Pennsylvania:* Bucknell University; Haverford College; Lafayette College; State Teachers College (West Chester); Swarthmore College; Temple University. *Rhode Island:* University of Rhode Island. *Vermont:* University of Vermont.

SOUTH (32)

Alabama: Birmingham-Southern College; State Teachers College (Florence); Talladega College. *Arkansas:* Arkansas State College (State College). *Florida:* Rollins College; University of Miami. *Georgia:* Agnes Scott College; Atlanta University. *Kentucky:* University of Louisville. *Louisiana:* Dillard University; Loyola University; Southwestern Louisiana Institute. *Mississippi:* Millsaps College; Mississippi Southern College; University of Mississippi. *North Carolina:* Davidson College; East Carolina College; North Carolina College (Durham); North Carolina State College. *South Carolina:* Clemson Agricultural College. *Tennessee:* East Tennessee State College; Memphis State College; Univerity of Chattanooga; University of the South. *Texas:* Agricultural and Mechanical College of Texas; Baylor University; North Texas State College; Southern Methodist University; University of Houston. *Virginia:* College of William and Mary; Sweet Briar College; Washington and Lee University.

MIDWEST (34)

Illinois: Bradley University; Illinois State Normal University; Wheaton College. *Indiana:* Ball State Teachers College; DePauw University. *Iowa:* Cornell College; Grinnell College; Iowa State University of Science and Technology; Iowa State Teachers College. *Kansas:* Kansas State University of Agriculture and Applied Science; University of Wichita; Washburn University. *Michigan:* Albion College; University of Detroit. *Minnesota:* State Teachers College (Moorhead). *Missouri:* Lincoln University. *Nebraska:* Creighton University; Municipal University of Omaha; Nebraska State Teachers College (Wayne). *Ohio:* Antioch College; Baldwin-Wallace College; Case Institute of Technology; College of Wooster; Kenyon College; Miami University; Oberlin College; Ohio University; University of Akron; University of Cincinnati; University of Dayton. *Wisconsin:* Lawrence College; Marquette University; Wisconsin State College (Oshkosh); Wisconsin State College (Superior).

WEST (22)

Arizona: University of Arizona. *California:* Chico State College; Mills College; Occidental College; San Diego State College; San Francisco State College; San Jose State College. *Colorado:* Colorado College; Colorado State University; U.S. Air Force Academy; University of Denver; Western State College of Colorado. *Hawaii:* University of Hawaii. *Montana:* Montana State University. *North Dakota:* State Teachers College (Minot). *Oregon:* Lewis and Clark College; Oregon State College (Corvallis); Reed College; University of Portland. *South Dakota:* State University of South Dakota. *Washington:* Western Washington College of Education. *Wyoming:* University of Wyoming.

APPENDIX B

A seven-page questionnaire on history in the colleges was sent in November, 1958, to 562 four-year colleges. This random sample included all four-year colleges (not junior colleges and not institutions offering the Ph.D. in history) listed in 1958 as members of the American Council on Education and not included in the sample of colleges noted in Appendix A. Two-thirds of the history faculties (67% or 376) returned usable questionnaires. The 376 questionnaires represent history programs in the following institutions:

EAST (133)

Connecticut: Fairfield University; Hillyer College; New Haven State Teachers College; Teachers College of Connecticut (New Britain); U.S. Coast Guard Academy; University of Bridgeport. *District of Columbia:* Gallaudet College; Trinity College; Washington Missionary College. *Maryland:* College of Notre Dame of Maryland; Hood College; Loyola College; Maryland State Teachers College (Frostburg); Mount St. Agnes College; Mount St. Mary's College; St. Joseph College; Western Maryland College. *Massachusetts:* Anna Maria College; Babson Institute; College of the Holy Cross; College of Our Lady of the Elms; Eastern Nazarene College; Emmanuel College; Hebrew Teachers College; Lesley College; Merrimack College; New England Conservatory of Music; Newton College of the Sacred Heart; Regis College; Simmons College; Springfield College; Wheaton College. *New Hampshire:* Mount St. Mary College; Rivier College; St. Anselm's College. *New Jersey:* Caldwell College; College of St. Elizabeth; Drew University; Georgian Court College; Monmouth College; Newark State College; New Jersey State Teachers College (Trenton); Newark College of Engineering, Rider College, Stevens Institute of Technology; Upsala College. *New York:* Alfred University; Canisius College; Clarkson College of Technology; College of Mount St. Vincent; College of New Rochelle; College of St. Rose; Cooper Union; Elmira College; Hamilton College; Iona College; Keuka College; Le Moyne College; Long Island University; Marymount College; Nazareth College of Rochester; Pace College; Mount St. Joseph Teachers College; Pratt Institute; Siena College; St. Joseph's College for Women; St. Lawrence University; Sarah Lawrence College; Harpur College; College for Teachers (Buffalo); Teachers College (Brockport); Teachers College (Cortland); Teachers College (Fredonia); Teachers College (Oneonta); Teachers College (Plattsburgh); Teachers College (Potsdam); Union College and University; U.S. Merchant Marine Academy; Wagner Lutheran College; Wells College; Yeshiva University. *Pennsylvania:* Allegheny College; Beaver College; Chatham College; Chestnut Hill College; College

APPENDIXES 217

Misericordia; Drexel Institute of Technology; Elizabethtown College; Franklin and Marshall College; Gannon College; Geneva College; Gettysburg College; Grove City College; Juniata College; King's College; La Salle College; Lebanon Valley College; Lincoln University; Mount Mercy College; Muhlenberg College; Philadelphia Textile Institute; St. Francis College; St. Joseph's College; St. Vincent College; Seton Hill College; State Teachers College (Bloomsburg); State Teachers College (East Stroudsburg); State Teachers College (Edinboro); State Teachers College (Indiana); State Teachers College (Kutztown); State Teachers College (Lock Haven); State Teachers College (Mansfield); State Teachers College (Millersville); State Teachers College (Shippensburg); State Teachers College (Slippery Rock); Susquehanna University; University of Scranton; Ursinus College; Washington and Jefferson College; Waynesburg College; Westminster College; Wilkes College; Wilson College. *Rhode Island:* Rhode Island School of Design. *Vermont:* Norwich University; St. Michael's College. *West Virginia:* Bethany College; Concord College; Marshall College; Shepherd College; West Liberty State College; West Virginia Wesleyan College. *Puerto Rico:* Inter-American University of Puerto Rico.

SOUTH (85)

Alabama: Alabama Polytechnic Institute; Howard College. *Arkansas:* Arkansas State Teachers College (Conway); Harding College; Hendrix College; Southern State College. *Florida:* Bethune-Cookman College; Florida Agricultural and Mechanical University; Stetson University; University of Tampa; Jacksonville University. *Georgia:* Brenau College; Georgia State College for Women; Mercer University; Savannah State College. *Kentucky:* Berea College; Centre College of Kentucky; Kentucky State College (Frankfort); Transylvania College. *Louisiana:* Grambling College; Louisiana College; Louisiana Polytechnic Institute; Northeast Louisiana State College; Southern University and Agricultural and Mechanical College; Xavier University. *Mississippi:* Alcorn Agricultural and Mechanical College; Delta State College; Mississippi College; Mississippi State College for Women. *North Carolina:* Agricultural and Technical College of North Carolina; Bennett College; Catawba College; Elon College; Johnson C. Smith University; Livingstone College; Meredith College; Queens College; St. Augustine's College. *Oklahoma:* Central State College; Langston University; Oklahoma College for Women; Panhandle Agricultural and Mechanical College; Phillips University; Southeastern State College. *South Carolina:* Erskine College; South Carolina State College (Orangeburg); Winthrop College. *Tennessee:* Austin Peay State College; David Lipscomb College; King College; Knoxville College; Le Moyne College; Lincoln Memorial University; Maryville College; Middle Tennessee State College; Siena College; Southwestern at Memphis; Tennessee Agricultural and Industrial State University; Union University; Belmont College; Tennessee Wesleyan College. *Texas:* Austin College; Incarnate Word College; Lamar State College of Technology; Mary Hardin-Baylor College; Prairie View Agricultural and Mechanical College; St. Mary's University of San Antonio; Southwestern University; Stephen F. Austin State College; Sul Ross State College; Texas Southern University; Texas Womens University; Texas Wesleyan College; West Texas State College; Wiley College. *Virginia:* Emory and Henry College; Hampden-Sydney College; Lynchburg College; Madison College; Randolph-Macon College; Randolph-Macon Woman's College; Roanoke College; University of Richmond; Virginia Polytechnic Institute; Virginia State College.

MIDWEST (117)

Illinois: Augustana College; Aurora College; Barat College of the Sacred Heart; Blackburn College; Carthage College; Chicago Teachers College; College of St. Francis; De Paul University; Eastern Illinois University; Elmhurst College; Illinois Institute of Technology; Illinois Wesleyan University; Knox College; Millikin University; Monmouth College; North Central College; Northern Baptist Theological Seminary; Northern Illinois University; Principia College; Quincy College; Rockford College; Roosevelt University; Rosary College; St. Procopius College; Shimer College. *Indiana:* Butler University; Evansville College; Franklin College of Indiana; Indiana State Teachers College; Marian College; St. Joseph's College; St. Mary's College; Taylor University; Valparaiso University; Wabash College. *Iowa:* Central College; Clarke College; Coe College; Loras College; Luther College; University of Dubuque; Wartburg College; Westmar College. *Kansas:* Bethany College; Fort Hays Kansas State College; Friends University; Kansas State Teachers College; Mount St. Scholastica College; St. Benedict's College; Southwestern College. *Michigan:* Calvin College; Central Michigan College; Kalamazoo College; Marygrove College; Michigan College of Mining and Technology; Northern Michigan College; Western Michigan College. *Minnesota:* Augsburg College and Theological

Seminary; College of St. Scholastica; College of St. Teresa; College of St. Thomas; Gustavus Adolphus College; Hamline University; Macalester College; St. John's University; St. Mary's College; St. Olaf College; State Teachers College (Bemidji); State Teachers College (Mankato); State Teachers College (St. Cloud); State Teachers College (Winona). *Missouri:* Central College; Drury College; Fontbonne College; Harris Teachers College; Lindenwood College; Maryville College of the Sacred Heart; Northwest Missouri State College; Southeast Missouri State College; Webster College; Westminster College; William Jewell College. *Nebraska:* College of Saint Mary; Doane College; Duchesne College; Hastings College; Midland College; Nebraska State Teachers College (Kearney); Nebraska Wesleyan University; Union College. *Ohio:* Ashland College; Capital University; Central State College; College of Mount St. Joseph-on-the-Ohio; Denison University; Fenn College; Heidelberg College; Hiram College; Kent State University; Lake Erie College; Marietta College; Muskingum College; Ohio Northern University; Otterbein College; Western College for Women; Wilmington College; Wittenberg College; Xavier University. *Wisconsin:* Alverno College; Mount Mary College; Northland College; Ripon College; Stout State College; Viterbo College; Wisconsin State College (Eau Claire); Wisconsin State College (River Falls); Wisconsin State College (Whitewater).

WEST (41)

Arizona: Arizona State College (Flagstaff); Arizona State College (Tempe). *California:* California State Polytechnic College; California Western University; College of the Holy Names; College of Notre Dame; Dominican College of San Rafael; George Pepperdine College; Golden Gate College; Humboldt State College; Immaculate Heart College; Loyola University of Los Angeles; Mount St. Mary's College; Pacific Union College; Pasadena College; Sacramento State College; San Diego College for Women; San Francisco College for Women; University of Redlands; Westmont College; Whittier College. *Colorado:* Colorado State College; Regis College. *Idaho:* Northwest Nazarene College. *Montana:* College of Great Falls; Eastern Montana College of Education; Montana School of Mines; Northern Montana College. *New Mexico:* New Mexico Institute of Mining and Technology. *North Dakota:* Jamestown College; State Normal and Industrial College (Ellendale); State Teachers College (Mayville); State Teachers College (Valley City). *Oregon:* Linfield College; Marylhurst College; Portland State College. *South Dakota:* Augustana College; South Dakota State College (Brookings); South Dakota School of Mines and Technology. *Washington:* Central Washington College of Education; Whitman College.

APPENDIX C

Questionnaires of the type noted in Appendixes A and B were also received from history faculties in 51 junior colleges. All the responding junior colleges are members of the American Council on Education. Institutions in all parts of the nation are represented in the sample. Listed alphabetically by name of college within a region, they are as follows:

EAST (16)

Bennett Junior College, Millbrook, New York; Briarcliff College, Briarcliff Manor, New York; Colby Junior College, New London, New Hampshire; Endicott Junior College, Beverley, Massachusetts; Gwynedd Mercy Junior College, Gwynedd, Pennsylvania; Hershey Junior College, Hershey, Pennsylvania; Jersey City Junior College, Jersey City, New Jersey; Keystone Junior College, La Plume, Pennsylvania; Montgomery Junior College, Takoma Park, Maryland; New York City Community College of Applied Arts and Sciences, Brooklyn, New York; Parker Collegiate Institute, Brooklyn, New York; Pine Manor Junior College, Wellesley, Massachusetts; Potomac State College of West Virginia University, Keyser, West Virginia; Valley Forge Military Junior College, Wayne, Pennsylvania; Wesley Junior College, Dover, Delaware; Worcester Polytechnic Institute, Worcester, Massachusetts.

SOUTH (11)

Amarillo College, Amarillo, Texas; Averett College, Danville, Virginia; Daniel Payne College, Birmingham, Alabama; Del Mar College, Corpus Christi, Texas; Eastern Oklahoma Agricultural and Mechanical College, Wilburton, Oklahoma; Jones County Junior College, Ellisville, Mississippi; Lee College, Baytown, Texas; Little Rock University, Little Rock, Arkansas; Northern Oklahoma Junior College, Tonkawa, Oklahoma; South Georgia College, Douglas, Georgia; Wharton County Junior College, Wharton, Texas.

MIDWEST (12)

Christian College, Columbia, Missouri; Gogebic Community College, Ironwood, Michigan; Graceland College, Lamoni, Iowa; Henry Ford Community College, Dearborn, Michigan; Highland Park Junior College, Highland Park, Michigan; Junior College of Kansas City, Kansas City, Missouri; La Salle-Peru Oglesby Junior College, La Salle, Illinois; Monticello College, Godfrey, Illinois; Stephens College, Columbia, Missouri; Vincennes University, Vincennes, Indiana; Virginia Junior College, Virginia, Minnesota; William Woods College, Fulton, Missouri.

WEST (12)

Colorado Woman's College, Denver, Colorado; Compton College, Compton, California; Dixie Junior College, St. George, Utah; Mesa College, Grand Junction, Colorado; Modesto Junior College, Modesto, California; Mount San Antonio College, Pomona, California; New Mexico Military Institute, Roswell, New Mexico; North Idaho Junior College, Coeur d'Alene, Idaho; Orange Coast College, Costa Mesa, California; Pasadena City College, Pasadena, California; San Bernardino Valley College, San Bernardino, California; Weber College, Ogden, Utah.

APPENDIX D

On November 2, 1959, Dexter Perkins sent a letter to presidents of 200 colleges, none of which then offered the Ph.D. in history, asking the following questions:

1. In adding historians to the faculty, how important to you is the proof or promise of teaching ability as compared with proof or promise of research scholarship?

2. How do you discover and evaluate the qualifications of candidates (and newly appointed faculty members) as teachers?

By December 18, 1959, the committee had received responses from a total of 134 presidents, academic vice-presidents, or deans. The letters came from 44 states (including the two newest ones) plus Puerto Rico and the District of Columbia. The letters were regionally distributed as follows: *East*, 37; *South*, 32; *Midwest*, 36; and *West*, 29. Almost all the letters were thoughtful and helpful, and many of them ran to two pages of single-spaced type. Letters were received from executives of most of the colleges named in Appendix A, plus a number of others.

The institutions from which the committee received replies are listed below. It will be noted that they include public and private colleges and that among the latter are institutions that are predominantly Negro, predominantly male, female, Protestant, Jewish, or Catholic. The list purposefully included a number of teacher-training colleges, but the great majority of the institutions are primarily arts and sciences colleges. While the colleges are representative in many ways, they are—by design—unrepresentative in one sense: they include a disproportionately large number of colleges that have considerable reputations for quality among institutions of their type.

EAST (37)

Connecticut: Connecticut College; Danbury State Teachers College; Trinity College; The University of Connecticut; Wesleyan University. *Delaware:* University of Delaware. *District of Columbia:* District of Columbia Teachers College; Howard University. *Maine:* Bowdoin College; Colby College; University of Maine. *Maryland:* Goucher College; Morgan State College; Washington College. *Massachusetts:* Amherst College; Brandeis University; Massachusetts Institute of Technology; Mount Holyoke College; University of Massachusetts; Wellesley College. *New Hampshire:* Dartmouth College; University of New Hampshire. *New York:* City College (New York); Colgate University; Hofstra College; Hunter College of the City of New York; Queens College; Rensselaer Polytechnic Institute; Skidmore College; Teachers College (New Paltz); Vassar College. *Pennsylvania:* Bucknell University; Carnegie Institute of

Technology; Haverford College; Temple University. *Vermont:* University of Vermont. *Puerto Rico:* Universidad de Puerto Rico.

SOUTH (32)

Alabama: Alabama College; Birmingham-Southern College; State Teachers College (Florence). *Arkansas:* Arkansas State College; Philander Smith College. *Florida:* Florida Southern College; Rollins College; University of Miami. *Georgia:* Agnes Scott College. *Kentucky:* Murray State College; University of Louisville; Western Kentucky State College. *Louisiana:* Loyola University; Southwestern Louisiana Institute. *Mississippi:* Millsaps College; Mississippi Southern College. *North Carolina:* Davidson College; East Carolina College; North Carolina College at Durham; North Carolina State College; Western Carolina College; Women's College, University of North Carolina. *South Carolina:* Clemson College. *Tennessee:* East Tennessee State College; University of Chattanooga. *Texas:* Agricultural and Mechanical College of Texas; North Texas State College; Sam Houston State Teachers College; Southern Methodist University; Trinity University. *Virginia:* College of William and Mary; Sweet Briar College.

MIDWEST (36)

Illinois: Illinois State Normal University; MacMurray College; Southern Illinois University; Wheaton College. *Indiana:* DePauw University; Hanover College; Purdue University. *Iowa:* Cornell College; Drake University; Grinnell College; Iowa State University of Science and Technology; Iowa State Teachers College. *Kansas:* Kansas State University of Agriculture and Applied Science; Washburn University. *Michigan:* Albion College; Eastern Michigan College. *Minnesota:* Carleton College; State College (Moorhead). *Missouri:* Park College. *Nebraska:* Creighton University; Municipal University of Omaha; Nebraska State Teachers College (Wayne). *Ohio:* Baldwin-Wallace College; Bowling Green State University; Case Institute of Technology; Kenyon College; Miami University; Oberlin College; Ohio University; University of Akron; University of Cincinnati; University of Toledo. *Wisconsin:* Beloit College; Lawrence College; Marquette University; Wisconsin State College (Oshkosh).

WEST (29)

Alaska: University of Alaska. *Arizona:* University of Arizona. *California:* California Institute of Technology; Chico State College; College of the Pacific; Mills College; Occidental College; San Diego State College; San Francisco State College; San Jose State College; University of Santa Clara; University of San Francisco. *Colorado:* Colorado State University; University of Denver; Western State College of Colorado. *Hawaii:* University of Hawaii. *Montana:* Montana State University. *Nevada:* University of Nevada. *North Dakota:* State Teachers College (Minot). *Oregon:* Lewis and Clark College; Oregon State College (Corvallis); Reed College; University of Portland. *South Dakota:* State University of South Dakota. *Utah:* Brigham Young University; Utah State University. *Washington:* Eastern Washington College of Education; Western Washington College of Education. *Wyoming:* University of Wyoming.

APPENDIX E

Twenty-eight Ph.D.-training history departments were visited by at least one member of the Committee on Graduate Education in History in 1959 or were represented by a member of the committee. Those marked by no footnote in the list below were visited by Professor Snell. On their campuses or at history conventions he interviewed more than 230 members of Ph.D.-training history faculties, taking notes during the interviews or dictating summaries of the interviews on the same day they occurred. Full summaries of these interviews were read by all members of the committee in 1959.

These interviews sought to find detailed and general answers to three fundamental questions: (1) What is wrong with doctoral training in history at your present institution? (2) What was wrong with it in the program where you took your Ph.D.? (3) What suggestions would you make for the improvement of Ph.D. training in history?

APPENDIXES 225

The 28 universities visited by or represented on the committee were: *East* (9): Columbia University, Cornell University,[1] University of Delaware,[1] Harvard University, Johns Hopkins University,[2] University of Pennsylvania, Princeton University, University of Rochester, and Yale University.[3] *South* (5): Duke University,[1] Florida State University, University of North Carolina,[1] University of Texas, and Tulane University. *Midwest* (6): University of Chicago, Indiana University, University of Minnesota, Northwestern University, University of Notre Dame, and the University of Wisconsin. *West* (8): University of California,[1] University of California at Los Angeles,[1] University of Colorado, Occidental College,[1] University of Oregon, University of Southern California,[1] Stanford University and the University of Washington.

APPENDIX F

Three types of questionnaires were completed by departments offering Ph.D. training in history. In November, 1958, a 21-page questionnaire was distributed to all history departments in the nation known to be offering doctoral training. Usable questionnaires were returned in time for tabulating by history departments in the 77 institutions listed below. One arrived later from the University of Delaware, which only inaugurated its Ph.D. program in history in 1960. From Vanderbilt University we received a carefully detailed letter that was most helpful in lieu of a questionnaire. Partially completed questionnaires were received from Fordham University, George Washington University, and the Hartford Seminary Foundation in addition to the 77 institutions noted below.

The basic questionnaire to departments with doctoral programs solicited information about: (1) scope and general character of the graduate program; (2) the discovery, encouragement, and recognition of able teachers of history; (3) the master's program; (4) length of time required for the Ph.D.; (5) faculty objectives

[1] Visited by Dexter Perkins.
[2] Visited by Boyd C. Shafer.
[3] Represented by Leonard Krieger.

in doctoral training, and faculty supervision of Ph.D. candidates; (6) anticipated changes; and (7) recommendations for the improvement of graduate training for college teachers of history.

A supplementary questionnaire, distributed in November, 1959, asked for a report on the number of Ph.D.s in history awarded in 1959, and for impressions of supply-demand relationships. It also asked the Ph.D.-training departments to list separately the top 20 centers for Ph.D. training in (1) United States history and (2) modern European history. By December 14, 1959, reports had been received from 71 departments, 54 of which presented rank lists as requested. The references in Chapters 1 to 9 of this report to "top-prestige" institutions are based upon composite rank lists compiled from the reports of these 54 Ph.D.-training departments, distributed as follows: *East,* 17 departments; *South,* 15; *Midwest,* 16; *West,* 6.

On May 15, 1960, a second supplementary questionnaire was distributed to all Ph.D.-training history departments. In this one they were asked to report "how many persons are virtually certain to be *awarded* the Ph.D. in history at your institution in June or August, 1960," and how many had already been *awarded* the degree in 1960, if any. On the basis of reports received from all but four Ph.D.-training history departments we have made our estimate of doctoral production in history for 1960 (Table 2-2).

Most of the data in the text from Ph.D. programs in history were supplied by departments in the following 77 institutions:

EAST (27)

American University; Boston College; Boston University; Brown University; Bryn Mawr College; University of Buffalo; Catholic University of America; Clark University; Columbia University; Cornell University; Georgetown University; Harvard University (including Radcliffe); Johns Hopkins University; Lehigh University; University of Maryland; New York University; Pennsylvania State University; University of Pennsylvania; University of Pittsburgh; Princeton University; University of Rochester; Rutgers University; St. John's University; Syracuse University; Tufts University; West Virginia University; and Yale University.

SOUTH (19)

University of Alabama; Duke University; Emory University; Florida State University; University of Florida; George Peabody College for Teachers; University of Georgia; University of Kentucky; Louisiana State University; Mississippi State University; University of North Carolina; University of Oklahoma; Rice Institute; University of South Carolina; University of Tennessee; Texas Technological College; University of Texas; Tulane University; and the University of Virginia.

MIDWEST (19)

University of Chicago; University of Illinois; Indiana University; State University of Iowa; University of Kansas; Loyola University (Chicago); Michigan State University; University of Michigan; University of Minnesota; University of Missouri; University of Nebraska; Northwestern University; University of Notre Dame; Ohio State University; St. Louis University; Washington University; Wayne State University; Western Reserve University; and the University of Wisconsin (including the History of Science Department).

WEST (12)

University of California; University of California at Los Angeles; University of Colorado; University of Idaho; University of New Mexico; University of North Dakota; University of Oregon; University of Southern California; Stanford University; University of Utah; Washington State University; and the University of Washington.

APPENDIX G

In a further attempt to estimate the changing relationship between supply of Ph.D.s in history and demand for them, a questionnaire was distributed in September, 1959, to the placement officers in all institutions in the nation known to offer Ph.D. training in history. They were asked to report on employment trends from 1954 through 1959.

Usable answers were returned by placement officers in the following 16 institutions: *East* (6): Columbia University; Cornell University; Harvard University; Lehigh University; University of Pennsylvania; and Yale University. *South* (4): Duke University; George Peabody College for Teachers; University of Kentucky; and University of Tennessee. *Midwest* (5): State University of Iowa; University of Kansas; University of Minnesota; University of Nebraska; and Washington University (Mo.). *West* (1): University of California (Berkeley).

APPENDIX H

In August, 1959, a 22-page questionnaire was distributed to 284 persons who were reported by 79 graduate schools to have been awarded the Ph.D. degree in history in 1958. Of these, 182 returned usable questionnaires in time for tabulation. A total of 49 institutions (83% of those awarding Ph.D.s in history in 1958) are represented by the Ph.D.s returning questionnaires. The sample represents all major producers of Ph.D.s in history and is otherwise representative. Thus, while the seven top-prestige programs awarded 34% of all Ph.D.s in history in the nation, 1955–1959, they are represented in our sample by 36% of all 182 questionnaires; regionally, 46% of the questionnaires are from graduates of Eastern universities, 24% are from Midwestern, 17% from Southern, and 13% from Western institutions.

The questionnaire to 1958 Ph.D.s solicited information about personal and academic background, almost all aspects of graduate training, job experience since 1958, and the qualities of good and poor teachers with whom they had studied. It also solicited suggestions for changes in graduate training in history.

The 49 institutions represented by the 182 questionnaires from Ph.D.s in history of 1958 are: *East* (18): Boston College; Boston University; Brown University; Catholic University of America; Columbia University; Teachers College of Columbia University; Cornell University; Fordham

University; Georgetown University; Harvard University; Johns Hopkins University; New York University; University of Pennsylvania; University of Pittsburgh; Princeton University; University of Rochester; St. John's University; and Yale University. *Midwest* (12): University of Chicago; University of Illinois; Indiana University; University of Michigan; University of Minnesota; University of Missouri; University of Nebraska; Northwestern University; Ohio State University; St. Louis University; Western Reserve University; University of Wisconsin. *South* (12): Duke University; University of Florida; George Peabody College for Teachers; University of Georgia; University of Kentucky; University of North Carolina; University of Oklahoma; Texas Technological College; University of Texas; Tulane University; Vanderbilt University; University of Virginia. *West* (7): University of California; University of California at Los Angeles; Claremont Graduate School; University of New Mexico; University of North Dakota; University of Southern California; and Stanford University.

APPENDIX I

As noted in the text, a considerable amount of questionnaire-collected and processed data on 306 graduate students in history (plus comparable data on 2,536 other graduate students) was provided this study by the National Opinion Research Center of the University of Chicago. The data on history graduate students from the South and West are not as adequate as are the data from the East and Midwest, because universities that are major producers of Ph.D.s in history were not included in the Eastern and Western samples. But as a national sample of history graduate students the NORC material was invaluable to this study.

The students questioned by the NORC were in residence in the year 1958–1959 in the following institutions: *East* (12): Boston College; Boston University; Brown University; Catholic University of America; Columbia University; Cornell University; Georgetown University; Harvard University; New York University; University of Pennsylvania; Pennsylvania State University; and Rennselaer Polytechnic Institute. *South* (3): University of Oklahoma; University of South Carolina; and

University of Tennessee. *Midwest* (8): University of Chicago; Indiana University; University of Kansas; University of Michigan; University of Minnesota; Ohio State University; University of Wisconsin; and Western Reserve University. *West* (2): University of California (Berkeley); and University of Oregon.

APPENDIX J

A special questionnaire on training for the master's degree in history was completed by history departments in 87 colleges that in 1958–1959 did not offer the Ph.D. degree in history. Information thus received supplemented that collected on the master's degree in history from the 77 Ph.D.-training departments (Appendix F). The following colleges are represented in our sample of institutions granting the master's degree in history:

EAST (27)

Connecticut: Connecticut College; St. Joseph College. *District of Columbia:* Trinity College; District of Columbia Teachers College. *Delaware:* University of Delaware. *Massachusetts:* Amherst College; University of Massachusetts. *New Hampshire:* University of New Hampshire; *New York:* Canisius College of Buffalo; Brooklyn College; Colgate University; College of Saint Rose; Hunter College; Hobart College; Long Island University; Mount St. Joseph Teachers College; Nazareth College of Rochester; St. Bonaventure University; Sarah Lawrence College. *Pennsylvania:* Bucknell University; Haverford College; Swarthmore College; Temple University; University of Scranton. *Rhode Island:* University of Rhode Island. *Vermont:* University of Vermont. *West Virginia:* Marshall College.

SOUTH (23)

Alabama: Auburn University. *Arkansas:* Henderson State Teachers College. *Florida:* Stetson University; University of Miami. *Georgia:* Atlanta University. *Kentucky:* University of Louisville. *Mississippi:* Mississippi Southern College. *North Carolina:* North Carolina College at Durham. *Oklahoma:* Oklahoma State University. *Tennessee:* Tennessee Agricultural and Industrial State University; Memphis State University. *Texas:* Baylor University; North Texas State College; Southern Methodist University; Stephen F. Austin State College; Sul Ross State College; Texas Christian University; Texas College of Arts and Industries; Texas Western College; University of Houston; West Texas State College. *Virginia:* College of William and Mary; University of Richmond.

MIDWEST (16)

Illinois: Roosevelt University. *Indiana:* Indiana State Teachers College. *Iowa:* Drake University. *Kansas:* Fort Hays Kansas State College; Kansas State University of Agriculture and Applied Science; Kansas State Teachers College of Emporia; University of Wichita. *Michigan:* University of Detroit. *Missouri:* Lincoln University. *Nebraska:* Creighton University; University of Omaha. *Ohio:* Kent State University; Miami University; Ohio University; Ohio Wesleyan University; University of Akron.

WEST (21)

Arizona: Arizona State College (Tempe); University of Arizona. *California:* Fresno State College; Mills College; Occidental College; Pacific Union College; Sacramento State College; San Francisco College for Women; San Jose State College; University of Santa Clara. *Colorado:* Colorado College; Colorado State University; University of Denver. *Idaho:* University of Idaho. *Montana:* Montana State University. *Nevada:* University of Nevada. *New Mexico:* New Mexico State University. *Oregon:* University of Portland. *Washington:* Gonzaga University. *Wyoming:* University of Wyoming. *Hawaii:* University of Hawaii.

APPENDIX K

In November, 1958, a questionnaire was distributed to the editors of six historical journals and the directors of eight university presses. This questionnaire solicited the impressions of training for research and writing in Ph.D. programs in history that these editors and directors may have formed from their examination of manuscripts prepared by many new Ph.D.s in history.

Editors of all six journals responded: *American Historical Review, Journal of Modern History, Mississippi Valley Historical Review, Pacific Historical Review, Speculum,* and the *William and Mary Quarterly.*

Directors of four university presses completed questionnaires: Harvard University Press, University of Kentucky Press, University of Oklahoma Press, and the Princeton University Press.

INDEX

Acceleration needed in Ph.D. training, 176–188, 193–199, 203–205
 (*See also* Ph.D. training, duration)
Accrediting associations, 104
Acton, Lord, 36
Adams, Herbert Baxter, 16, 29
Admission policies (*see* Graduate students; Master's training; Ph.D. training)
African history, 31, 32, 76–77, 123
Agriculture (as discipline), 49
AGS (Association of Graduate Schools), 102
Air Force Academy, 63
Alabama, University of, 43, 104, 112, 120
Albion, Robert G., 146
Allegheny College, 43
Allen, Paul M., viii
Alpert, Harry, 103
American Association of Colleges for Teacher Education, viii
American Bar Association, 54
American civilization (*see* United States)
American colonies, history, 57
American Historical Association, vii, 1, 73, 165, 174–175, 201
 (*See also* Committee on Graduate Education in History)
American Historical Review, 175
American history (*see* United States)

American Medical Association, Council on Medical Education and Hospitals of, 167
American Slavic and East European Review, 175
American University, 112, 113, 119
Amherst College, 43, 63, 77
Ancient history, 31, 32, 74–78, 118–125
Anthropology, 40, 144, 150
Antioch College, 80
Arizona, University of, 111
Arkansas, University of, 43, 112
Art illustrations, 80
Asian history, 31, 32, 74–77, 119–125, 212
 (*See also* Far Eastern, Indian, and Near Eastern history; Non-Western areas)
Association of American Universities, 106, 138
Association of Graduate Schools (AGS), proposals of Committee on Policies in Graduate Education of, 102
Association of Medical Colleges, 54
Augustana College, 43

Bachelor's degrees, 19, 21, 66
 (*See also* Undergraduate studies)
Barzun, Jacques, v, 56, 88, 169
Baylor University, 43

Becker, Carl, 2, 5
Berelson, Bernard, viii, 23, 26, 34, 44, 53, 56, 67, 106, 138, 149, 151, 173, 176, 179, 180
Biological sciences (as disciplines), 54
Birmingham-Southern College, 43
Black, C. E., 136
Bonn Republic, 186
Boston College, 43, 112, 119
Boston University, 43, 112, 113, 119
Botany (as discipline), 50
Bowdoin College, 43
Bowen, Clarence, 16
Brandeis University, 113
Breadth (*see* Master's training; Ph.D. training; Undergraduate studies)
British history, 30–33, 35, 74–78, 118–125
Brogan, A. P., 103
Brooklyn College, 43
Brown University, 43, 99, 112, 113, 119, 156, 157
Bryn Mawr College, 43, 112, 113, 119
Budgets for library purchases, 136–137
Buffalo, University of, 112, 113, 119
Butler University, 43
Byrnes, Robert, 136

California, University of, Berkeley, 43, 47, 78, 112–114, 122, 154, 193, 194, 199
  Los Angeles, 43, 112, 113, 122
Calvinism, 57
Caplow, Theodore, 132, 133
Career aims (*see* Graduate students)
Carleton College, 43
Carman, Harry J., 64
Carmichael, Oliver C., 103–104
Carnegie Corporation, vii, 1
Carnegie Foundation for the Advancement of Teaching, 103
Carnegie Institute of Technology, 80
Cartwright, W. H., 99
Catholic University, 43, 112, 113, 119
Catholics as history Ph.D.s, 42, 44
CCNY, 43

Central Missouri State College, 43
Chairmen of departments (*see* College faculties; Ph.D. programs)
Chase, John L., viii, 48
Chemistry (as discipline), 48, 50, 173, 174
Chicago, University of, 43, 47, 112–114, 121, 153, 155, 229
Cincinnati, University of, 43, 112, 113
City College, New York, 43
Claremont Graduate School, 78, 112, 113, 192
Clark University, 43, 112, 119, 156
Classes, size, 33, 130, 131
Classics, historical, 8, 84
Cognate studies (*see* Master's training; Ph.D. training; Undergraduate studies)
Colgate University, 43, 63, 99
College executives, consultation for this study, 221–224
  opinions, 61–65, 104–105, 163–185
College faculties, consultation for this study, 213–220
  degree qualifications, 22, 64–66
  opinions, 31–33, 61, 62, 65, 71, 93, 163–185
  publication, 70–71
  in recruiting students, 55–56
  research, 70–71
  teaching loads, 70–72, 84
  travel, 67
  (*See also* Colleges)
College teaching as career aim, 53–54
Colleges, courses, 73–79, 84–85
  enrollments, 74
  forms of instruction, 79–81, 84–85
  graduation requirements, 73
  history instruction, 61–85
    fields taught, 73–78
  leaves of absence, 72
  libraries, 67–68
  Master's training, 86–107
  size of classes, 70
  teaching loads, 68–72, 211–212
Colorado, University of, 43, 112, 113, 122

INDEX 235

Columbia University, 43, 47, 87, 111–114, 119, 178, 180
 Teachers College, 3
Committee of Fifteen, 165, 169
Committee on Graduate Education in History, American Historical Association, recommendations, 200–212
 summarized, 4–14
Committees, service on, 72, 131, 211
Comprehensive examinations (*see* Ph.D. training; Undergraduate studies)
Conant, James B., 4
Concordia Seminary, 43
Constitutional history, 76, 77, 123, 169
Cornell University, 43, 79, 112, 113, 119, 154
Course credits and requirements (*see* Master's training; Ph.D. training; Undergraduate studies)
Creighton University, 43
Cultural history, 74–77, 123, 124
Curti, Merle, 186

Dartmouth College, 43
Davidson College, 43
Debts of history graduate students, 51–52
Delaware, University of, 111
Demand for Ph.D.s (*see* Ph.D. training; Ph.D.s)
Denver, University of, 43
DePauw University, 43
Dickinson College, 43, 58
Dilthey, Wilhelm, 144*n*.
Diplomatic history, 76, 77, 122–124
Directed reading courses (*see* Master's training; Ph.D. training; Undergraduate studies)
Discussion sections (*see* Master's training; Ph.D. training; Undergraduate studies)
Dissertation (*see* Ph.D. training)
District of Columbia, 51
Doctorate in teaching discouraged, 201
Dramatic arts (as discipline), 49, 158
Dropsie College, 112

Duke University, 43, 99, 122, 113, 120, 190–191
Durant, Will, 52
Duration of training (*see* Master's training; Ph.D. training)

Earlham College, 43
East (United States region), college faculties, 66
 definition, 27*n*.
 faculty travel, 118
 history, enrollments, 70, 126
  types taught, 76–78
 library resources, 136–137
 master's training, 89, 94–96
 Ph.D. training, 27–29, 114, 115, 177
 publication of faculties, 117
 teaching loads, 129–131
 undergraduate majors, 126
East Carolina College, 63
Eastern European history, 28, 30–32, 41, 74–78, 118–125, 135–136
Economic history, 74–77, 123, 124
Economics (as discipline), 6, 19, 20, 40, 50, 93, 144, 150, 160, 179
Editors, consultation for this study, 231–232
 recommendations, 171–174
Education (as discipline), 18, 19, 46, 49, 96, 99, 111, 144, 158, 165
Educational television, 34, 79, 81
Elder, J. P., 106
Emory University, 43, 112, 113, 120, 197
Engineering (as discipline), 54
England, 57
English (as discipline), 18, 19, 38, 49–51, 150, 158, 160, 173, 174, 179
English history (*see* British history)
Enrollment trends (*see* Colleges; Ph.D. training)
European history, 29–31, 78, 82
 (*See also* Medieval history; Modern European history)
European History Section, Southern Historical Association, 175

Examinations (*see* Master's training; Ph.D. training; Undergraduate studies)
Expansion, discouraged, in Ph.D. programs, 138–140, 201
  encouraged, in Ph.D. training (*see* Ph.D. training)

Faculties (*see* College faculties; Junior colleges; Ph.D. programs)
Families, prolongation of training by, 12
Far Eastern history, 32, 74–78, 118–125
  (*See also* Asian history; Non-Western areas)
Fellowships (*see* Ph.D. training, financing)
Field requirements (*see* Master's training; Ph.D. training; Undergraduate studies)
Field trips, 80
Film, 208
Financial needs (*see* Graduate students; Ph.D. training)
Fine, Benjamin, 73
Florida, University of, 43, 112, 120
Florida State University, 111
Folger, John K., viii
Fordham University, 43, 112, 113, 119
Foreign languages, as discipline, 178
  in master's training, 89, 91, 92, 96
  in Ph.D. training, 153, 154, 158, 159, 193, 194, 202
  in undergraduate study, 40–41, 84
Foreign students, 207
Forestry (as discipline), 49
France, 29, 172, 186
Franklin and Marshall College, 43
French (as discipline), 153, 195
Fulbright Fellowships, 47
Fund for the Advancement of Education, 103–104

General education courses, 76, 77
  (*See also* Western civilization)

General examinations (*see* Ph.D. training)
George Peabody College, 112, 120
George Washington University, 43, 112, 113, 119
Georgetown University, 43, 112, 113, 119
Georgia, University of, 43, 112, 120
German (as discipline), 153, 195
Germany, 57, 186
Gettysburg College, 43
"G.I. Bill," 19
Gonzaga University, 43
Gordon, A. R., 88, 106
Grade requirements (*see* Master's training; Ph.D. training)
Graduate Record Examination (GRE), 38–39, 202
Graduate students, ability, 37–41
  academic origins, 41–43
  admission, 38, 39, 55, 56, 181, 198, 200–202
  career aims, 53, 54, 163
  consultation for this study, 229–230
  faculty neglect, 133–134
  financing, 41, 45–53, 59, 127, 188, 200–201
  guidance, 113–134, 181–184, 198
  numbers, 23–25, 29, 36, 37
  opinions, 12, 13, 31–33, 151, 162, 163, 169
  progress delayed by work, 50, 51
  recruiting, 5, 6, 35, 54–59, 180, 186, 200–201
  screening, 88–89, 154–155, 159, 183, 194–198, 201–202
  social origins and characteristics, 42–46
  undergraduate records, 37–41
Graduate study (*see* Master's training; Ph.D. training)
Graduation requirements, colleges, 73
GRE, 38–39, 202
Grinnell College, 43
Guidance (*see* Graduate students; Master's training; Ph.D. training)

Hamilton College, 43
Harrington, Fred Harvey, v
Harvard Guide to Historical Literature, 7
Harvard University, 43, 47, 58, 99, 111–114, 119, 153, 157, 178, 189, 193
Haverford College, 43
Hesseltine, William B., 173
High schools, 55, 58
Hiram College, 43
Historian, The, 175
Historians, number, per college, 65
  per Ph.D. training program, 114
Historiography, 76–78, 80, 122–125, 145, 158, 198, 202, 204, 206
History (as discipline), nature, 1–14, 36
History Department Newsletter (Harvard), 146
Hobart and William Smith Colleges, 43
Hobbs, M. E., 88, 106
Holt, W. Stull, 75
Honors work (*see* Undergraduate studies)
Howard University, 43
Hubbard, Richard B., 91
Humanities (as disciplines), 40, 41, 54, 161
Hunter College, 43, 63

Idaho, University of, 111
Illinois, University of, 43, 112, 113, 121
Independent study as form of instruction, 79, 81, 84, 85
Indian history, 76, 77, 123
  (*See also* Asian history; Non-Western areas)
Indiana, 77
Indiana Central College, 43
Indiana University, 43, 112, 113, 121, 191–192
Individual instruction, 127
Intellectual history, 74–77, 123, 124

INDEX 237

Intercollegiate Program of Graduate Studies, 192
Interdisciplinary courses, 76, 77, 123, 192
Interviews, need in appointing teachers, 209
Iowa, State University of, 43, 112, 113, 121, 156
Iowa State Teachers College, 43

Jameson, John F., 16, 185
Jernegan, Marcus W., 17, 132, 157, 173
Jews, Ph.D.s earned by, 42
Johns Hopkins University, 16, 43, 99, 112–144, 119
Journal of Central European Affairs, 175
Journal of Modern History, 175
Journal of Southern History, 175
Junior colleges, consultation for this study, 220–221
  degree qualifications of faculty, 83
  history instruction, 65–66, 75

Kansas, University of, 43, 112, 113, 121
Kaplan, Louis, 173
Keeney, Barnaby, 169
Kemp, Mrs. James B., vii
Keniston, Hayward, 164, 185
Kentucky, University of, 43, 112, 120
Kirkland, Edward C., v
Kittredge, George Lyman, 156
Knox College, 43
Krieger, Leonard, v, 225
Ktsanes, Virginia, vii

Langer, William L., 144n.
Large institutions, origins of most history graduate students, 42, 43
Latin-American history, 30–33, 35, 74–78, 118–125
Law students, 44
Leaves of absence, 72, 134, 174, 212
Lecky, William E. H., 14

Lecture courses, 79, 81, 84, 127, 145, 146, 158, 181, 208
Lehigh University, 112, 119
Levels of instruction, 121–123
Library resources, in colleges, 67–68, 84
  in Ph.D. programs, 47, 108, 135–137, 157, 201–202, 212
Literature (as discipline), 93, 144
Loads, teaching (*see* College faculties; Ph.D. programs)
Loan-scholarships suggestion, 52–53, 59
Loans to graduate students, 51–53, 200
Louisiana State University, 43, 112, 120
Loyola University (Illinois), 43, 90, 112, 121
Lumiansky, R. M., 99
Lyons, William P., 90

M.A. degree, history (*see* Master's training)
M.A.T. degree, 96–101
M.Ed. degree, 101
M.S. degree, history (*see* Master's training)
McGee, Reece J., 132, 133
McGill University, 113
McGrath, Earl J., 3, 4
Maine, University of, 43
Majors, history (*see* Undergraduate studies)
Manhattan College, 43
Married graduate students, 12, 44
Marxism, 57
Maryland, Unversity of, 12, 119
Mason, Henry L., 170
Massachusetts, University of, 78, 99
Master of Arts in Teaching (M.A.T.) degree, 96–101
Master's degree, history, 19, 86–107, 181
  two types, 101
  uses, 33, 65–66, 97, 98, 100
Master's training, 12, 19, 21, 33, 86–107, 203
  admission, 88, 105
  breadth, 92–94

Master's training, cognate studies, 93, 96
  duration, 94–95, 106
  examinations, 94, 96, 105, 154
  foreign languages, 89, 91, 92, 96, 105
  growth, 21, 86–87
  prevalence, 86, 87
  proposed reforms, 97–107
  regional variations, 89, 92, 94–96
  requirements, course, 92, 93, 96, 106
    credit hours, 89
    grade, 88, 89, 96, 105
    residence, 89, 105
  screening of students, 88–89
  seminar courses, 80–81, 84–85
  thesis, 12, 89–91, 96, 105, 106, 151, 175, 181, 183, 203
Mathematics (as discipline), 48, 150
Maul, Ray C., 22n.
Medicine as field of study, 44, 54, 55
Medieval history, 30–32, 74–77, 118–125
Methodology, historical, 76–78, 84, 122, 123, 145
Methods of teaching, 79–81
Miami University, 43
Michigan, University of, 43, 112, 113, 121, 156, 157, 196, 197
Michigan State University, 43, 112, 121
Midwest (United States region), college faculties, 66
  definition, 27–28n.
  faculty travel, 118
  history enrollments, 70, 126
  library resources, 136, 137
  master's training, 89, 92, 94, 95
  publication of faculties, 117
  teaching loads, 129–131
  types of history taught, 75, 76
  undergraduate history majors, 126
Military history, 74–77, 123
Millsaps College, 43
Minnesota, University of, 43, 112, 113, 121
Mississippi, University of, 43, 111

INDEX 239

Mississippi State University, 111
Mississippi Valley Historical Association, 73, 175
Mississippi Valley Historical Review, 175
Missouri, University of, 43, 112, 113, 121
Mitchell, Robert, vii
Modern European history, 30–33, 74–77, 118–125, 135, 143, 144
Morningside College, 43
Morrison, Donald, 69
Mount Holyoke College, 43, 77, 99
Moving pictures, 80
Musical recordings, 80

National Council for the Social Studies, 73
National Defense Educational Act Fellowships (NDEA), 16, 35, 47, 48, 111
National Education Association (NEA), 23, 26, 34
National Merit Scholarships, 68
National Opinion Research Center (NORC), viii, 44, 45, 48–50, 53, 54, 180, 229
National Science Foundation, 45
Natural sciences (as disciplines), 45, 48–50, 161, 202
Nazism, 57
NDEA, 16, 35, 47, 48, 111
NEA, 23, 26, 34
Near Eastern history, 74–77, 123
(*See also* Asian history)
Nebraska, University of, 43, 112, 121
Negroes, Ph.D.s earned by, 42
Nevins, Allan, 172
New Deal, 57
New England, 44
New Mexico, University of, 43, 112, 113, 122
New York University, 43, 112, 119
Non-Western areas, 74–78, 84
NORC, 45, 48–50, 161, 202
North Carolina, University of, 43, 112, 113, 120, 128, 136n., 156

North Dakota, University of, 112, 122
North Texas State University, 43
Northeast Missouri State Teachers College, 43
Northwestern University, 43, 112, 113, 121, 153
Notre Dame, University of, 43, 112, 113, 121, 151
NYU, 43, 112, 119

Oberlin College, 43
Occidental College, 43, 64, 78, 111, 192
Office of Education, viii, 48, 158
Ohio State University, 43, 112, 113, 121
Ohio Wesleyan University, 43
Oklahoma, University of, 43, 112, 113, 120, 128
Oregon, University of, 43, 103, 112, 122, 128
Orientals, Ph.D.s earned by, 42

Pacific Coast Branch, American Historical Association, 175
Pacific Historical Review, 175
Paperback booklets, 80
Parents of history graduate students, 44–46, 49, 55
Parsons College, 72
Pennsylvania, University of, 43, 112, 113, 119, 128
Pennsylvania State University, 43, 112, 119
Perkins, Dexter, v, 85, 161, 165, 167, 170, 221, 224–225
 summary of views, 1–14
Ph.D. candidates (*see* Graduate students; Ph.D. training)
Ph.D. programs, history, 1–14, 108–140, 200–212
 capacities for expansion, 139–140
 consultation for this study, 224–227
 courses, 121–126
 faculty appointments, 116–117, 128

Ph.D. programs, history, faculty degree qualifications, 116–117
faculty research and publication, 117, 128, 132–135
faculty travel, 117–118
growth, 109–111
increase discouraged, 136–140, 201
leaves of absence, 134
levels of instruction, 121–123
library resources, 47, 108, 135–137, 157, 201–202
minimum assets, 138, 201–202
opinions of faculties, 31–33, 146–185
promotions, 132–133
recruiting, 54–59
size, 109–116
specialized teaching, 117
teaching loads and conditions, 127–137, 211–212
undergraduate major, 126
Ph.D. training, general, growth, 15–23, 36
history, 1–14, 141–159, 200–212
ability of students, 37–41
acceleration needed, 35, 176–188, 193–199, 203–207
admission, 37–41, 88, 181, 193–199, 200–202, 204
breadth, 1–2, 7, 8, 84, 142–144, 161, 162, 169–171, 186, 187, 205–207
cognate studies, 6, 144, 153, 158, 170, 171, 195, 196, 205
course credits, 184, 204–205
course loads, 142
courses, 122, 127, 142, 158, 181, 193–199, 206–207
criticism, 1–14, 160–187
delay by student work, 179
directed readings, 127, 145, 148, 194, 206–207
dissertation, 12, 47, 145, 148–152, 157–158, 169, 173, 180, 181, 183, 185, 193–199, 204–205, 207

Ph.D. training, history, duration, 11–12, 16, 176–187, 203–205
examinations, 7–8, 152–159, 181, 184, 193, 194, 196–198, 205
field requirements, 142–144, 158, 181, 184, 193–199, 205, 206
fields of specialization, 28–31, 35, 118–126
variations, 28
financing, 16, 26, 35, 39, 45–53, 58–60, 108, 111, 113, 114, 116, 179–180, 188, 200–202, 204
foreign languages, 153–154, 158, 159, 181, 184, 193–198, 202, 204, 206
foreign students, 207
forms of instruction, 145–152
growth, 17–22, 31–33, 109–111
guidance of students, 133, 134, 181–184, 198, 206
historiography, 145, 158, 198, 204, 206
honors work, 127
independent study, 195, 198, 205
individual instruction, 127
interdisciplinary seminars, 192
lecture courses, 158, 181, 193–199, 206–207
need for deadlines, 181
neglect of students, 133–134
philosophies of history, 8, 145, 158, 171
projected needs, 23–27, 31–33, 200–202
publication emphasized, 171–175
reading, 148–149
recruiting, 5, 6, 35, 54–59, 180, 186, 200–201
regional variations, 27–28, 110–137, 177–179, 185
research training, 3, 4, 59, 65, 127, 141, 145–148, 161, 171–176, 204, 206, 208
residence requirements, 141
screening of students, 88–89, 154–155, 159, 183, 193–199, 201–202

Ph.D. training, history, seminars, 80–81, 84–85, 90, 127, 146–148, 151, 152, 158, 183, 193–199, 203, 204
  specialization, 142–144, 169–171, 186, 187, 205–207, 211
  teacher training, 4–5, 8–11, 50, 59, 64, 127, 141, 145, 159–168, 186, 188–193, 198–199, 208–210
  travel, 47, 135
  tutorials, 127, 206
  women in, 20, 42
  writing training, 171–173, 187, 206
  (See also Graduate students; Ph.D. programs)
Ph.D.s, history, 15
  in colleges, 21, 61, 66, 83
  in junior colleges, 66, 83
  need for more, 31–32
  of 1958, age when degree awarded, 44, 203
  consultation for this study, 228–229
  opinions, 52, 61, 146–185
  in Ph.D. training departments, 114
  social characteristics, 42, 44–46
Philosophies of history, study needed, 8, 76–77, 84, 123–125, 145, 158, 171
Philosophy (as discipline), 50, 144, 150, 173, 174, 202
Physical sciences (as disciplines), 54
Physics (as discipline), 38, 48, 50, 173
Pierson, G. W., 187*n*.
Pittsburgh, University of, 43, 59, 112, 113, 119
Pittsburgh Plan, 59
Placement officers, consultation for this study, 227–228
  estimate of supply and demand by, 24
Political science (as discipline), 19, 20, 49, 50, 54, 93, 144, 150, 160, 170, 178, 179
Pomona College, 43

Postdoctoral study, 174
Preliminary examination (*see* Ph.D. training)
Preparation for teaching (*see* Ph.D. training)
Prestige as factor in selection of Ph.D. program, 108
Prestigious institutions, 47, 114
Princeton University, 43, 47, 102, 104, 112–114, 119, 151–152, 155, 156, 189–190, 193, 198–199
Prizes for teaching excellence, 212
Procedures in this study, 213–232
Professional associations, 212
Prolonged studies (*see* Ph.D. training)
Promotion criteria, 132–133, 203, 212
Protestants, Ph.D.s earned by, 42, 44
Psychology (as discipline), 38, 41, 49, 93, 144, 150
Publication, emphasis on, 11, 70–72, 117, 128, 132–133, 171–175, 210
Pusey, Nathan D., 135*n*.
"Putz's Ancient History," 79

Qualifying examinations (*see* Master's training; Ph.D. training)

Radcliffe College (*see* Harvard University)
Ranke, Leopold von, 142
Recent history, 124
Recommendations, Committee on Graduate Education, AHA, 200–212
Recordings, musical, 80
Recruiting (*see* Graduate students; Ph.D. training)
Redlands, University of, 78, 192
Reed College, 42, 43, 80
Regional variations, 27–29
  (*See also* specific regions)
Religious history, 76–77, 123, 144
Research (*see* College faculties; Ph.D. programs; Ph.D. training)
Research scholarship, importance, 65, 210, 212
Reserve Officers Training Corps, 52

Residence requirements, 89, 105, 141
Rice University, 43, 112, 120
Richmond, University of, 43
Rochester, University of, 43, 112, 113, 119, 190, 199
Roland, Mrs. Charles P., vii
Roman Empire, 57
Rosenhaupt, Hans, 180
ROTC, 52
Ruml, Beardsley, 69
Russian history (*see* Eastern European history)
Russian language, 153
Rutgers University, 43, 112, 113, 119

Sabbaticals, 72, 134, 174, 212
Saint John's University, 43, 112, 119
Saint Louis University, 43, 112, 113, 121
Saint Olaf College, 43
Salaries, need for higher, 59, 60, 84, 212
San Jose State College, 43
Scholarships (*see* Ph.D. training, financing)
Science, history of, 76, 77, 123, 124
Sciences (as disciplines), 38, 39, 54, 55
Screening of students (*see* Ph.D. training)
Secretarial assistance, 72, 212
Seminar courses (*see* Master's training; Ph.D. training; Undergraduate training)
SHA, 175
Shafer, Boyd C., v, 60, 224–225
Sibley, Elbridge, 45, 139, 178
Size, history classes, 68–72, 74, 127–137
Slavic history (*see* Eastern European history)
Slavic Review, 175
Slide projectors, 80
Smith College, 43, 78
Snell, John L., v, vii, 12, 224–225
Snell, Maxine P., vii
Social history, 76, 77, 123, 124

Social sciences (as disciplines), 39–41, 45, 48–50, 54, 82, 96, 180, 202
Sociology (as discipline), 19, 20, 50, 87, 144, 150, 160, 179
South (United States region), college faculties, 66
  definition of, 27*n*.
  faculty travel, 118
  history of, 28
  history enrollments, 70, 126
  library resources, 136–137
  master's training, 89, 94–95
  Ph.D. training, 27–29, 110, 111, 114, 115, 127, 177–179, 185
  publication by faculties, 117
  teaching loads, 129–131
  types of history taught, 75–76
  undergraduate majors, 126
South Carolina, University of, 43, 112, 113, 120
South Dakota, State University of, 64
Southern California, University of, 43, 112, 122
Southern Historical Association (SHA), 175
Southern Illinois University, 43, 63
Southern Methodist University, 43
Southern Regional Education Board, viii, 50, 53
Southwest Missouri State College, 43
Southwestern Social Science Quarterly, 175
Soviet Union, 99, 153 *n*., 186
Spaeth, Joe, vii
Specialization (*see* College faculties; Master's training; Ph.D. training; Undergraduate studies)
Standardization problems, master's degree, 97–107
Standards in history graduate study, 37–41
Stanford University, 43, 112, 113, 122, 153, 193–195
State history, 76, 77, 123
Stipends (*see* Ph.D. training, financing)
Student ratings of teachers, 64, 128

Summer study, stipends needed, 47
Supervised teaching, 9–11, 64, 128, 165, 189, 190, 208–210
Survey courses, 76, 77, 93
  (*See also* Modern European history; United States; Western civilization)
Swarthmore College, 42, 43
Syracuse University, 43, 112, 113, 119

Tape recorders, 208
Taylor, George V., 135
Teacher training, experiments, 188–193, 198–199
Teachers, history, career aim of graduate students, 53–56
  characteristics desired, 56–57, 62–63
Teaching assistantships, 50
Teaching doctorate discouragement, 201
Teaching excellence, discovering, fostering, and rewarding, 209–212
Teaching loads (*see* College faculties; Ph.D. programs)
Television, 34, 79, 81
Temple University, 43, 63
Tennessee, University of, 111
Term papers, 80
Texas, University of, 43, 103, 112, 113, 120, 197
Texas Technological College, 112, 120
Thesis, for master's degree, 12, 89–91, 96, 105, 106, 151, 175, 181, 183, 203
  for Ph.D. degree (dissertation), 12, 47, 145, 148–152, 157–158, 169, 173, 180, 181, 183, 185, 193–199, 204–205, 207
  for undergraduate honors, 80–81
Thompson, John M., 136
Tightened programs, 188, 193–199
Tolstoy, Leo, 57
Topical approach, in college history courses, 75–77
  in Ph.D. programs, 123–126
Toronto, University of, 113

Travel, by college faculties, 67
  for dissertation research, 47, 135
  faculty need for, 212
  financial problems, 47, 135
  by Ph.D.-training faculties, 117, 118
Tufts University, 112, 113, 119, 156
Tulane University, v, vii, 43, 52, 59, 99, 112, 113, 120, 156, 192, 196
Turner, Frederick J., 8
Tutorials (*see* Ph.D. training; Undergraduate studies)

Undergraduate studies, history, bachelor's degree, 19
  breadth, 40–41, 202
  cognate studies, 40–41, 202
  courses, 39–41, 73–79, 81, 82, 84–85, 202
  credit hour requirements, 82, 202
  directed readings, 81, 84
  examinations, 84, 202
  fields of history, 74–77, 81, 82, 202
  foreign language study, 40–41, 202
  forms of instruction, 34, 79–81, 84, 85, 208
  honors theses, 80–81
  in large institutions, 42–43
  majors, 20, 21, 37–41, 58, 126
  research training, 39, 40, 83, 202
  in small colleges, 41–43
  specialization, 40–41, 202
  tutorials, 81, 84–85
  writing training, 40–41
Union of Soviet Socialist Republics (U.S.S.R.), 99, 153*n.*, 186
  (*See also* Eastern European history)
Union College (Nebraska), 43
United States, history, 29–33, 35, 73–78, 82, 118–126, 136, 143, 159, 169
U.S. Air Force Academy, 63
U.S. Department of Health, Education, and Welfare, Office of Education, viii, 48, 158

Universities, undergraduate origins of most graduate students, 42–43
Urban history, 125
Utah, University of, 43, 112, 122

Vanderbilt University, 43, 99, 112, 113, 120
Vassar College, 43
Vermont, University of, 43
Vines, Mrs. Kenneth, vii
Virginia, University of, 43, 112, 113, 120

Wabash College, 43
Wake Forest College, 43
Walla Walla College, 43
Washington, University of, 43, 112, 113, 122, 151, 197–198
Washington and Lee University, 43
Washington State University, 112, 122
Washington University (Saint Louis), 43, 112
Wayne State University, 43, 111
Wellemeyer, Fletcher, 21
Wellesley College, 43
Wesleyan University, 43, 80, 99
West (United States region), college faculties, 66
  definition, 28n.
  faculty travel, 118
  history enrollments, 70, 126
  library resources, 136–137
  master's training, 89
  Ph.D. training, 27–29, 110, 111, 114, 115, 177
  publication of faculies, 117
  teaching loads, 129–131
  types of history taught, 76
  undergraduate majors, 126

West Germany, 186
West Virginia University, 43, 112, 119
Western civilization, history, 74–77, 123–125
Western Kentucky State College, 43
Western Reserve University, 43, 112, 113, 121
Wheaton College, 43
White, Andrew D., 79
Whitehead, Alfred N., 57
Whittier College, 78, 192
William P. Lyons Essay Award, 90
Williams College, 43
Wilson, Kenneth M., viii
Wilson, Logan, 138
Wilson, Meredith, 103
Wisconsin, University of, 43, 47, 112–114, 121, 128, 189
Women, as history undergraduates, 20
  Ph.D.s earned by, 20, 42
  as professional historians, 20
Woodrow Wilson Fellowships, 16, 35, 39, 41, 47, 48, 59, 114, 116
Wooster, College of, 43
Work, prolongation of doctoral training by, 12, 50–52, 179
World history, 74–77, 123–125
World War II, 18, 82, 110
Wright, Benjamin, 176
Writing training, 85, 171–173

Xavier University, 113

Yale University, 16, 43, 47, 79, 99, 112–114, 119, 176, 187n., 193, 195–196
Yalta Conference, 57

Zoology (as discipline), 150